Information Technology and the Teaching of History

T0383620

Information Technology and the Teaching of History

International Perspectives

Edited by
Allan Martin
University of Glasgow, UK
Lez Smart
Roehampton Institute, London, UK
David Yeomans
University of Leeds, UK

harwood academic publishers
Australia • Canada • China • France • Germany • India • Japan
Luxembourg • Malaysia • The Netherlands • Russia • Singapore
Switzerland • Thailand • United Kingdom

Amsteldijk 166
1st Floor
1079 LH Amsterdam
The Netherlands

British Library Cataloguing in Publication data

Information technology and the teaching of history
    1. History — Study and teaching   2. History —
    Computer-assisted instruction
    I. Martin, Allan   II. Smart, Lez   III. Yeomans, David
    907

    ISBN 90-5702-024-6 (Softcover)

Contents

List of Figures   ix

List of Tables   xi

Foreword   xiii

Notes on Contributors   xv

Introduction   Perspectives on Teaching History with
               Information Technology
               Allan Martin   1

PART I   THE HISTORY CURRICULUM AND IT
           Introduction to Part 1   9

Chapter 1   The Future of the Survey Course in
            American History
            James Schick   13

Chapter 2   Information Technology in the Curriculum
            in the UK: Past, Present and Future
            Alaric Dickinson   29

Chapter 3   History and Computing:
            The Example of Luxembourg
            Jean-Paul Lehners   37

Chapter 4   The Use of Computers in Portuguese
            History Curricula
            Maria da Conceição Canavilhas   45

Chapter 5   Computing in French Secondary Schools
            Daniel Letouzey   57

Chapter 6   The Use of IT in the Danish History
            Curriculum
            Sten Larsen and Lars Bluhme   63

Chapter 7   IT and History: A Whole School Approach
            Wayne Birks   69

Chapter 8   History and Computing with Sixth Formers
              Jane Jenkins   75

Chapter 9   A Longitudinal Study of the Provision of
              Information Technology in Ten Schools:
              Implications for Computers in the History
              Classroom
              David Yeomans   83

**PART II   THE PRACTICE OF TEACHING AND
            LEARNING**
            Introduction to Part II   95

Chapter 10   The History Teacher and the Computer:
              A Case Study from The Netherlands
              *A.C.M. Peek, W. Veen, I.V.D. Neut and
              P. Spoon*   97

Chapter 11   Teaching Strategy and the Management
              of IT in the History Classroom
              Isobel Jenkins   105

Chapter 12   Progression in Children's Thinking and
              Understanding in History
              Alaric Dickinson   109

Chapter 13   Sturt and Pericles: Two Computer-Based
              Inquiry Units
              Lee Wright   127

Chapter 14   The Hobbs of Havant:
              Local History Brought to Life
              Nicola Gosling   133

Chapter 15   Spanish Armada: The Classroom Use
              of a Database
              David Martin   139

Chapter 16   Facilitate and Enhance
              Lez Smart   147

Chapter 17   Initial Teaching Education and Student
              Understanding of IT in the History
              Classroom
              Graeme Easdown   155

PART III   TECHNOLOGIES FOR LEARNING
Introduction to Part III   163

Chapter 18   History CAL at a Turning Point:
A Quantum Leap Ahead? New Horizons for
History Teaching in the Nineties
Marie-Elise Bitter-Rijpkema   167

Chapter 19   Canton, New York: An Interactive Computer
Project for the History Classroom
*Cornel J. Reinhart, Michael O. Sedore and
Isamu Ochiai*   175

Chapter 20   Recycling History:
A CD-ROM Project on the Cheap
Robin McLachlan and John Messing   179

Chapter 21   Moving House: A Computer Package
Analysing Migration within a 19th Century
Urban Area: Glasgow
Peter Hillis   191

Chapter 22   A Comparison of Three Computer-Assisted
Case Studies in Historical Decision-Making
Yta Beetsma   203

Chapter 23   Computer-Based Modelling in School History
Mary Webb   211

Chapter 24   HiDES in the Sixth Form: Exemplars from
the HiDES Project, 1990
Frank Colson and Neil Thompson   219

Chapter 25   The Sygap Package: Its Application in
the Practice and Teaching of Historical
Demography
Alain Bideau and Guy Brunet   225

Chapter 26   IT, ET and Beyond: Rethinking How
Allan Martin   233

Bibliography   243

Index   249

List of Figures

1	History's Stakeholders	2
2	The IT Threshold	6
6.1	Recommended Weekly Distribution of Lessons	64
6.2	Language Line: Number of Lessons per Week per Subject	65
7.1	History and Technology Attainment Target Comparison	71
12.1	Causal Relations: An Additive Response by a Year 6 Pupil	112
12.2	Causal Relations: A Narrativizing Response by a Year 9 Pupil	113
12.3	Causal Relations: An Analytical Response by a Year 7 Pupil	114
12.4	Causal Relations and Causal Structure: Schematic Provisional Model	115
12.5	Causal Relations: Response from a Teacher (1)	116
12.6	Causal Relations: Response from a Teacher (2)	117
12.7	Causal Relations: Response from a Teacher (3)	118
12.8	Causal Relations: Response from a Teacher (4)	119
12.9	Causal Relations: Response from a Teacher (5)	120
12.10	Causal Relations: Response from a Teacher (6)	121
12.11	Causal Relations: Response from a Teacher (7)	122
12.12	Causal Relations: Response from a Teacher (8)	123
12.13	Causal Relations: Response from a Teacher (9)	124
12.14	Causal Relations: Response from a Teacher (10)	125
15.1	Spanish Flagship: San Martin	140
15.2	Tokenised Fields	140
15.3	English Flagship: Ark	141
15.4	Venn Diagram Comparing Tonnage and Fate	142
15.5	Venn Diagram to Compare Frontline Ships and Fate	143
15.6	Bar Graph Showing Ports of Return	143
15.7	Pie Chart Showing Fate of Missing Ships	144
16.1	Key Questions and Activities	150
20.1	Organisation of the Gallipoli Stacks	181
20.2	Sample Page from the Diary Stack	183
20.3	Example from the Map Stack	184

20.4   Entry from the Dictionary of Slang Words
and Military Terms   185
20.5   Drawing from the Statistics Stack   186
20.6   Frame from a 1915 Film Clip in the Film Stack   187
20.7   Sample Card from the Biography Stack   188
21.1   *Moving House* Main Menu   195
21.2   Module: People and the Past   195
21.3   Primary Sources: Post-Office Directories   196
21.4   1 Park Terrace: Details of the Owner   196
21.5   No. 1 Park Terrace   197
21.6   Census Data: 1 Park Terrace (1)   197
21.7   Census Data: 1 Park Terrace (2)   198
21.8   The Baillie   198
21.9   Mr Peter Clouston   199
21.10   1 Monteith Row, 1832   200
21.11   1 Monteith Row, 1861   200
21.12   1 Monteith Row, 1931   201
22.1   Specific Structure of the Case Studies   204
22.2   Time Spent on the Case Studies and
Number of Sessions and Schools   207
23.1   Modus – The Integrated Modelling System   211
23.2   The 'Expert Builder' Program   214
23.3   The Model of the Battle of Hastings   216
26.1   Technological Revolutions in History   234

List of Tables

2.1   IT in Primary Schools in England – Summary   30
2.2   IT in Secondary Schools in England – Summary   30
2.3   Use of Software in Primary and Secondary Schools in England: All Subjects   31
2.4   Areas of the Curriculum where IT is Used   32
2.5   Use of Computers in Teaching Periods   32
2.6   Percentage of Secondary Schools/Departments Reporting Contribution of IT to Teaching and Learning   33
2.7   Percentage of Staff Shown at their Highest Level of Training in the Use of IT   34
9.1   IT Provision in the Ten Schools in Years 10 and 11 in 1985/86 and 1991/92   87
9.2   IT Co-ordinators in the Ten Schools   89

Foreword

At its heart, the computer deals with starkly clear distinctions in a completely unambiguous fashion. Either a bit of information is a zero or a one, a plus or a minus, a yes or a no, a truth or a falsity. Computers offer no room for degrees of difference, for shades of distinction, for uncertainty.

The heart of history as disciplined inquiry is a very different thing. As Allan Nevins taught us, history is interpretation, to be written by each generation as it struggles to understand itself in the light of its past. Historians don't focus on 'yes or no' but on 'why'. Interpretations are not right or wrong but are more or less valid, their validity to be judged by the amount and quality of data that can be marshaled in their support.

What then might be the role of the computer, and the information technology it supports, in improving history education? I find the answer both ironic and exciting. There is certainly some irony in the notion that computers, with their 'binary epistemology', are seen by the authors in this volume as having the potential for moving history teaching away from an emphasis on telling students what happened as fact and toward engaging students in thought that is interpretative, tentative and concerned with shades of meaning.

I also find the prospect of applying information technology to history education exciting, because I think the authors in this volume are on to something! At least until the last few years, a characteristic of schooling in general, and history education in particular, has been that it occurs in an information-impoverished environment. Of all the information pertinent to a historical issue, a very small percentage has typically been available to students. Thus, for economy's sake, the few sources of information that were available, primarily text books and teachers' lectures, were designed to deliver conclusions which had been developed by others and which were generally perceived as factual by students.

Beyond their dependence on binary data, computers have another key characteristic, their speed. They can process their zeros and ones VERY fast, and, as speed increases, so does the volume of information that those zeros and ones represent to the user. With its increase in information volume, information technology thus offers the potential for making schooling environments information-rich, and it is this potential that the authors in this volume are exploring. Rather than yield to an old epistemology of 'if-not-right-then-wrong, if-not-true-then-false' they are striving to engage history students in the building and judging of interpretations, and that building and judging is supported by information made accessible and plentiful by computer technology. The students' task is transformed from recalling as fact what others have determined to be historical truth, to understanding historical 'truth' as interpretation which is created with and must stand or fall on the foundation of its supporting information.

How might students be engaged in such a task? How might information technology be bent to the support of their 'doing' history? Will the broad base of history teachers be willing to abandon their role of telling students what happened in favor of accepting a vision of history as dynamic, interpretative and information-based? The authors in this volume do not present answers to such questions. Rather, they offer a variety of cases of struggles with questions such as these, and in the offering they endow their readers with experience, with insights and with examples that inspire yet further development and exploration. As such, this volume is a relatively early step in what must surely prove to be a long and complicated journey, but one that holds considerable potential for reforming and improving the teaching of history in the schools.

Willis D. Copeland, Professor and Chair
Department of Education
University of California, Santa Barbara

Notes on Contributors

Yta Beetsma has been a courseware designer at the University of Groningen since 1982. She is currently working on projects in biology, statistics and psychology.

Alain Bideau is a doctor of history at the Centre Pierre Léon at the Université Lumière in Lyon, where his research is focused on historical demography and population genetics.

Wayne Birks is head of the history department at Cheslyn Hay High School, in the English Midlands.

Marie-Elise Bitter-Rijpkema is a researcher and project manager in the Educational Expertise Centre (OTEC) of the Dutch Open University. Her expertise is in educational technology, educational consultancy and research.

Lars Bluhme works at the Ministry of Education in Copenhagen, Denmark, in the Department for Upper Secondary Education.

Guy Brunet is doctor of history and doctor of science at the Institute Européen des Genomutations at the Université Lumière in Lyon, where his research is focused on historical demography and population genetics.

Maria da Conceição Canavilhas has been a history teacher and now works at the Institute for Multimedia Communication at the Open University of Portugal, based in Lisbon.

Frank Colson is director of the Digital Libraries Research Centre at the University of Southampton. He has been working with and developing HiDES packages since 1987 when prototypes were built.

Alaric Dickinson is senior lecturer with responsibility for history education at the Institute of Education, University of London. He is currently co-director of the CHATA (Concepts of History and Teaching Approaches for children aged 7–13) Project, and is one of the editors of the *International Yearbook of History Education*.

Graeme Easdown is a tutor in history education in the Department of Educational Studies at the University of Oxford. He has been involved in a number of research projects focused on the development of student teachers' understanding and use of IT in the history classroom.

Nicola Gosling has recently retired as advisory teacher for resources in history to the county of Hampshire. As such she helped to increase awareness of the contribution IT can make to the teaching and learning of history and to support classroom colleagues.

Peter Hillis taught history in several Scottish schools. He is now head of history and social studies education at the Jordanhill Campus of the University of Strathclyde.

Isobel Jenkins is lecturer in education at the University of Leeds. She has been head of Humanities in a secondary school and an advisory teacher for IT, has worked on national projects applying IT to history teaching and has produced software for classroom use.

Jane Jenkins is head of history and flexible learning co-ordinator at Itchen College, Southampton. She has worked for some time with the HiDES team.

Sten Larsen works at the Ministry of Education, in Copenhagen, Denmark, in the Department for Primary and Lower Secondary Education.

Jean-Paul Lehners has lectured in history at the Universities of Trier and Saarbrücken, and is now professor of history at the Centre Universitaire de Luxembourg; he also teaches at the Lycée Michel-Rodange, Luxembourg.

Daniel Letouzey is a teacher of history at the Lycée de Vire (Calvados), and in charge of training history teachers in Southern Normandy.

Robin McLachlan is a senior lecturer in history at the Bathurst campus of Charles Sturt University, Australia. His main interests in history education are the application of information technology and the making of historical information more accessible to the public.

Allan Martin has taught history in schools and sociology and IT in higher education, as well as training IT teachers. He is now academic co-ordinator in the Office of Information Technology at the University of Glasgow. He is education editor of *History and Computing*.

David Martin is adviser team leader for humanities in Dorset Education Professional Development Services. He has been involved in a series of research projects and publications exploring how IT can support good history teaching for pupils in the post-11 age range.

John Messing is a senior lecturer in information technology at the Wagga Wagga campus of Charles Sturt University, Australia. He has been involved in computer education for over a decade, focusing on multimedia in recent years.

Isamu Ochiai is presently completing his undergraduate degree at Notre Dame University in South Bend, Indiana.

A.C.M. Peek is a teacher trainer at IVLOS, Institute of Education of the University of Utrecht. He has been involved in projects involving research and development of IT in secondary education, and has been editor of *KLEIO*, the national magazine for history teachers.

Cornel J. Reinhart has taught history in universities, and is now director of the University Without Walls programme at Skidmore College in Saratoga Springs, New York, where he is developing computer based distance learning.

James Schick is professor of history at Pittsburg State University, Pittsburg, Kansas. He is also editor of *History Microcomputer Review*.

Michael O. Sedore is director of instructional technology at St. Lawrence University, New York, where he specialises in developing computer-related pedagogies.

Lez Smart is senior lecturer in primary education at Roehampton Institute, London, having been a primary school teacher. He is currently investigating the impact of CD-ROM in the teaching of history with young children.

Mary Webb taught in secondary and middle schools before moving to the Advisory Unit for Microtechnology in Education in 1987. She was co-ordinator of the Modus Project from 1990 to 1994 and is now teaching in a primary school as well as continuing her research into computer based modelling.

Lee Wright is a teacher of history at the Wagga Wagga Technology High School in rural New South Wales, Australia. He works with pupils aged 7–12. He is involved in exploring how IT can contribute to the storing of and access to local historical information.

David Yeomans has taught in schools in Zambia and England, and is now senior research fellow at the School of Education of the University of Leeds, where he has been involved in a number of major research projects.

Introduction

The study of history is memorable. The vast majority of adults can remember the history lessons they attended when they were at school, either because they were interesting, or because they were not. History lessons are remembered, even when they are boring. Is there then an expectation that history should be interesting, that makes the boredom more blameworthy than if it characterised a chemistry lesson, that makes the teacher more culpable for the failure to excite? Indeed, the excitement of history is ingrained in popular culture, and underlined again and again in films, novels, biographies, TV documentaries and magazines. With all this going for their subject, one might expect that history teachers would have an easy time peddling their wares. And yet, all too often, pupils still find history lessons tedious and uninspiring.

This volume deals with the contribution which information technology (usually abbreviated to IT) can make to ensuring that the experience of history in school can be a fulfilling and an exciting one. However, the computer does not descend into a vacuum; it arrives into a world already well-peopled, and well-established in its habits and its daily round. To adopt the new because it is new is the worst of reasons, and history teachers often regard themselves as well-armoured against the lances of fashion. Yet to reject the new because it is new may also be unwise, for the difference that is worthwhile may be overlooked. In this volume we look at the difference which IT can make to the teaching of history. Although most of the authors are persuaded that IT has indeed something valuable to offer teaching and learning in history, this is not a volume by uncritical enthusiasts. The message which emerges is that IT is indeed an enhancing addition to the teacher's armoury and the student's toolkit, but that its adoption may not be easy, and its success cannot be taken for granted.

History's Stakeholders

History is a peculiarly public subject for study, in a way in which many other academic subjects are not. Most of the population of the advanced Western countries will at some point in their lives take an interest in history. Many will have studied it at school, and a few of these will later take an academic course in the subject. More will take daytime, weekend or evening classes in historical subjects as a leisure interest. Much greater numbers will involve themselves in history in less systematic ways; looking at historical sites; visiting "heritage centres" where history may be offered as reconstruction and marketing opportunity; or by reading historical novels or non-fiction. Even more will watch historical subjects presented through film, either at the cinema or on television; the latter is probably the most powerful exposure to history that most of the population will have. We will pass over the quality of some of that exposure.

History thus attracts many stakeholders (see Figure 1). The interests of those groups in studying or propagating history will vary, and there will be considerable variations within them, about how history should be studied, about the deductions

1

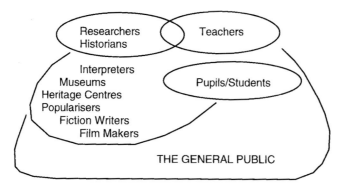

Figure 1   History's Stakeholders

to be made, about the segments to be selected for presentation, and about how they should be presented. This makes for a lively public interest in historical matters, but it also means that the academic historians are a small minority amongst those who take part in the debate.

History is not only widely available to the population, it is also publicly meaningful in a way that other subjects are not. Historical images are powerful reflectors of identities. Thus, in Scotland the recent films *Rob Roy* and especially *Braveheart* have found a widespread resonance amongst a population for most of whom an essential element of their identity as Scots is the resistance to and defeat of an imperialistic southern neighbour. The political potency of historical images makes them of profound interest to those who would determine how we think and act. Thus the setting out of the National Curriculum for History for England became a politicised process unlike that for any of the other National Curriculum subjects.

The implication is that, in considering how information technology can enhance the teaching of history, we are dealing with topics and activities in which most of the population may have an interest, and which may attract meaning and interpretation far beyond what we intend. Through the work of teachers, perceptions of history can be influenced, and IT can enhance that influence, and make public interaction with history significantly more powerful. For us this is both a challenge and an opportunity. It is a challenge because it has to be handled responsibly, so that history is not misread or misused. It is an opportunity because it can help to nurture an interest in history, a curiosity about the past and its relevance to the present and the future, that can make better citizens and better people.

Dynamics of Change

Over the last twenty years the teaching of history has undergone major changes, and the computer has been employed very much on the side of those changes, by teachers who are largely themselves in favour of "new" approaches to history. The computer has been itself an agent in the process of innovation, in stimulating the development of new assumptions about how history is learned and about how history is done.

The three main carriers of innovation have been changes in historical methods, teaching methods, and technology, and we should recognise that each has some influence on the other. Developments in historical method, and in teaching methods are crucial. But the technology itself has also been of some significance, in making possible activities which were once regarded as almost impossible. The best example of this is the interrogation of large databases, which has enabled historians to expect rapid answers to questions which would twenty years previously have been the work of weeks or months. This is not to say that the answers are necessarily conclusive, only that the debate over their significance is carried out in an arena where more evidence is available. The activities of the historians have influenced those of the teachers, particularly in the light of the changing emphasis in teaching towards doing the sorts of things that historians do as well as learning about what the historians have found. Thus, with the availability of relatively cheap desktop computers at the beginning of the 1980s pupils in schools could follow the historians in using IT to interrogate databases.

The difficulty with innovation is always that of moving it beyond the circle of the innovators. In this respect, as the papers in this volume demonstrate, we have moved forward in four key areas: developing materials, training teachers, publishing case studies of usage, and persuading teachers to take IT on board. There is now a large amount of material, including some of very high quality, which enables IT to be used effectively in teaching history. Technical advances, in for instance the use of sound and video stored on CD, are being imaginatively taken on board. Teacher educators are becoming more aware of the importance of IT and are drawing it into courses of tuition for would-be history teachers. There are now a good number of reported case-studies of how teachers use IT in the classroom, which can be used to demonstrate that it does work, and that it does not need to be complicated or technical. And the process of persuading teachers themselves to adopt IT into their practices goes on. We are now aware that persuasion does not stem from an official instruction, or from a mass-meeting at which they are harangued by an enthusiast, but from the gradual awareness of what others are doing, and the taking of simple and hesitant steps, which, if successful, will be repeated.

Innovation is a slow process. In the heady days of the late sixties and the seventies, and again in the eighties with the arrival of the microcomputer, and again in the nineties with CD-ROM and multimedia, it was easy to assume that everything will would change overnight, that the blind must see, and walk away rejoicing. History should teach us that this is not what people are like, perhaps especially teachers of history, since one of the great gifts of history is to give us a healthy scepticism for plans to change the world. But the dynamic is there, the innovative process is moving forward, and it seems that teachers of history are gradually being convinced that IT can make their teaching better.

The Curriculum

Enough evidence is beginning to become available from a number of countries to enable some perspective to be gained on IT adoption into school history curricula. From this evidence emerges a considerable overlap in the issues seen as important.

The first, and fundamental, issue is that of identifying the place and function of IT input into history curricula; this implies considering both the IT applications or programs and the teaching methods and classroom situations which will enable their effectiveness to be maximised, in the context of existent curricular structures. A process of focusing was evident in the UK, in which initial wide-ranging surveys of the possible (Blow and Dickinson, 1986), accompanied by enthusiastic anecdotal accounts of particular applications (e.g. those in Wilkes, 1985) gave way, after a period of experiment, to the identification of relevant applications placed precisely into the context of a national curriculum for England and Wales (Martin, 1992), and the exploration of the curricular relevance and pedagogical implications of particular applications or genres (e.g. Blow, 1989; Bennett, 1990; Martin, 1993). This process was complicated by the fact that during this period the curriculum itself was being restructured. The restructuring process provided an opportunity for IT input to be offered to the curriculum developers (HABET, 1991), opportunities which similarly arose in Portugal, Luxembourg and the Netherlands (see, respectively, the chapters by Canavilhas and Lehners in this volume, and Bitter, 1990). Despite detailed proposals being submitted incorporating specific uses of IT in History classrooms, only the most generalised statements regarding IT were adopted into new curricula; nevertheless these statements were positive, and endorsed the view of IT as an essential tool for the study of history.

It is possible to see two different curricular strategies in the adoption of IT into school history teaching. What we might call the "enhancement" strategy asks how history is being taught (including ongoing changes in this process) and seeks to enhance this process using IT. This was the approach adopted in the UK. A more cautious "percolation" strategy seeks to identify the ways in which IT is used by professional historians, introduce these at the upper levels of the school system, and see how far it is appropriate to let them permeate downwards; Cerman (1990) describes this process in Austria, and the experience recounted by Lehners in Luxembourg is not dissimilar. The two views are of course not exclusive: changes in the history curriculum in the UK were being powerfully influenced by the view that activities undertaken by pupils in history classrooms should more closely resemble those undertaken by historians; and the "British experience" of the use of IT in the context of the "New History" in schools offers an important model to be considered in the course of policy formulation — thus Eder (1989) bases much of his discussion of the implications of IT for the teaching of history in Austria on British developments.

Curricular intentions can however only be realised in the context of the resources provided, either from schools' own capabilities or through support and intervention by local, regional or national government. It is clear that support from national governments was often very limited in scale, and in no cases adequate to meet the level of provision considered necessary by both classroom teachers and those involved in teacher education and in materials development.

In several countries specific programmes were implemented to develop IT in schools and to identify appropriate applications and develop new software. Materials development has followed two courses: first, the identification and provision of software which already exists and can be effectively used in history teaching and second, the identification of areas in which new software needs to be developed. The first strategy formed a major feature of work carried out under the Portuguese MINERVA programme, through which a bundle of generic software was supplied free to all participating schools, as the basic resources for classroom IT work — this provided an effective basis for the production of easily exchangeable additional resources in the form of data files. The second was practised by MEP in England and Wales, and generated a very large amount of software, of very variable quality, and, in a more targeted manner by the Dutch government's INSP and NIVO projects. Despite the rows of zeroes at the end of the global sums however, the funding available to individual participating units developing history materials turn out to be very small, and much history IT material has been developed on a very low cost basis. The Australian Biographical Dictionary Database serves as a good example of a major classroom resource generated at, perforce, minimum cost (McLachlan, 1990). Hardware provision is also a key constraint on what can be done in the classroom, and one of the strands in IT boosting programmes has always been hardware standardisation. Unfortunately, hardware provision issues have sometimes been distorted by political decisions to tie them to economic policies, usually by insisting , as in France (Wolff, 1990; Letouzey in this volume) and the Netherlands, that subsidised hardware must be domestically produced. The most notorious case here must be that of the UK, where a policy of supporting domestic computer builders resulted in the majority of UK schools becoming tied to computers incompatible not only with the rest of British society, but with the rest of the world.

Resource provision will be ineffective in achieving penetration of IT usage unless it is linked to the development of teacher competence and confidence in choosing and using IT applications in history. The scale of training needs, in all countries which have been reported on, is enormous. Even in the UK, where the earliest and possibly most well-funded IT boosting programme was implemented, penetration of IT into history classrooms has been limited (see the chapter by Dickinson in Part I of this volume). Wolff indicates that in France "there was virtually no articulation between equipment and training and much of the equipment remained unused simply because staff were not trained to use it" (Wolff, 1990:37). There is plenty of evidence that teachers involved in funded projects have made great strides in using IT in the classroom and in developing materials for others to use (e.g. Wills, 1990; Canavilhas in this volume), but there remains a problem of stimulating usage beyond projects which provide resources and training and perhaps also select only the more dynamic and innovation-friendly teachers to work with.

There is plenty of evidence that teachers need first of all to be convinced that IT can enhance their history teaching; then they require sufficient training in the operation of relevant software and the most appropriate ways in which to employ it in the classroom, so that the intense caution which many teachers of the humanities feel towards technological developments can be overcome. Ideally, a level of competence in the operation of hardware and software is required which will enable teachers to focus on their teaching goals rather than IT skills. The admittedly small-scale study by Peek *et al.* in this volume illustrates in detail the effort and time required, in terms of hardware and software provision, and training in usage and in classroom implementation.

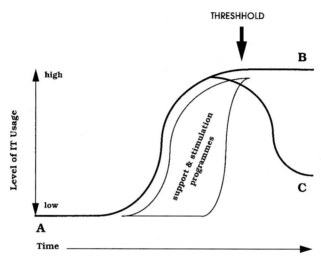

Figure 2   The IT Threshhold

Achieving Transparency

It will be clear from the preceding discussion that government — local, regional or national — has an important role to play in stimulating and supporting the adoption of IT into school curricula, and that different strategies may have different results. In no case has a completely successful strategy been identified for stimulating IT use in history, and even in those countries where the process is now beyond the inception stage, the depressing fact emerges that there is still a very great distance to go before the majority of history teachers use IT confidently and appropriately. There are real dangers that IT usage across the curriculum will fail to achieve that threshhold beyond which heavy stimulus and support from government is no longer necessary, or that it may achieve the threshhold and then fall away. This has implications for the type of stimulus and support which is required and we need more knowledge of what types and forms of support are effective in different national and school contexts in achieving the IT threshhold and in ensuring that IT use is sustained once the stimulus and support is withdrawn. Getting from A to B (see Figure 2) rather than from A to C represents a massive challenge. There is clearly a need to get over the crucial threshhold into the unsupported and confident use of IT in history; but how long this will take (assuming that at some point it will happen) is at present unclear.

Varieties of Experience

Identifying some of the similarities of experience that have emerged should not blind us to the great variety of what is being achieved. The chapters in this book demonstrate just something of what the range of the possible can include.

The variety of possibilities extends through the levels of the educational system. In primary schools history may be submerged within integrated social studies or "topic" activities, and a problem which arises before considering IT may well be the ensuring that teachers who have little or no academic training in history appreciate the sorts of activities which are considered historically worthwhile. The training which this involves offers a good opportunity to deal with the way in which IT can enable those activities. The integrated form of much primary school work has a beneficial side, in that more time may be spent on a historical topic, and relevant connections may be made with geographical, economic, cultural and other approaches and materials. Smart (1995) describes some of the possibilities for primary history activities which can be supported by IT, and the continuity with secondary school activities considered in several of the chapters in this book is clear.

A difficulty however which many primary schools face is the lack of hardware and of IT-confident staff, a problem exacerbated by the lack of specialist IT personnel in primary schools. Specialist support in secondary schools is identified (e.g. by Yeomans, 1995 and Martin, 1995) as a major factor in assisting the confident use of IT across the curriculum. Thus, in the UK at least, the IT experience which pupils will gain, whilst it is variable in secondary schools, will be dramatically variable in primary schools with, in many primary schools, none at all. IT learning often has to begin again in the secondary school.

A minority of the chapters in this book touch upon the use of IT in history in higher education, where the computer is now well-established as a tool of historical research, and is increasingly being used in the course of teaching. Specialist historical or humanities computing courses are being established, whilst computer-facilitated investigative activity is being incorporated into the usual topic or period based history courses (Spaeth, 1996, gives a good overview of current activities; Davis *et al.* 1993, is a collection papers on Historical Computing Courses). Textbooks on historical computing have recently become available (Mawdsley & Munck, 1993; Greenstein, 1994) giving detailed accounts of activities which are now possible. Schick (1990) offered a survey of the sorts of activities undertaken in the 1980s, and it is clear that now, as one might expect, the range is greater, that the facilities are more powerful, and that we have moved away from a need to be versed in technical aspects such as computer programming.

As historians, of course, we should expect things to change. Change is, after all, our business. Whilst historical researchers seek more powerful and more subtle tools to carry out the mechanisable parts of their investigations, history teachers seek tools which, for their own students, at whatever level, will give a flavour of those investigations, as well as a feel for the past, and will enable students of whatever age to think about and to enjoy their history.

Part I

The History Curriculum and IT

The first part of this volume focuses upon the impact of IT upon the history curriculum. It opens with a powerful statement of the possible from Jim Schick. Schick begins by speculating on the characteristics of the IT-using history course in higher education. He then goes on to outline the whole range of resources which just one facility — the compact disk — will enable the history student to have at his/her disposal for the study of just one course. The example serves to emphasise that IT is more than "yet another gadget" being pressed upon the teacher and the student. The power of the medium is able to astonish again and again. Schick also reminds us — what we should never forget — that the study of history is absorbing, fascinating and enjoyable, and that a big part of the reason we are involved with history is that we like it. If using IT can make it more absorbing, more fascinating and more enjoyable, so much the better.

In chapters 2 to 6 the curricular significance of IT in five different countries is considered. The UK was probably the first country to address the role of IT in schools, and Alaric Dickinson considers the fate of IT in history teaching in England and Wales in the period 1985–90. He provides evidence of the substantial increase in hardware; yet there is no evidence of a corresponding increease in the use of computers in history classrooms or in teachers' confidence in their use of IT. Terry Haydn (1996) has shown recently that even those statistics seeming to show a high level of usage can be very misleading. It seems that in order to convince many more teachers that IT can make a substantial contribution to the teaching and learning of history there needs to be much more provided than just initial awareness training for teachers, and much more rigorous and public evaluation of the value of IT in history classrooms. The approach adopted in Luxembourg, outlined by Jean-Paul Lehners, is more tentative than that in the UK, and is focused on particular pieces of software which it was felt would be of particular use in the history classroom, and would help to persuade both teachers and students of the value of IT. Once again, the need to bring both teachers and pupils along with innovative practice is emphasised.

The necessity of working with and through the average teacher in the classroom (as opposed to the computer enthusiast) is directly addressed by Conceição Canavilhas in her exposition of the way in which IT usage within the curriculum can be nurtured and developed. Mass programmes of innovation are notoriously unsuccessful: short-term and superficial adoptions peter out as soon as the boosting support is removed. This chapter demonstrates the success of the alternative strategy: working on a long-term basis alongside teachers until they are confident in their own right. It may take longer, but it has the advantage of working. Canavilhas also brings out the strategies available in software choice. Whilst other programmes chose to develop or adopt history-specific software, the approach taken in her work was to make use of generic software tools, which could be turned to good account across the whole curriculum. This is not to suggest that this is a more successful approach; only that both approaches have viability and can be used to achieve history teachers' goals.

The chapters by Daniel Letouzey and by Sten Larsen and Lars Bluhme discussing computing in history in French and Danish schools respectively serve to indicate that whilst each country has its own approach, the elements and the choices involved in each approach are common. Letouzey notes the skewing of policy through political strategies, the notion that teachers will have the time and knowledge to write educationally successful computer programs, the desire to boost domestic computer products, the variability in quality of software, the constant over-expectation. Often the same mistakes are made, the same lessons learned. In identifying data handling and simulation as elements for particular emphasis, Larsen and Bluhme are consistent with colleagues internationally in considering first the facility which most historians and history teachers see as the most useful IT technique to be applied in history teaching, and then that which they would consider the most contentious.

Wayne Birks and David Yeomans focus upon characteristics of the school itself, and show how important is the organisational and resource context in enabling the adoption of innovation. Birks considers how the computer-using history teacher can be made much more effective in the context of an IT-using culture within the school. This culture is rooted within an organisational strategy which incorporates a clear impression both of how IT will be developed and supported across the whole curriculum, and of the contribution which each subject area, including history, can make to this. In face of an organisational culture which is negative, or even merely indifferent, to the role of IT in learning, the lone enthusiast, whether in history or any other department will achieve only very limited success. Yeomans opens up in detail the institutional contexts within which history teachers are being encouraged to adopt IT into their classroom practice. Resourcing and support are factors of crucial significance in allowing IT to be diffused across the curriculum, and without adequate resourcing and specialist support, the actions and achievements of individual departments are restricted in effectiveness. In the conclusion that the advances gained have been disappointing compared with the predictions made, there are echoes of Alaric Dickinson's chapter in this volume. Evidence from various sources suggests that there is still a good way to go before the IT-using culture is a common feature of the school.

The theme of culture is taken in a different direction by Jane Jenkins. Developing IT usage within history involves constructing an understanding on the part of teachers and pupils of the role of IT applications within a culture of history, that set of assumptions and aspirations, questions and issues, and mode of discourse, which are uniquely associated with the study of history. By the time they have reached the upper part of the secondary school, pupils have begun to enter the world of the discourse of historical inquiry. A goal of the HiDES work has been to permit worthwhile interaction with the computer to be carried out in the language and on the terms of serious historical discourse. To such aspirations, the proper response must be cautious but open-ended: it is not difficult to write computer programs which can engage in a superficially believable conversation. The computer can in no sense "be" a real teacher of history; but it can be programmed to draw the student through the process of historical inquiry, and oblige him/her to make use of the language of historical discourse. The inquiry and the language can be reinforced, made more meaningful and taken forward in face to face interaction with a teacher in the classroom. Whilst the computer may be a powerful facilitator, we return again to the crucial role of the teacher.

Chapter 1

The Future of the Survey Course in American History

James Schick

Introduction

As one who has spent many hours worshipping history in the British Library and the British Museum, I always welcome the opportunity to mingle with the tourists gawking at the Rosetta Stone or Egyptian depictions of the Afterlife or to sit under that magnificent dome reading an 18th-century tract dealing with the American Revolution. For a teacher of history, even a teacher of United States' history, there is much from which to profit, for much of what we do as teachers is teasing evidence from unlikely sources or trying to understand some new thing from looking at some old thing.

The Assyrian reliefs are one of my special places in that magnificent collection. They are inviting of themselves, of course, but as I looked at these objects with my son — then 12, now 24 — we tried to find as many insights about the people who made these monuments as we could. We could see a state and a faith triumphant, how to bring humans and animals and mythical beings to life in such subtle ways, how to conduct siege warfare and what was new in military technology, how to confirm Biblical history and see events as they might have happened, how an artist conveyed an interpretation of the past through size and detail, what victory and defeat meant in cold stone (sometimes shown by a subsequent ruler who had the face of a rival chipped away to make him a non-person), what the absence of women in these reliefs might tell us about the society, what hubris means, how governments use public art for self-inflation and propaganda, how the persistence of memory and the very human attempt to shape the future's understanding of the past can be seen from the distance of time and cultural change, and how governments today pursue similar goals. All these are to be found there. These reliefs demand — invoke — a teacher.

In fact, they stand in relation to us in the same way history stands in relation to the student: while scholarship can tell us something about the lives of the people who carved and looked upon these reliefs, there are many questions we can ask and there is more we can find on our own if we but look. Much of what I am about in teaching revolves around helping others find out for themselves. Being a midwife, if you will, to knowledge, rather than its father. Someone with experience to serve as guide, interlocutor, mentor, Boswell, Socratic gadfly, Diogenes, collaborator, conscience, and best friend who will listen to one's silly notions and sound ideas and say what needs to be said even if it might hurt. Midwife seems about right as a metaphor to sum up all of these guises the teacher must assume. Someone who will never forget that the important person here is the student and the reason everyone is here gathered is to attend the student's birth of knowledge.

My remarks concern the survey course in American history, the basic undergraduate course taken by history majors and non-majors in the United States, most often together and with a significant majority of the latter in most colleges. My time frame is 2006 or ten years from now. Let me begin by listing my assumptions about trends influential in the next decade.

Part I

First, that some form of the compact disk (CD-ROM, CD-I, etc.) will be the preferred medium for publication, and such works will contain text, still and motion images, and sound, when appropriate. Present disks hold about 275,000 pages of text, so space will be available for complete citations, perhaps whole books or chapters, articles, and other relevant data. 'Editions' of articles and books will change frequently to update research, respond to critics, or add new topics; instead of 'second edition', it will be 'edition 2.0924.04' to designate the month, day, and year of the change. It will become common, after the fashion of *Who Built America?*, to publish both a printed edition and an expanded CD version.

Second, that the teacher's role will shift away from an emphasis on lecture. Rather than serving as the fact provider, I think college history teachers will work with students to find facts, analyze facts, and relate facts across a spectrum of time and place. Teachers will come to rely on computer-based tutors to build basic competency and on videotape and computerized tutorials to tell the story of the past. These computer assistants may well be created by the teacher by means of authoring programs that rely on the principles of cognitive theory. Videotape histories will be available in hour-long surveys and shorter, more focused modules. (I assume that teachers will continue to do that which they do best. If the professor in question delivers powerful lectures, then it would be criminal not to do so. If the professor, instead, orchestrates discussions in the manner of a symphony conductor, then by all means I would want this teacher to emphasize that talent. I am thinking here of the rest of us who may do many things well, but not spectacularly so.) Class time will primarily involve multi-media mini-lectures (10–20 minutes), videotapes, discussion, Socratic dialogue, computer simulations, student presentations, and other mind-stretching activities. The search for meaning will be a key part of what we do.

Third, that teachers will emphasize skills transference at all levels. Building on the success of 'writing across the curriculum' and similar activities, teachers will be asked to sharpen students' skills in thinking, communicating, and information processing. Bringing all the cognitive skills into play will become more important in education and relatively less effort will be devoted to short-term memory. Teachers will also attempt to address alternative ways of learning. If the purpose of college is to become educated, these skills are a key component of that enterprise. Of course familiarity with a broad range of fields and their insights is an important aspect of education, history certainly near or at the top. But because historians have remained relatively free of jargon and emphasize nuanced prose and careful think-ing, we have a major responsibility to undertake in the survey course, and I believe computers can play an important part in meeting this challenge effectively.

Fourth, that 'focus groups' will become common in teaching history. Based on the ability to tailor readings for individual needs, I think teaching survey courses may evolve into a multi-track smörgåsbord. For instance, while all students would be responsible for the basic information, such as that found in today's textbooks, they would also choose one or more topics for special emphasis. Those which come to mind are gender studies (both male and female), Africans in America, the Hispanic heritage, the core of English institutions and culture, Europe in America and America in Europe, the Asian connection, popular culture, the arts curri-culum (literature, music, theater, art), science and technology, historiography, and research methods. These tracks may be dictated by the student's major or simply by interest. In this way we will be able to serve students more effectively and pro-vide enrichment for all of them, and will make the survey course more stimulating and rewarding for the student and the professor as well.

Fifth, that most schools will divide this course into thirds from the present two parts. I think the breaks should occur at about 1789/1815/1828 and 1898/1914, so we have a 16–18th century course, a 19th-century course, and a 20th-century course. This will mean the teacher can dig more deeply into the past being cov-ered, demonstrate firsthand what it means to be a historian, and expect students to try their hands at it as well, all in an undergraduate survey course. Learning history takes time, time for reflection and time for reading more widely. While changing the time frame might simply allow the teacher to add more depth to the entire course and thus more closely resemble an upper-level period course, I would hope, instead, to provide both the sweep of the past and extensive looks at a few interesting topics, what is often called 'post-holing.'

Sixth, that custom-built readers drawing on articles from virtually any journal published in the world, book chapters, and newspapers and newsmagazines, along with images from photo archives, full-color artwork, and sound libraries, will be widely used for ancillary readers and for composing the basic textbook. Increasingly, I think these will be used in electronic form shown on large, high resolution desktop and laptop monitors, not on paper. This will mean the teacher can add and subtract readings at any time during the school term in response to recent discoveries or student interest in a particular subject, or to the focus groups I have mentioned above. It is possible today for an individual to order a music compact disk entirely made up of selections taken from a master list, a disk unlike that created for anyone else. It seems likely the same could be assembled for text documents.

Seventh, that history teachers will borrow the format of in-class student presen-tations from their colleagues in the Business School. These will be multi-media discourses on topics related to the student's interest area and will feature original research undertaken in conjunction with the class. It may be given wholly on the computer screen or simply feature computer-based segments. Shifting some of the responsibility for teaching to the students themselves will immeasurably aid their education. As teachers know, the most effective way to learn a subject is to have to teach it.

Eighth, that conflicting operating systems will have become a thing of the past as the big companies (if there are any big companies) compete in the area of enhancements and not in the world of DOS, Windows, Macintosh, UNIX, and the rest. The parts for Ford, Jaguar, Mazda, and BMW may not be interchangeable, but the same gasoline and oil works in all of them and they travel the same highways. If you buy a compact disk, it will work in any of the boxes. Manufacturers will compete by offering new whiz-bangs and peripherals to make one brand of computer preferable to another. In turn, this change in hardware will alter competition in software and make the decision to move from one brand to another relatively simple. Modular construction will facilitate software tailored specifically for an academic discipline or individual needs.

Ninth, that networking with colleagues will become as ubiquitous a resource for teachers as videotapes. Teachers will invite 'guests' into their classrooms regularly, whether from other parts of the campus or other parts of the world. Sometimes they will respond to student questions, at others to student presentations. Sometimes they will be part of a 'dig' for facts, at others will offer hypotheses to frame analysis, fruitful avenues for comparison across cultures or eras, and interpretations differing from those of the class or instructor. Students will 'publish' essays on undergraduate electronic journals, will critique the work of other students on campuses all over the globe, and will research in the libraries of the world without leaving the classroom. Students from different colleges will connect with a leading authority at a given time, and the historian can truly be in many places at the same time. Perhaps, like debate, we will have one or two questions to which history students will devote the year in research and writing, and then share the results (and even the research) via network. In many ways this will build new bonds between students and historians that could not have been developed before. Distance-learning techniques producing cooperative courses will be increasingly common. If, for example, historians from the University of Minnesota at Crookston, Pittsburg State in Kansas, and Texas A & M University at Kingsville, can schedule classes for the same hour (adjusted for time zones, of course), they could cooperatively teach a single course on American history, perhaps even with a comparative dimension, such as the history of the frontier, borderlands, slavery and servitude, and the like. These contacts by means of two-way television would also allow, via fax or network connections, written interaction as well as on-screen verbal interaction among professors and students. I see no reason why, in ten years' time, this will not be possible for historians within the United States, but costs may well be prohibitive for international hookups until the following decade or so. The interactive media highway now being promoted by the Clinton administration should have become a reality, a development which will facilitate both the concept of realtime, cross-distance contacts and the means by which to accomplish them.

Tenth, that LCD overhead projection devices will become more widely available as they become less expensive. Because even history departments will have daily access to these wonderful gadgets, a roomful of students will be able to participate in computer-based activities without requiring multiple monitors or multiple computers. For instance, composing a collaborative essay with an outliner or word processor will be readily do-able. If used with networked 'guests,' for example, the whole class could share the comments and propose responses. This type of dynamic blackboard will liven and sharpen class research and writing projects, can provide on-screen lecture notes that can be changed just before or even during the class period, and can give more flexibility than a laser-printed overhead transparency.

Eleventh, that the younger generation will have come of age in college class-rooms — on the teacher's side of the desk. Consider the cliché about young children knowing how to program the VCR and operate the new technology. For now these young people sit in front of us. In ten years they will have PhDs and occupy tenure-earning positions. Will administrators continue to deny advance-ment to teachers, particularly to computer-using teachers? I doubt it. In ten years those who have been in the first vanguard of this movement will have retired to the sidelines. This new generation of leaders, more comfortable with this techno-logy, will push the discipline beyond the reluctance which characterizes the present moment.

Twelfth, that the problems borne of 'inclusion' will be a thing of the past. Over the past several decades, from the time when 'history' meant the political and dip-lomatic history of white, Anglo-Saxon males, to today when African-Americans, women, social history, native American history, and other necessary additions have subtracted from the story of the past much that was valuable. Dictated by cost, publishers have decreed that textbooks will remain at about 400 pages, so everything brought in meant something left out. The CD textbook can include everything relevant to providing a thoughtful account of what happened and why.

Thirteenth, that the Mount Everest phenomenon ("because it was there") which has marked the last dozen years — remember the first IBM pc came out in 1981 — will continue unabated. So far potential and imagination have dominated this in-dustry. Witness the new givens of business: spreadsheets, faxes, scanners, multi-media presentations, and the word processor. If a bigger, faster computer chip can be made, it is. If there is a feature you need, someone will offer it. If someone dreams a new dream others share, it will sell; but if a product is too derivative, clunky, no corporate logo, no expensive advertising campaign will save it from failure. Listening to consumers, providing support for customers, these have become the watchwords of the computer world, and in few other industries. And as business goes, so goes education. In history, however, we seldom make this connection because other departments, business, psychology, economics, the sciences, even the social sciences, see the changes first. If we could but articulate our desires, we would have them fulfilled. This means that those with vision, those who write and speak about academic computing in history and those who use computers in the classroom, have a vital responsibility to carry this change forward. I believe it will happen and that every phase of the historian's labors, from researching to writing to teaching, will be transformed by computing far beyond that which is common today.

Before I go on to my specific proposals, I want to emphasize just how basic the computer is to these assumptions. Only the division of the survey into thirds does not depend upon the computer. I would anticipate, however, that computer use will increase as a result of professors having more time and fewer years to cover in the survey of American history. In short, I think the computer will be the key to a radical transformation of the basic survey course. Academic computing will become even more basic to what college teachers of history do than it is today. The concept of interactivity will effect a fundamental change in what history teachers do and how they do it.

Futurists have one failing above all others, and that is an insufficiency of daring. Rather than wild-eyed iconoclasts, most in fact turn out, upon examination, to be rather more conservative than far-seeing. So the future may well be strikingly different from the one I have outlined. These changes I have sketched will not be adopted uniformly, and some may not be accepted by a majority of college history teachers by 2006, but I believe in ten years they will have appeared on many campuses. It may be, however, that this will be a top-down revolution where we first witness these changes taking place in upper-level period courses, but that will only make them more likely to occur in the undergraduate survey.

Part II

With this as a background I now want to provide examples of the software I would like to have available for my use in teaching the undergraduate survey of American history. I have not tried to cover all time periods or topics, only my own interest areas and the types of software that could be developed. Some overlap in approach or subject matter does occur; these examples are intended only to suggest fruitful history CDs. While I have provided examples for titles in a CD series, I am certain readers will readily suggest other applications of the concept. Each description is followed by a brief justification.

SourceBook Editions™: the complete text, related images and charts, generous quotations from all sources cited in the book, plus extensive critiques by scholars in the field — an example of how historians think and work, this disk could include research diaries (if available from the historian) to explain where decisions were made and how they were arrived at. These are expanded books. Examples of books suitable for this possibility might be David Hackett Fischer's *Albion's Seed*, Charles A. Beard's *An Economic Interpretation of the Constitution*, Frederick Jackson Turner's frontier thesis, Bernard Bailyn's *Ideological Origins of the American Revolution*, Paul Kennedy's *The Rise and Fall of the Great Powers*. My purpose here is to provide both the sources used in key books on American history, and also comments by the author (when possible) about the decision-making process and critiques by established historians. This sort of activity can be found currently on programs of national historical conventions and occasionally in scholarly journals. Students at every level could benefit by evaluating how historians work. James Davidson and Mark Lytle's *After the Fact* has this as its justification, and by carefully choosing works for study the same excitement in tracking down evidence and making a judgment could be demonstrated with this compact disk.

Challenge of the Past™ series: episodes which challenge historians to interpret their cause and meaning, with full documentary and secondary readings. Examples: Hernan Cortes and Moctezuma; Witchcraft at Salem, Massachusetts; The Boston Massacre or Tea Party; Sectionalism from Jay-Gardoqui to Secession; Why did the U.S. enter World War I?; How successful was the New Deal? Taking the old D.C. Heath series of readers as an example, I would select important issues and include the major schools of interpretation and the sources necessary to form an opinion about their rightness or wrongness. I would allow the author (if living) to participate in the selection of documentary evidence so as to give as fair a hearing as possible. While historiographical in nature, these topics would, I hope, have a universal appeal because they focus on key issues of the American past. Because the author would have the opportunity to go more deeply into the evidence considered in reaching the conclusion, writers would have the time to develop their case more fully and students could share the process of interpretation.

Topics In Focus™ series: groupings of primary and secondary accounts of experiences many "ordinary Americans" shared, including still and motion images, taped interviews, and other sources. Examples: Great Awakenings, 18th century to the Born Again movement; The frontier experience, from colonization to sodbuster; The first ten years in each of the colonies; Slave narratives, the master's view, visitors reflections; The Great Depression; Civil Rights in the 20th century; Opposition to war throughout American history; Women's history. Too often writings by and about the "common" man and woman consist of an isolated letter or diary entry, or a few selections over a period of time. The compact disk edition would have the space to provide a very ample collection from a wide variety of individuals, so that complete diaries or a full run of letters could be included, thus allowing the writer to become a real person. It might be possible to include fictional accounts as well; for instance Upton Sinclair's *Jungle* or John Steinbeck's *Grapes of Wrath* could be used as the starting point for a reader on the Progressive era or the Great Depression. Studs Terkel's oral history of the 1930s, *Hard Times*, is an another model of the resources that could be collected on this disk.

You Decide™ series: topical groupings of sources and historians' essays based on these documents intended as a learn-by-example activity for students of history. Examples: Were cotton plantations profitable before the Civil War?; Did the Seven Years' War bring on the American Revolution?; What ended the Depression, the New Deal or World War II?; Was the War of 1812 the 'second War for Independence'? For many teachers of history, the way to reach students who have become disenchanted through previous bad experiences in history classes is to provide them an opportunity to be their own historians. The compact disk in this case could serve for both the lower-level survey and upper-level period courses. For example, Kenneth Stampp's *Causes of the Civil War* provides only brief examples of seven different interpretations of the coming of sectional conflict; this compact disk would have space for a hundred times more documentation, thus providing any interpretation with firm grounding on the evidence.

Where History Lives™ series: still and motion video providing a look at still-extant historical sites, plus complete background history, and selections from key primary and secondary sources relevant to the location. Examples: Martin's Hundred in Virginia; The Alamo, San Antonio, Texas; Gettysburg, Pennsylvania; Pullman, Illinois; Pearl Harbor, Hawaii. Next to holding an artifact in their hands, seeing where an important historical event occurred has an immediacy that can transport students to the time being studied and make learning more exciting and rewarding. Having a historian or archeologist as a guide to the site will not only enrich a history course, it will become another means of preserving the past from the inroads of developers and time. Ivor Noël Hume's investigation of Martin's Hundred is an excellent example of historical archeology and sleuthing.

Great Battles™ series: full accounts of the key battles or wars which have shaped history, including primary sources, still and motion pictures, discussions by historians, animated color maps, what-if speculations on the decisions made or not made, demonstrations of the weapons in use, biographies of the participants, and bibliography. Examples: Saratoga; New Orleans; Gettysburg; D-Day or the Battle of the Bulge; Tet Offensive. I would use William Seymour's *Decisions in Battle* for a model of what-if scenarios, panoramic map-paintings such as those found in American Heritage's *Battle Maps of the Civil War*, the sort of computer tools available on the *Universal Military Simulator*, plus videos of reenactments, contemporary and modern location shots, and historical accounts of the key battles of American history. Diaries of participants would also have an important place in this collection of military history resources. My overriding purpose would be to provide materials which would appeal to both peace- and war-mongers.

Echoes of Our Past™ series: diaries or histories offering first-person insight on key events; these would be grouped by time period and event, cross-indexed to historians' accounts of these events. Examples: Bernal Diaz del Castillo on the conquest of Mexico; Civil War — North, South, and West; World War I — in the trenches and in the air; World War II — European and Pacific theaters, home front; Vietnam — those who served, exiles, home front. The letters of Hernan Cortes and contemporary historians of the Spanish conquest of the Aztecs cannot match the power, romance, insight, and drama of Bernal Diaz, who held a subordinate officer's position in Cortes's army. Much of the same could be said of the accounts of military history found in George F. Scheer and Hugh Rankin's *Rebels & Redcoats*, Henry Steele Commager and Richard B. Morris's *The Spirit of 'Seventy-Six'*, and Commager's *The Blue and the Gray*. Many other episodes in American history, from immigrant life to the frontier experience, women and work, anti-German propaganda during World War I, and many other topics could benefit student readers.

Epic Journeys™ series: journals and accounts of European exploration and the migration of settlers, in South and Central America as well as North America. Native Americans certainly engaged in such journeys, as the Cherokee's Trail of Tears and the Aztecs' sojourn from the northern desert scrublands to eventual magnificence in Tenochtitlan both attest, and their accounts would have a place in this sort of collection. Examples: Bernal Diaz del Castillo; Lewis and Clark expedition; Trail of Tears; Mormon saga. Students have a fascination for this topic because (for most) their ancestors made such a decision, endured the same hardships, faced these bewildering choices, and persevered against unforgiving nature and hostile natives (earlier transplanters or Indians). By juxtaposing the stories from and to different continents and about different populations, students would gain a valuable perspective and information necessary to assess the importance of immigration to the United States and relate it to their own lives.

Westward to the Pacific™: diaries of the cross-continent journeys to Oregon and California, collected and collated so that relevant portions of many different diaries covering the same situations or locations are grouped. J.S. Holliday's *The World Rushed In* should be the foundation of this collection. This extraordinary account combines a 'Forty-Niner's letters recounting his travails sent to his wife back home and his wife's letters about coping on the farm without her husband. It would be my intention to give full treatment to all sides of this story, those who went to "see the elephant" and stayed in California, those who were left behind to wonder and wait, and those who died along the way, turned back, or those who, having found little gold, returned richer for the experience.

The Founders™: essential letters and essays on public issues by Americans in the age of the American Revolution: Franklin, Jefferson, Adams, Washington, *et al.*, arranged chronologically and topically. While these letters have much to tell us about the coming of revolution, they reach students either as scattered individual letters or as part of multi-volume collections students seldom consult. By collating these letters and organizing them thematically, this compact disk will provide a sampling broad enough to tell the story of American history from the 'rising empire' of the 1750s to the successful ratification campaigns of the 1787–1788 and Washington's inauguration as first President.

Ruffles and Flourishes™ series: the leaders, speeches, platforms, and scholarly essays on every major and minor political party which mounted a national or statewide campaign, and on each national election, plus the iconography of campaigning for the Presidency, with political buttons, banners, ballots, and the rest. Examples: Thomas Jefferson's 'Revolution of 1800'; Andrew Jackson's popular politics; 'Tippecanoe and Tyler, Too'; 'Rum, Romanism, and Rebellion'; 'Unlimited coinage of silver at a ratio of 16 to 1'; 'Two chickens in every pot, and a car in every garage'; 'Nixon's the One'. Among the subjects lost in the translation of time are the issues which divided Americans during the political campaigns of the past. Al Smith's pronunciation of 'radio,' Grover Cleveland's illegitimate child, the 'bloody shirt of rebellion'. Republican campaigns of the late 19th century, the momentous 1860 campaign in which the eventual victor followed the common wisdom of staying at home, and William Henry Harrison's popular politics, to Andy Jackson's democracy, Tom Jefferson's French radicalism, and John Adams's airs, all have something to tell students about how ordinary Americans related to the people who have become much reverenced and little understood figures from their past. Arthur Schlesinger, Jr., put together a multi-volume account of electoral history that could become a model for this series. The political Americana displayed by the Museum of American History in Washington, D.C., or the Hartford collection of political items would provide some of the artifacts to illustrate the story of politics in America. The slogans, phrases, and other images from past campaigns can bring into focus the issues that have polarized and attracted Americans.

Front Page™ series: centering on key events in modern history, these disks examine how newspapers and other periodicals covered the story, together with historians' essays. These are intended primarily as sources for student papers. They could be expanded to include radio, film, and television news coverage as well for modern events. Examples: The Twenties; The Crash and Great Depression; The Cuban Missile Crisis; The 'armed conflict' in Vietnam; Watergate scandal. Most Americans today get their news from newspapers and television news programs. In the last decades of the 20th century, public opinion has certainly been shaped by media (opposition to the war in Vietnam, for instance; Ross Perot's talk-show campaign in 1992). Politics in the 1790s was similarly framed by the new national Federalist and Democratic-Republican newspapers. Telling this story so that students can vicariously share events as Americans came to know them can provide students with crucial insights about the past. For example, reading the Virginia Gazette from the 1730s and 1770s graphically reveals the development of an American consciousness and gives a multi-dimensional picture of life in another time and place.

I Hear America Singing™: historical songs from colonial days to the present, plus introductions dealing with their meaning, alternative verses, and place in history. Songs have powerfully affected modern times ("Blowin' in the Wind," Dylan's "weatherman" line, the crippled Vietnam vet pleading "Ruby, Don't Take Your Love to Town"). "The World Turned Upside Down" was reputedly played as the British surrendered at Yorktown. "Dixie" and "The Battle Hymn of the Republic" can still stir an audience in the late 20th century. Sea chanties, "Yankee Doodle," "The Hunters of Kentucky," "Over There," and many more are part of the nation's heritage and provide a perspective useful to tell the story of ordinary Americans. From minstrel shows to "race music," white singers "covering" black rock and roll tunes in the 1950s, and rap, the story of black music has much to tell us about discrimination and the black consciousness. This CD would feature the words and music, plus photographs, drawings, and cartoons relevant to the topic.

Hooray for Hollywood™: a history of motion pictures from the invention of moving images to the present day, with still and motion video clips, interviews with directors, writers, and actors, original and shooting scripts, and historians' assessments. Hollywood has shaped America's image of itself and how the world sees America, and is worthy of study for itself. D.W. Griffith's *Birth of a Nation* remains a powerful statement of racism. Movie shorts and newsreels have also given us glimpses of the early part of the 20th century that are worth preserving in this fashion. Film is a medium students are comfortable with and one they have no problem relating to, and as such it can be an effective way of raising issues important in American life. John Wayne's *Green Berets* is one example of Hollywood's attempted didacticism, as was *Reds* for another point of view. The blacklist of suspected communists and the 1930s 'Code' for film censorship are also worthy of study. Technological improvements will make the compact disk of 2006 equivalent to today's videodisc for showing motion pictures.

Sound and Fury™ series: primary source documents offered as dramatic readings or as captured on audio- or videotape. Examples: Benjamin Franklin's essays; Letters and speeches of Abraham Lincoln; Franklin D. Roosevelt's Inaugural Address and "Day of Infamy" speech; Watergate hearings. Before these resources are lost to us, historians must make every effort to collect the images which have shaped the recent past. The Kefauver crime hearings and the Army-McCarthy hearings are other examples of television's impact, as are the classic radio broadcasts of the Hindenburg airship disaster or Orson Welles's *War of the Worlds*. Seeing Richard Nixon's "Checkers" speech or the announcement of the taping system in President Nixon's Oval Office have a drama best captured in the live television broadcast. This material is an important resource for teachers of modern American history.

The Historian's Bible™: a collection of necessary tools and sources useful to historians, including the DAB, economic statistics, formulas for converting prices, fully indexed historical maps, encyclopedia, online MLA and Kate Turabian style sheets, and a grammar handbook, a 'Swiss Army knife' for historians. Grouping these writing aids in one place would be a boon for every history student who has writing problems or a style that needs work.

Lay of the Land™: a historical atlas with layered, animated maps of single events and events over time, political overlays on geographical maps, economic maps, social maps, plus maps that can be copied for use with drawing programs and made into classroom displays. At present there are no historical map sets on computer. Since American students are deficient in geographical knowledge, this resource will prove an invaluable aid for them and for the teacher.

The Great Works of History™ series: the important books and seminal articles that have shaped history and our understanding of American and world history. Examples: Frederick Jackson Turner's frontier thesis; Charles A. Beard's economic interpretation; Upton Sinclair's *The Jungle*; George Frost Kennan on containment of communism. Not only could students of historiography profit from this collection, students in survey courses could be directed to these works as examples of scholarship. These books could be organized chronologically and topically to provide an interpretive history of the United States.

Historical Decisions™ series: interpretive articles or book chapters together with essays on the sources and the decision-making process used to reach a conclusion. Any topic from biographies of 'ordinary' Americans to local history, cliometric studies, historiographical essays, and traditional works would be suitable. The purpose of this collection is to show would-be historians how practitioners frame questions, develop evidence, weigh the sources, and make decisions based on the evidence. It might also be possible to provide more than one level of interpretive rigor, suitable for beginning survey courses, upper-level period courses, and graduate research seminars.

Topical History™ series: designed for use with lower-level survey courses and advanced undergraduate period courses, this series would include documents, images, interviews with historians, statistical information, maps, paper topics, selected articles from scholarly journals and popular history publications, and other resources for classroom discussion and short papers. Examples: Women in American history; War and dissent; Radicalism and the American Revolution;

Abolitionism and the anti-slavery movement; Rise of the city; The West comes of age; Boom and bust in American history; Inventions which have shaped America. Intended as a supplement for any college history textbook, this collection would correspond to the "focus groups" mentioned above and be aimed at students in the survey course. Articles would be selected for their appeal to this audience.

Material Culture™: selections from Godey's Lady's Book to the Sears Roebuck catalogue, advertisements for Stanley Steamers and Pierce Arrows, radio and television program guides, fashions found in motion pictures, and inventories of personal property. There is much students can learn about the lives of ordinary Americans from these sources, but they are seldom available in one place.

So You Want to be a Historian™

Volume 1: Starter Set: First, this disk would contain a series of articles (3–6 on the compact disk). Also included would be the author's notes on the sources consulted, with the areas of the notes highlighted so the student could see where the material came from, how the author formed his/her ideas (the author would provide commentary on the major issues, how a decisions were reached). Students would be expected to examine these papers for style, methodology, and use of sources. Second, this disk would contain other 'papers' to edit, proofread for spelling and grammar, comment on sources, and the sorts of things a seminar is supposed to do. The advantage: no individual will feel bad if the paper is criticized; the student will get practice in doing thorough critiques. These papers would be of varying quality, some very good and some very bad, with gradations in between; some would have technical problems, others methodological problems, historiographical problems, some questionable conclusions, and the like. Third, this disk would also contain sufficient documents for other papers, ones to be written by the student, on topics similar to those of the historians' essays. The disk might also contained (in locked files not available to the student until the professor unlocked them) essays by historians on these topics; these would be used for comparison and further study of how historians work.

Volume 2: Documents on Disk: Supplemental disks would also be available with documents for papers on specific topics: slavery, radicalism, World War II, Sacco-Vanzetti, etc. *Documents on Disk* should become a separate publishing venture with periodic revisions, updates, and the like. While Volume 1 would present the skills and thinking component, Volume 2 would carry the student forward. Since these disks would provide complete sources, students could easily find and comment on others' use of the sources. The disk might use an expert system or Socratic dialogue to probe the students' knowledge of a specific topic or to guide students through conceptualizing, organizing, and evaluating the sources and the resulting paper. Volume 2 would provide students with the opportunity to apply the skills they gained with Volume 1, and would offer them a number of learn-by-doing activities, all with a historian 'looking over their shoulders' at their original work.

Being There™: simulations covering all periods of American history from the age of discovery to the end of the Cold War. Examples: Columbus and the New World;

James Towne in Virginia; Boston Merchant; The Decision for Independence; United states: Confederation and Constitution; Bill of Rights; Economic Policy, 1790s–1820s; Foreign Policy, 1790s–1820s; Gold Rush; Lincoln's Decisions; Reconstruction; Protest and Reform; The Road to War, World War I and World War II; The New Deal; The Vietnam Quagmire; Fighting the Evil Empire. Grouping a comprehensive set of simulations on one disk would allow the teacher to choose the most relevant experiences for students in that class. These might vary from relatively short activities (15–30 minutes) to much longer simulations (1–2 hours), and they should be accompanied with sufficient instructions to be used in class or by individual students in a laboratory setting unsupervised by the teacher.

How Things Work™: explanation of inventions and systems that have affected history, with animated diagrams. Examples: Eli Whitney's cotton gin; Samuel Slater's textile factory; Underground Railroad; Pyramid monopoly; Internal combustion engine; A computer. When students encounter an invention or system ("American manufacturing" for example), there should be some source they can turn to which will provide a step-by-step explanation, animated diagram of the device in action, and discussion of its significance.

Origins™: decade-by-decade history of countries from which immigrants came, the ocean journey and Ellis Island, plus diaries of those who traveled to America and within America searching their new home. This would be detailed enough to cover regions or districts within each country (Württemburg in Germany, for instance), include relevant ship's logs, representative passenger lists, procedures at Ellis Island, photographs illustrating the immigrant's journey, and first-person materials providing insight about the America of their dreams and the reality. "Great Expectations"? Examples: Africans in bondage; Puritan migrations; Scots-Irish outpouring; Moravians; Revolutions of 1848; Irish Potato Famine; The 'New Immigration'; Anti-immigrant enactments. When the subject of immigration to America becomes important, being able to access these short histories will help students understand why people left their homes, gave up their past for an uncertain future, and endured many hardships and doubts before settling in America. Students of family history also need this sort of comprehensive reference.

Everyday Life™: information on how people lived their lives from pre-Columbian America to today. The emphasis is on 'ordinary' people, farmers, shopkeepers, laborers, and the like, with discussion of working, the home, food, leisure, books they read, community activities, marriage and family, customs, folklore, and language. Examples: life on the frontier; Big-city America in the 1920s. The last generation of historians has built up a detailed picture of what life was like for ordinary Americans, but pulling it together and telling the story from the Indians to the present day is difficult. Having a single source for this information would make it available for students who wanted to know how their ancestors lived their lives or how a particular time and place differed from their own in the rhythms and givens of everyday life.

Imagined History™: works of poetry and fiction illuminating American history, including books which have affected history. Examples: Parson Weem's life of

George Washington; Upton Sinclair's *The Jungle*; John Dos Passos' trilogy on the 20th century; John Steinbeck's *Grapes of Wrath*; Robert Penn Warren's *All the King's Men*. Grouping works of fiction or imagination which present history three-dimensionally would be of great benefit to teachers and students in understanding the American experience.

American Lives™: biographical dictionary of individuals great and small who have affected American history. This comprehensive source will contain brief entries and, where available, images and sound, relating to the lives of memorable individuals who have something to tell students about American history. Examples: John Smith; Richard Frethorne; Anne Hutchinson; Abigail Adams; Sojourner Truth; Mary Elizabeth Lease. Having this information instantly available would help teachers preparing lectures and students wanting to know more about the people they encounter in a textbook. With so much space available, this resource could be quite complete.

Roundtable™ series: the leading historians on key historiographical subjects have a face-to-face discussion of present understanding and future directions of research regarding their fields of expertise. These would be supplemented by far-ranging historiographical essays relevant to the era by each of the participants. The purpose would be to have students understand how historians work and think, why they perceive events as they do, and to respond to questions by other knowledgeable historians.

One Piece of Evidence™: historians would discuss crucial documents that changed the way we think about the past by examining previous views, how this document came to light, and how it unlocked the past. The purpose of this set is to offer students case studies in the use of evidence and in critical thinking.

Plus four journals:

The Great Issues of the Past™: topical articles on a common theme featuring the major interpretive schools, the authors writing in full knowledge of the other participants, perhaps even sharing their initial drafts; to be revised and expanded annually. Examples: The many facets of Puritanism; Witchcraft at Salem; Revolution from the Bottom Up; Commercial democracy; Reconstruction; Robber Barons or great men of capital; Farmers, Laborers, and reform; Origins of the Progressive movement; The decision to drop the atomic bomb; Was the Cold War won? While some scholarly journals will devote a single issue to one topic, there is simply not space enough to provide a full discussion of ideas. Festscrifts seldom have sufficient thematic unity. An editor having up to 250,000 pages to fill could certainly create a body of writing that could explore every significant issue in depth. Lower-level students might read only the core essays, while advanced history students would be expected to investigate one of the sub-topics.

The American Museum™ series: guided tours of temporary exhibits (art, historical, ethnological, archeological) and sites (digs, newly opened preservation buildings, etc.), with reviews, catalogues. Permanent collections should also be covered. Examples: "Circa 1492" or "Seeds of Change" organized for the Columbus quincentenary. Documenting and preserving these essential visual displays for future generations will make them available to students long after the artifacts are returned to the many collections from which they were drawn. Time and distance make it difficult to visit the nation's permanent collections that tell the story of the colonial past (Winterthur, for instance), native Americans (Denver and Los Angeles Country Art Museums have impressive ethnological collections, as do other museums across the country), or World War II (the German U-boat at Chicago's Museum of Science and Industry, for example). By capturing them on compact disk, any student could quickly find what a Swedish log cabin looked like (museum in New Castle, Delaware) or a Pony Express mail bag (museum in St. Joseph, Missouri). This series will be an important addition to the study of American history.

The CD History Journal™: essays and full-length citations, plus complete reviews by scholars in the field. For many publications the cost of production necessarily restricts the length of an issue or even of the number of pages for an article. The compact disk edition will allow authors to explain themselves fully, plus provide appropriate citation by reprinting the source itself. It might be possible to publish a dozen topically or chronologically themed scholarly journals under this one title and on a single disk.

Dissertation Quarterly™: a collection of significant doctoral dissertations presented in full, with an index to names and key subjects. This would include dissertations from the past, plus recent contributions to scholarship. Finding the gems among the dross is very difficult today, although there is a printed index to dissertations. With editors charged with discovering the good ones, scholars and students could benefit from easy access to works that might never appear in print.

Part III

The titles suggested here represent possible compact disks for use as supplements to traditional textbooks by accommodating the changes in education mentioned previously. For the past decade in academic computing, historians have been content with letting software publishers decide what might be useful for them. As we enter the age of the CD, it might be helpful if we decided instead to tell them what we need.

The bottom line question is, would I ask my library to stock these titles? Price would have a place in the decision, but CDs, once the master has been created, are very inexpensive when compared to printed books, raise fewer ecological concerns, conserve space on shelves, can be quickly searched, and contain mountains of material on a single disk. Yes, I would buy most of these titles, some with more enthusiasm than others, of course, but if each were $14.95, I would see that as an amazing bargain. Even if I thought only 250 of 250,000 pages were of real benefit to my students — as I conceive of the course this year, for I cannot anticipate how my needs will change, nor can I know what will interest my students in future — I would think it money well spent.

We are on the brink of an exciting future in history education. If the coming years are in fact to be interactive, I hope historians will themselves become more active at this significant stage in the evolution of history education.

Chapter 2

Information Technology in the Curriculum in the UK: Past, Present and Future

Alaric Dickinson

Introduction

In many countries at present there is much emphasis on innovation and change in education. Therefore, perhaps more than ever, there is a need to consider both intended and unintended outcomes of these changes, and also to establish and maintain good working relationships between teachers, researchers and policy makers. It is important that teachers have opportunities to share their ideas and experiences with each other, and that policy makers do not ignore the practical wisdom of teachers or the findings of educational research. The CHC (Computers in the History Classroom) conferences have a significant role and value in this situation; they provides a forum for developing interaction between teachers and researchers and policy makers at both a national and an international level. The conferences, and the publications and e-mail exchanges which follow from them, provide opportunities for a widespread exchange of information about major developments and for critical and constructive consideration of pertinent issues. The main aims of this chapter are to provide evidence of what has been happening in practice in terms of IT in schools in England, to highlight some issues and implications, and to offer some suggestions about possible ways forward.

Findings and Trends in Recent Statistical Bulletins

The 1992 survey of IT in schools in England, prepared by the British Government Statistical Service and published by the Department for Education (DFE, 1993), was based on a representative sample of over 800 primary schools and over 500 secondary schools. The purpose of the survey was to determine the level of provision, the use being made of IT in schools and its contribution across the curriculum. The survey was carried out in the academic year 1992 and published in February 1993. Many of the questions asked were the same as those posed in the surveys completed in 1985, 1988 and 1990. Thus it is possible to identify trends and changes over a number of years.

What Seem to be the Most Significant Findings and Trends?

Certainly one major feature is the very considerable increase in expenditure on IT in primary schools (for pupils from 5 to 11 years of age). As indicated in Table 2.1, total expenditure on IT in primary schools rose from £6 million in 1985 to £10 million in 1988, £18 million in 1990 and then £50 million in 1992. These increases in expenditure on IT have meant a very considerable increase in the total number of computers in schools, and therefore a significant reduction in the number of pupils per microcomputer (from one computer per 107 pupils in 1985 to one computer per 25 pupils in 1992). The 1992 survey also provides evidence that the percentage of teachers who said they were confident about using IT themselves had risen

Table 2.1 IT in Primary Schools in England — Summary*

	1985	1988	1990	1992
Expenditure				
Average IT expenditure per pupil	£2	£3	£6	£15
Average IT expenditure per school	£300	£500	£950	£2,600
Total expenditure on IT (millions)	£6.0m	£9.6m	£18.2m	£49.5m
Computers				
Microcomputers per school	1.7	2.5	4.3	7
Pupils per microcomputer	107	67	40	25
Total microcomputers available	33,500	48,300	82,400	132,500
Teachers				
% of staff confident in use of IT	*	56	65	72
% of staff making regular use of IT	*	50	62	62

• Details from Department of Education, *Statistical Bulletin* 1993, and 1989 and 1991.
* Information not available.

Table 2.2 IT in Secondary Schools in England — Summary*

	1985	1988	1990	1992
Expenditure				
Average IT expenditure per pupil	£3	£6	£21	£21
Average IT expenditure per school	£2,250	£4,850	£15,000	£15,500
Total expenditure on IT (millions)	£9.8m	£20.2m	£60.1m	£59.5m
Computers				
Microcomputers per school	13	23	41	58
Pupils per microcomputer	60	32	18	13
Total microcomputers available	58,700	96,300	163,400	223,100
Teachers				
% of staff confident in use of IT	*	48	50	52
% of staff making regular use of IT	*	30	31	32

• Details from Department of Education, *Statistical Bulletin* 1993, and 1989 and 1991.
* Information not available.

(to 72%) but that the percentage of staff making regular use of IT in 1992 was the same (62%) as that reported in the 1990 survey.

Regarding secondary schools (for pupils aged 12 to 16 or 12 to 18), the survey reported that total expenditure on IT was slightly less than it had been two years earlier (See Table 2.2). Nevertheless the level of expenditure meant that the total number of computers available in schools had increased by 25% between 1990 and 1992. This also meant that the average number of computers per school had risen; the survey found that there was now on average one computer per 13 pupils. (Of course, some of these computers were now old models!) With regard to teachers' confidence and classroom use of IT, the survey found the same trends among secondary teachers as were evident with their primary counterparts. Thus there was evidence of a slight increase in the number of secondary school teachers stating that they were confident about using IT themselves, and a smaller (minimal) increase in the number making regular use of computers in their teaching (defined, for the survey, as using computers at least twice per week in their teaching).

What did Pupils do During their Time Using the Computer?

The schools involved in the survey were asked to record for one week exactly which software packages and programs were being used. The findings (summarised in Table 2.3) provide clear evidence that word-processing was the most common activity at all ages, accounting for more than one-third of all activity and showing a further, small increase on the figures recorded two years earlier. The

Table 2.3   Use of Software in Primary and Secondary Schools in England: All Subjects

Application	Year							
			Percentage Frequency of Use by Age Group					
			{Primary School}			{Secondary School}		
		Age						
		5	7	9	11	12	14	16
Word Processing	1992	39	43	45	38	30	28	35
	1990	33	41	41	39	26	29	32
Data Handling	1992	8	16	14	12	15	17	16
	1990	5	11	16	16	15	17	17
Simulation	1992	3	3	4	6	5	7	6
	1990	6	7	8	6	8	9	9
	1988	6	13	13	12	15	14	12
Practice Exercises	1992	32	16	10	5	13	10	6
and Puzzles	1990	42	24	16	12	20	11	9
	1988	56	39	27	22	26	15	11
Desk Top Publishing	1992	2	5	7	9	7	8	8
	1990	2	3	5	7	5	6	4
Others		(Computer-aided Design and Musical Composition, etc.)						

survey also found a small increase in Desk Top Publishing (DTP), and in the use of data handling facilities with primary school children.

How Much Variation in Use in Different Areas of the Curriculum?

The survey revealed that only one out of every five secondary school history teachers used IT regularly (See Table 2.4). In secondary as well as primary schools it seems from the survey that there is less use of IT in history classrooms than in any other main areas of the curriculum. Indeed the survey found that on average IT was being used in only 5% of history sessions, one session out of every twenty (See Table 2.5). This means that pupils studying history are likely to have, on average, just four hours of history per year in which some use is made of IT. It is also interesting to note that this amounts to a decline (of as much as 50%) since the previous

Table 2.4   Areas of the Curriculum Where IT Used

Subject area	Secondary Schools: % of Staff who used IT Regularly*		
	1988	1990	1992
English	19	27	31
Mathematics	24	31	34
Science	23	28	30
Art	31	30	32
Technology	38	50	53
Geography	15	19	25
History	11	20	22
Computere Studies	84	92	93

* At least twice a week on average.

Table 2.5   Use of Computers in Teaching Periods (As Reported by Heads of Department)

		Percentage of Teaching Periods at age					
		12	13	14	15	16	17+
History	1992	5	6	6	5	5	5
	1990	11	11	8	7	6	4
Geography	1992	7	6	5	5	5	5
	1990	6	6	6	7	7	6
All Departments	1992	12	11	11	15	16	16
	1990	13	10	18	22	20	20

Table 2.6   Percentage of Secondary Schools/Departments Reporting Contribution of IT to Teaching and Learning

	Substantial Teaching Learning		Some Teaching Learning		Little Teaching Learning		None Teaching Learning	
Computer Studies	96	95	3	5	1	0	0	0
Geography	4	4	38	41	42	41	16	14
History	8	3	33	37	40	42	19	18
Mathematics	7	9	47	58	39	28	7	5
Science	6	2	41	44	44	46	9	8

survey in 1990, a decline which is probably due to the introduction of the new national curriculum history requirements from 1991 onwards.

Do Teachers Think IT Makes a Substantial Contribution to Their Work?

The findings summarised in Table 2.6 indicate that only a small minority of teachers (except those who teach Computer Studies!) consider that IT is at present making a substantial contribution to the teaching and learning of their subject. Indeed, the survey found that six out of every ten history teachers questioned in the survey expressed the view that IT was at present making little or no contribution to the teaching and learning of history.

Some Observations and Suggestions

This appears to be a rather disappointing outcome given the potential value of IT for teaching and learning in school, and the very considerable expenditure on IT that has been achieved in the UK in recent years. Of course these findings apply to just one country at a particular point in time. Perhaps the situation will be very different at different points in time as well as in different countries.

A key to understanding much of what is happening regarding IT in classrooms is the tendency so far of policy makers and teachers consistently to overestimate what can be accomplished quickly by providing computers and to underestimate not only the long term consequences but also the immediate practical problems facing teachers. In Britain the Government has done much to encourage the use of IT in classrooms, greatly increasing the IT facilities in schools. But most teachers have received little more than initial training in the use of IT for teaching and learning. The figures in Table 2.7 reveal that the 1992 survey found that only one out of every five history teachers had received more than brief, introductory training in the use of IT. Banks, hotels and other businesses aiming to make substantial use of IT invariably have staff development programmes which include providing relevant and systematic training in the use and capabilities of the equipment which

Table 2.7 Percentage of Staff Shown at Their Highest Level of Training in the Use of IT

	No training	Initial Awareness Training	Additional In-service Course	More Than One Such Course	An Award-Bearing Course
History	14	42	24	19	1
Geography	12	40	24	23	1
Mathematics	9	30	22	35	4
All Departments	14	37	22	24	3

staff have to use. Surely appropriate training for teachers would bring more confidence, and a greater appreciation of the possible benefits of IT for teaching and learning.

Of course such training is costly in terms of time and money, so where should we go from here with regard to the use of IT in history classrooms? Whatever is done, the paramount concern should be to maintain and develop the quality of history teaching provided in our schools. Professor Marwick has eloquently emphasised the importance of helping pupils to acquire historical knowledge and understanding by saying that a person without knowledge of the past is like a person living in a house without windows.

In terms of longer-term developments for IT in the curriculum, there is clearly a need for teachers to be involved with, or as, researchers and authors in state-of-the-art developments in Artificial Intelligence, modelling and expert systems. In terms of the immediate future it seems from the evidence now available to us that one need is for teachers and policy makers to be alert to the possibility of unintentionally misleading others through overestimating what can be accomplished simply by providing IT equipment and underestimating the immediate practical problems that are likely to arise.

Further evidence of the fact that effective and substantial use of IT in history classrooms should not be expected to occur instantly can be found in the evolving City Technology Colleges (CTCs) in the UK. The British Government has encouraged the creation of a small number of CTCs, each very rich in IT resources. In one newly created CTC the history department was provided from the beginning with access to a computer for every pupil when required, a multimedia authoring system, and CD-ROM packages, including one based on *The Times* newspaper (enabling access to a broad range of pictures and text covering 200 years). In their first year the department chose, understandably, to concentrate on the use of word-processing and data handling facilities, prior to embarking on more adventurous uses of the rich IT resources available to them.

Dissemination also merits further attention, including dissemination of the practical wisdom of teachers, and the findings of research. More evaluation of teaching approaches and the role of IT in the teaching and learning of history would be welcome, plus further consideration of how best to disseminate such findings. It seems appropriate here to mention the seminal work of the ImpacT Project (Watson, 1993), and to commend the articles and research reviews published in the *Journal of Computer Assisted Learning*, and also the many useful articles and teaching suggestions to be found in *Teaching History* and *Primary History*. But surely there is also a need to exploit the use of IT further with regard to dissemination as we approach the 21st century?

Another useful development is the clarification of the IT knowledge and capability ideally to be achieved by teachers at various stages of their career. At a time when radical reforms of schools and curricula have led to so much change in the life and work of teachers, many teachers may find it difficult at first to be enthusiastic about such suggestions or requirements with regard to IT skills, knowledge and understanding. The authors of the Trotter Report (DES, 1989) have stated that experienced teachers in the United Kingdom should have appropriate expertise in terms of:

1. **Practical IT skills**: the ability to use with confidence, within an educational context, a range of appropriate packages and devices relating to a teacher's curriculum area and phase.
2. **Relating IT to the curriculum**: understanding how these and other packages and devices apply to the teacher's curriculum area and phase; and how their use and more generally the existence of IT affects the content of schemes of work, styles of teaching and pupils' learning.
3. **Managing and evaluating IT use**: the ability to implement this knowledge and understanding within everyday classroom teaching, to manage the consequent activities, and to evaluate the quality of pupils' learning with IT and other resources.

Such lists of the expertise now expected of teachers constitute a formidable and challenging agenda. Teachers should not be under-valued or their abilities underestimated as we approach the 21st century; indeed teachers have the ability to respond more flexibly than any computer to the intent of pupils' questions. However, history is a developing subject and should make use of developing technology at all levels, including classrooms. It seems, therefore, that there is a need to do whatever is possible and appropriate now and into the 21st century in order to make the best possible use of our teachers and of the developing technology.

Chapter 3
History and Computing: The Example of Luxembourg
Jean-Paul Lehners

Introduction

Before developing the main ideas of this chapter, it may prove useful to make some general remarks about the geographical situation of Luxembourg and also about the Luxembourg school system as a whole. The Grand-Duchy of Luxembourg is situated in the (perhaps former) heart of Europe, surrounded by France, Belgium and Germany. Since 1839 it has occupied its current area of 2,586 square kilometres (999 square miles), only a quarter of the area of the country in the 14th century. Three partitions — in 1659, 1815 and 1839 — have cut Luxembourg down to its present-day boundaries. Luxembourg has been participating in the construction of the European Community since the first day, because it chose to but also because it had to. The capital (pop. 80,000) is today the seat of several European institutions, including the European Court of Justice, the European Bank of Investment and the secretariat of the European Parliament. After a high rate of emigration in the 19th century, the country has known since 1890 a high rate of immigration too, due to late industrialisation in Luxembourg (late in comparison with England for example). Today 27% of the Luxembourg population are foreigners.

This geographical and social situation between two important European civilisations explains the particularities of our school system. Besides their own native tongue (Luxembourgish) which became a national language by a law passed in 1984, every Luxembourger has to be able to speak two other languages: German and French. This is one reason why primary education in Luxembourg lasts for 6 years, longer than in many other countries in Europe. It is preceded by 2 years of kindergarten, the second being compulsory. During their 6 years of primary education children study German, French, elementary mathematics, the history of Luxembourg, the geography of Luxembourg and the surrounding European countries, and several other subjects including physical education, music or religion. After a national test taken at the age of 12, the pupils must choose between three types of school, Études secondaires, Études secondaires techniques or Enseignement complémentaire. Courses at the Études secondaires (grammar schools) last for 7 years and prepare pupils mainly for university studies. Courses at the Études secondaires techniques (secondary technical schools) lead to different qualifications, one of which, also after 7 years, allows access to Polytechnics or Technical Colleges. Pupils who do not qualify for these two types of school attend the enseignement complémentaire from the age of 12 to 15 when compulsory schooling ends.

Luxembourg students, and also students of other countries of course, may continue their studies in a limited number of subjects in Luxembourg. Among these possibilities is the Centre Universitaire which offers a one-year course for beginners to enable the transition from secondary education to further education abroad. The successful completion of this course gives students admission to the second year of undergraduate studies at most foreign universities. The Centre Universitaire is of course interested in co-operating with other universities. (A law allowing the CU to offer courses covering two years is in preparation.) Luxembourg students then continue their university or polytechnic studies abroad, in France, Belgium, Germany, Switzerland, England, Scotland, etc. However, if they want to become primary school teachers they attend the teacher training college in Luxembourg (ISERP — Higher Institute for Studies and Research in Pedagogy) for three years. It is also possible for students to continue their studies at a level between secondary school and university, for example becoming a technical engineer or a specialist in IT after studying for several years at the Higher Institute of Technology or completing a two-year course at the Centre Universitaire.

Computers in the Classroom

Before considering the use of the computer in history classrooms, we have to take into consideration the general use of the computer in our schools. As a matter of fact the place of the computer in history is closely linked to the general philosophy of computer teaching in Luxembourg. In 1989 there was a reorganisation of the syllabus for elementary schools (children between 6 and 12 years of age). The documentation included the statement: "Considering the overloading of the syllabus, IT should not be introduced as an additional activity. IT should be instrumental in teaching languages, mathematics, sciences, technology, ..." History is not mentioned *expressis verbis*. Is that indicative of the present low status of the computer in the history classroom, or do the authors of the school syllabus think that history ranks among the sciences? Why not?!

Hardware and software are paid for by the local authorities but only a limited number of elementary schools are adequately equipped. In the beginning the equipment consisted of BBC machines; now the schools participating in the pilot programs have several PCs with double disk drives and one PC with a hard disk per school. The pilot projects focus on writing workshops using word processing, graphic design and desktop publishing; creating and searching databases; simulation; logo; and drill & practice programs. In the enseignement complémentaire the computer is used in the same way, i.e. integrated into different subjects as a project in years 8e and 9e (pupils aged 14 and 15 years old).

Regarding the Études secondaires (secondary grammar schools for pupils aged 12 to 19), it is necessary to distinguish between the first 3 and the last 4 years of schooling. During the first three years there is one computer course in the third year with an average of 1.5 lessons per week (in fact one lesson in the first semester and two lessons in the second, the semestrial division being somewhat artificial because our school year is divided into three terms). In these courses three units are compulsory: an introduction to the use of the computer with Logo, an introduction to word processing, and finally an introduction to computer programs for information handling. Three other units are optional: an introduction to BASIC; technical applications including Robotics; and notions of telematics (e-mail). For several years there have been computer courses for students specialising in economics: two lessons per week during one year (2e). From September 1990 the organisation of the last 4 years of our secondary schools will be changed to include one weekly computer course in 4e, the first year of the upper division. The software used in this year will probably be the integrated package, *Works*.

In secondary technical schools the situation is the same for the first three years, after which — as the secondary technical school prepares for a specific profession — we have computer courses adapted to the general aim of the section (for example, robotics in engineering and computer assisted design in the graphics section). Concerning equipment in both secondary and secondary technical schools, at first there were the different BBC-Acorn generations (32K, 64K, then the Master). Each school has a computer room with about 12 computers, which means one workstation for two pupils. From September 1990 each school will be equipped with a second computer room containing 12 Bull PCs with a hard disk (30 MB) and MS-DOS 4.0. We shall probably also have some laptops for each school so that teachers will be more independent of the occupancy of the computer rooms.

Computer Training for Teachers

The students who want to become primary school teachers have to take a compulsory course in IT. In the past some secondary school teachers have followed a part-time program in IT for a period of two years, first in Luxembourg, and then abroad in Nancy, Liege or London. A new concept is elaborated for what is called *formation lourde*, the aim of which is to have teachers specialising in IT. In addition, in-service training is organised in Luxembourg by the Ministry of Education for teachers in their free time, for example introductory courses for BASIC and Pascal, but also in the use of the computer in subjects like history and geography. Moreover, in the Teacher Training College, primary school teachers can attend special courses for further qualifications. All these courses are co-ordinated in the Ministry of Education by a national co-ordinator.

A new structure, aiming at the integration of IT into the general framework of education, has been set up with a new law on the reorganisation of the Pedagogical Innovation and Research Service (SIRP). However, experience in Luxembourg as well as in other countries seems to suggest that it is necessary to start IT teaching as early as possible. One argument in favour of this is that at a later stage the classes are too heterogeneous concerning children's knowledge of computers, so from September 1990, in several secondary and secondary technical schools, there are different projects in class 7e. The principles underlying these projects have been outlined in a paper prepared by a commission under the direction of Dominique Portante, national coordinator of the Technologies of Information and Communication at the Ministry of Education, and are as follows:

1. Didactic projects enable children to use in an active way informatic tools such as word processing, database analyses, calculation programs, electronic mail and robotics.
2. Those informatic tools are integrated into a project defined in relation with the program of 7e. These projects may be of different kinds; school or class newspaper, exchange between schools on specific subjects, and interdisciplinary projects etc.
3. These didactic projects also have to give the pupils the opportunity to develop various skills, especially exploring skills, autonomous work or team work, problem solving abilities, and oral and written communication.

Schools are linked together by the electronic mail system of the Ministry of Education called *Restena,* and also by the system *Videotex* of the Post and Telecommunication system.

History Classrooms

Turning now to history, some general information is again relevant. As our history teachers begin their studies in Luxembourg but finish them abroad, their knowledge of IT depends on the programs of the different universities which they attend. As far as Luxembourg is concerned, the Centre Universitaire offers two computer-assisted courses, the first in Academic English and the second in Quantitative Methods for Human Scientists. These courses commenced in the academic year 1990/91 and cover 30 lessons a year each. When the students return from their universities and want to become history teachers in Luxembourg, they first have to follow courses in general didactics and also in didactics of history. In both courses they are introduced to IT. In history this course unfortunately totals only four lessons. The historians who are already secondary school teachers may attend a special course on the use of computers in history classrooms (for 15 lessons a year). This course was held for the first time in May 1990. Only 4 teachers attended the course (four half days) and they wanted to find out about the possibilities of using IT not only in the history classroom, but also in historical research. Their interest in KLEIO, the database management program developed by Manfred Thaller of the Max Planck Institute for History in Göttingen, was at least as great as their interest in specific software for the history classroom.

This special training for teachers of history takes into account the changing focus of interest in history courses. For too long the aim of our history courses has been to learn hundreds of events and dates by heart. It is time now to change. Unfortunately the board charged with establishing the syllabuses tends to define these syllabuses by the numbers of pages to learn in a book. Surely, however, the goal of history courses should be to get the pupils to handle different kinds of information in a critical way? So the general aim is not only to know, but to know *how*, to know *where* and to know *why*. The computer can help us do that.

This means we should encourage the use of computer software which enables pupils to ask questions and to determine the sequences of their questions, not "drill and practice" programs which would only reinforce the more or less mindless learning by heart. We also wanted a database close to the every-day life of the children. Thus we came to use census lists and the *Quest* and *Qstats* programs. Why census lists of inhabitants? First because the classification unit is the house or the household, a notion familiar to the pupils; second because we have many of these census lists for many villages and towns of our country in the 19th century. (We are not allowed to use 20th centur nominal lists because of the protection of the individual against infringement of his rights through storage of computerised data.) It is possible to have about 20 of these lists of inhabitants for each village or town of the country in the second half of the 19th century, which was an important transitional period from an agrarian to an industrial society. Because of the great number of these lists, the history teachers can chose from a number of possibilities, taking for instance one or several lists of the city where the school is situated, or where most of the pupils come from, or which is well known to almost all of the pupils. With the help of *Quest* or *Qstats*, or another information handling program, pupils can do their own research, coming into contact with an original source in history and also with the problems typical of an historian's work (too many or too few documents, gaps in the information, difficulties of classification, for instance of the different occupations etc.). They can also make a statistical interpretation of their sources, provided the mathematics teacher has taught them some elementary statistics.

Other software now in use includes an Austrian program called *Histo* which pursues identical aims and was presented at the first CHC conference (Leeds, 1988). A big advantage of *Histo* is the documentation about the place from which the census list came. The program is user-friendly and allows many significant cross-tabulations. Three minor disadvant-ages perhaps are that the database is relatively small, it is not always easy to see the link between the documentation and the computer program, and the graphic display could be improved.

A second kind of software presented in the in-service training has been simulation. The first computer simulation to be considered was *Palestine 1947*, which is based on the plan of the United Nations for the partition of Palestine in 1947. The pupils have hundreds of possibilities to combine the policy of the different states or nations involved in the conflict, but only 4 outcomes are possible, among them the outbreak of World War III (but not the foundation of an Arab state). The pupils like the "game" and have many questions about the program, about the relationships between the different states, and so become interested in the subject.

A second simulation program is called *Saheli* and concerns geography and history. This program focuses on financial help for so-called developing countries. Pupils have a certain amount of money and several possibilities for helping the Sahelis. Two examples of general goals to achieve are:

1. The Sahelis are constantly hungry, because their cattle are killed under the influence of the Tse-tse fly. Avoid this during the next ten years!

2. The population of the Sahelis must increase in the next ten years to prevent the invasion by foreign nomadic populations.

The program tells the pupils if they have achieved their aim. This program, which was awarded the Förderpreis des deutschen Schulsoftwarepreises (a prize to promote German school software), has several disadvantages. First, the Sahelis do not exist. They are fictitious, though the information given seems to fit a real situation in the south of the state of Niger; and it is not possible for pupils to obtain supplementary information about the different countries of the Sahel zone. Second, we have almost no information about the mathematical model behind the software. For instance the program calculates the bio-mass, taking into consideration the pastureland, ground water level and precipitation as well as the number of wells. It does not tell us how it calculates this index. Third, we have to ask ourselves if the use of contraception is really the solution to the problem of population explosion in the so-called Third World. Fourth, it is undignified to compare stocks of cattle with stocks of human beings. But even the greatest critics of simulation programs can see at least one advantage in them: they raise questions interesting enough for pupils to benefit from them even if the simulation does not give direct answers to them.

Pupils' Reactions

One of our problems concerning the use of IT in history classrooms is the motivation of the teachers who often make such comments as: "Our program is large enough. We have no time to organise supplementary sessions." or "The computer doesn't take into consideration the individual, but history is mainly concerned with individual personalities." Perhaps these will soon be views held by only a minority of history teachers. The reactions of the pupils themselves — and let us not forget that they are our first concern — are quite different. Even if they do not see any sense in the use of Logo for instance, they are enthusiastic about finding out how many children are named Jean or Nicolas or Marie or Elisabeth, and exploring possible links between the age of the people and their occupations. They are glad to be able to sort out names alphabetically or to see the age pyramid of a village at the beginning and at the end of the 19th century, making comparisons possible.

The comments below are some of the reactions of pupils in 5e of the Lycée Michel-Rodange in Luxembourg to whom the author taught history, geography and IT in addition to his work at the Centre Universitaire. (This school participated in 1989 in an international project grouping 100 schools in Europe and the United States and using E-mail to exchange information on specific subjects. The Lycée is willing to repeat this experience which may be the first step to a more intensive collaboration with another school). Here are some comments picked up at random.

First, some of the advantages of the computer:

"We ourselves can do some work in history and not only listen to the teachers."

"By using the computer in history we learn many things about computers per se."

"It is a lesson without stress, without preparations at home."

"We can experiment."

"We can work together with friends."

"Through the simulations we are able to understand the problems of other people and we can help to solve these problems."

"The only computer lessons I still remember are the lessons in history and geography."

"It is also a good change for the teacher."

"It is nice that sometimes we have two teachers in the classroom in these computer lessons."

"It is good to see not only the advantages, but also the disadvantages of the computer."

Now some of the disadvantages:

"We learn on old BBC computers which don't exist in every-day life."

"Learning something about the computer when we are already 15 is too late."

"If we used the computer in many subjects, we wouldn't have enough computer rooms."

"Those of the pupils who don't have a computer at home are disadvantaged."

"We are no longer capable of freely expressing our own ideas; we become lazier."

So much for the reactions of the pupils. We hope that with our new projects in the class of 7e we shall take into account some of these comments and also motivate more and more teachers to use IT in their history classes.

Pilot Projects

It is intended that three projects will be offered to history teachers (starting in 1990/91) and that these projects will be organised at first during two consecutive days in several secondary schools and during 30 lessons a year in several secondary technical schools. The first project concerns the census lists and the computer programs Quest and Qstats as mentioned earlier. The second project concerns oral history. Here the general aim is to bring the pupils into contact with historical method and to ensure that they take an active part in the realisation of an historical project. The second aim is to familiarise pupils with a word processor. The data gathering can be realised in two ways, with the pupils either conducting the interviews themselves with a sample of persons on a specific subject (and after preparing or discussing them in the classroom), or using interviews which already exist and are available in the archives (for instance in the Centre National de l'Audio-Visuel in Dudelange or in the National Archives in Luxembourg). These interviews concern every-day life in agrarian and industrial regions of our country, but also bear witness to the Second World War. The final aim will be to write texts on a word processor and to produce either a small brochure or a series of articles for a newspaper. The third project will be realised together with a teacher specialised in the use of hypertext programs. With a program called *Thinksheet* it is possible to prepare tree structures into which the pupils feed their data. In some ways this work resembles drill and practice, except that the pupils can set up their own tree structures. These programs may however appeal to teachers less familiar with computers in general.

There will also be several interdisciplinary projects where the participation of an historian is desirable. One of these is a project on the different calendars existing around the world, where the geographer explains what a year is, where the historian explains the origin of the different kinds of calendars, where the mathematician develops the algorithm to calculate leap years for the next century, and where finally the pupils have to find out why the October Revolution took place in November, or why Saint Theresa of Avila died in the night from the fourth to the fifteenth of October 1582. For all these projects the pupils may have recourse to the e-mailbox to get more information and to exchange results with other schools.

Conclusion

What are the main ideas underlying this paper? In the view of the author they are as follows:

1. As the principle underlying the use of IT in classrooms is no longer to provide separate courses but to integrate the computer as a tool into existing subjects, the use of computer software in those subjects, including history, becomes more and more important.
2. Thus the use of the computer has different objectives:
   - It is a tool which allows more efficient use of quantitative methods and better handling of historical data, especially in social and economic history.
   - It gives access to large databases.
   - It stimulates the critical mind of the pupils by the use of simulations.
3. It allows the realisation of integrated, interdisciplinary project oriented units.

What specifically characterises our situation in Luxembourg? First it must be stressed that we have no development of computer educational software of our own, that we therefore use the programs of other countries. A second characteristic is that our hardware was Acorn-BBC, but is being replaced more and more by PCs. A third significant feature is that our pupils are multi-lingual and we do not, therefore, normally need a translation of the different computer programs (but this is mainly true for the pupils aged at least 15). All this means, finally, that international contacts are of extreme importance for us.

Note: I should like to thank Gary and Lony Legerin-Lambert and also Jean-Jacques Weber for their helpful advice in translation. Thanks are also due to Dominique Portante for the information about the general use of computers in our schools.

Chapter 4
The Use of Computers in Portuguese History Curricula
Maria da Conceição Canavilhas

The Minerva Project

This project, approved by the Ministry of Education in October 1985, aimed to introduce information technologies into all levels of education except for higher education. The project started with a pilot phase, from 1985 to 1989, and operated in a highly decentralised manner, with the cooperation of many Portuguese universities, the Ministry Department of Planning (GEP) and the Schools of Education. All these institutions are charged with teacher training, curriculum development, and its evaluation, and operated with wide autonomy and a diversity of approaches to establish objectives, deciding what kind of work to do with schools. In 1985–86 the Project involved 40 schools and by the end of the pilot phase, 1988–89, involved 235 schools. It then moved into a dissemination phase until 1992. In 1992 it was expected that all Secondary, Preparatory, and about 15% of Primary Schools, would be provided with the means of actually using information technologies.

My own role in this project is to offer in-service courses to teachers of Social Studies, History and Geography in the Department of Education of the University of Lisbon. This training concerns both the technical component, referring to the use of computers and other technologies (like video), and its pedagogic and didactic use in activities developing either in the classroom or in extra-curricular activities. Thus I support the conception, development, evaluation and dissemination of work developed in this area. [Note: only the work which I developed (coordinated by Prof. Dr. João Pedro da Ponte) in the Department of Education, University of Lisbon, is considered in this chapter.]

The Computer in the Classroom

Throughout 1986 some history teachers (including myself) were encouraged to use computers in their classrooms, and with some specific groups as extra-curricular activities (club activities). We knew the great interest that pupils took in computers, as in TV, video and cinema. We had no doubt that the computer would be an element of motivation to our pupils. But we expected more than that from it. As our work advanced, we became aware that the computer offered different potentialities from the other resources usually employed, and it could be the starting point for pupils becoming more autonomous in the learning process. We know that today's pupils, the citizens of tomorrow, live in a world where information is increasing and they will have to develop skills and aptitudes which enable them to manage information and develop a critical attitude, to be able to solve the innumerable problems that they are going to face. Nowadays, pupils need to develop attitudes to locate them within the community where they will have an active and intervening role. Moreover, we are aware they will need to be ready to deal with change.

We felt that the traditional way of teaching did not convey these skills. The school cannot forget the fact that it does not play its role in a satisfactory way, if it is only a vehicle to transmit knowledge. Children, working in groups, have to develop an interest for research, organisation, exchange and discussion of ideas, cooperative work, responsibility and deliberation, which will be indispensable if they are to proceed with successful scholarship and adequate integration into the ever-changing world.

For these reasons we could not consider the computer as a powerful machine able to do everything, a kind of medicine for every illness, a teacher in miniature, more efficient but as judicious as the traditional teacher. We therefore put aside the idea of the computer as a tutor and rejected the use of crude tutorial software, often referred to as 'drill and practice' or 'skill and drill' software. Rather, we consider it as a powerful tool, which, managed by pupils, should help them to provide a variety of learning facilities. We had in mind to propose to the pupil some activities which could give them a greater independence and autonomy regarding the teacher, to hold them responsible for the accomplishment of the various tasks, making easier the development of a critical stance towards information, as well as the possibility of developing problem solving within the classroom.

We do not believe that the introduction of the information technologies as a tool is the single factor to take us to a renovation of the teaching of the human sciences, which we all feel as necessary. On the contrary, we think this renewal is mainly dependent on the methods employed in the teaching and learning environment. The computer, as a tool, will be just a powerful means, among many others, through which it can be achieved. This was our perspective when we introduced the computer into the classroom.

Software Applications in the History Classroom

Preliminary work 1985–87

The first work we carried out was the use of the computer in Social Studies, which belongs to the curriculum of the 5th grade (pupils of 10–11 years old), during years 1985–86 and 1986–87. Nine history teachers (only women), teaching in different Preparatory Schools in Lisbon, were involved in this work, each one with one class. Teacher training regarding technical aspects, the organisation of work units, and materials development (worksheets for pupils and software requirements such as datafiles), took place both during three weeks of intensive preparatory work and regular meetings every week during the two years of the study. Analysis of the results achieved, and continued revision of methods, strategies, classroom management and materials was an integral part of the whole procedure. For this work the computer was used as a resource for the treatment of the curricular subjects. The children used the computers in the classroom and in other activities outside the classroom as a tool for drawing, graphics, word processing and database work. The results of the experiment were positive. This formed the starting point for the work accomplished in the human sciences area, and it enabled us to gain experience and reach conclusions which had decisive influence on the work we did afterwards on the subject of history.

From the year 1987–88 the same group of teachers, and another group constituted later, had decided to introduce the computer into the history curriculum. The work previously developed enabled us to foresee that:

1. By utilising packages of maps created by drawing application software, pupils could acquire a more correct idea of the geographical space in which our history took place.

2. Manipulation of the notion of time could be facilitated by means of referring to datafiles whose core would be historical facts, chronologically indexed, which would permit incursions into past times, in both a synchronic and diachronic way.

3. Every item of quantitative data may be dealt with in a uniform way, through the representation of information in graphical form.

4. The use of software like word processing and desk top publishing could be a powerful source for the processing and communication of information collected by pupils in their learning and project work, for elaboration and synthesis of results, and even for interpretation of historical documents.

In short, the whole investigation process would be easier, more organised and would allow production of materials generated by the pupils themselves. We can now ask, how have these software applications been used in the history classroom?

Drawing Software in the History Classroom

Based on our experience with age-levels from 10 to 15, we concluded that pupils have some difficulties in dealing with categories such as space and time, though these difficulties are more evident among pupils between 10 and 12 years old.

Concerning space, the pupil advances more easily in his comprehension and apprehension if we give him the opportunity to visualise different geographical spaces and work on them. To achieve this purpose the teacher used to make use of outline maps, printed using the equipment available in the school, and pens and coloured pencils. Instead of that, mainly during the work done at the Preparatory Schools with pupils of 10 to 12 years old, we used the *Gem Paint* application software to build a package of outline maps, use of which is incorporated in the following work plan:

1. Statement of the problem.   (whole class activity)

2. Research and information collecting.   (small groups)

3. Treatment of information on computer   (small groups)
   using the package of outline maps.

4. Discussion of work accomplished,   (whole class)
   elaborating and registering of conclusions.
5. Eventual identification of new questions   (whole class)
   to investigate.

Following this plan, we have carried out, using the package of outline maps, among others, the following activities:

1. Localising spaces using shadings.
2. Creating drawings to illustrate the subject-matter of learning.
3. Drawings of routes.
4. Inserting the names of regions, towns, dates, and commercial products.
5. Elaborating legends.
6. Limiting the areas to be considered.

We must say that all this work has been very attractive to the pupils, enabling them to develop skills in the manipulation of this application software, greater precision in the treatment of space, and more correct apprehension of it. The production of a dossier of class work, and visual display material for wall exposure were some of the activities which followed up the work.

Database Management in the History Classroom

At the beginning of this experience it seemed very important to us to use database software in the history classroom. The management of databases and their use in the learning process have not been in any way an easy task. We chose to use *Superbase* which, in relation to other commercial databases, offers the advantage of being an easier software application for children. Despite this advantage *Superbase* is not as easy to manipulate as the drawing or word processing software we also used. To enable pupils to use it in an independent way, it is necessary that they understand fully the structure of the datafile, how to create it, and the way to select information. This type of software enables pupils to:

1. Create their own datafiles.
2. Access, search, select, interpret, correlate and evaluate information on previously constructed datafiles.
3. Store, organise and change information on a datafile structure previously constructed by teachers.

Each of these functions will now be considered in more detail.

Creating Datafiles

The construction of datafiles by the pupils was neither seen by us, teachers, nor presented to them, pupils, as an end in itself, but as an integral part of the larger project work. We must, however, emphasise that this process of creating a datafile structure requires of the learner the capacity to search, analyse and synthesise the information. They have to examine carefully the current conceptualisation of the way in which knowledge is structured, because they have to arrive at a set of logical categories into which they can place the information they have gathered, if the datafile is going to be of any value to them. This work favoured the development of logical capacities, since it obliges the learner to organise and structure concepts, and it seems to be a valuable learning strategy. However, because it is a very slow learning process, it would be easier to realise through activities with a less tight timetable such as, for instance, those which are accomplished in club activities (curriculum extending hours).

To exemplify, we will refer to one of those projects, beginning in the classroom and developed during club activities: "Portugal and World Cultural Exchanges". This project was developed in two Lisbon secondary schools, "Azevedo Neves" and "Camões", by the teachers Graça Pastor and Norberta Falcão, with pupils between 14 and 16 years old. The pupils, many of them from Africa, were motivated by teachers using resources like pupils' knowledge, video tapes and slides, to research the cultural exchanges consequent upon the Portuguese Discoveries. The initial questions were:

1. What cultural traces could they find in Portugal originally from their countries?
2. What cultural traces have been left in their countries by the Portuguese?

They developed together a worksheet for collecting data and began fieldwork researching the families of the African pupils. Afterwards they visited museums, the zoo, the Botanic Garden, embassies, and libraries. As a result of this work, they collected a large amount of data and completed more than a hundred worksheets concerned with food, on topics such as fruits, utensils, furniture, cooking, words used, etc. They also began to think about the datafile structure, which developed into one of 15 fields, one of them with external text and another with an external image. So a datafile was developed called "Exchanges", which includes at the moment about 100 records, and which will go on during the next school year, eventually being extended to more teachers, classes and schools.

With a methodology similar to this project, other datafiles were created. Examples are, in Preparatory schools: Toponymy of Alfama (an old quarter of Lisbon); Portuguese Monuments; Personalities from Portuguese History; Technical Innovations through Time; Festivals, Fairs and Pilgrimages; Typical Portuguese Food; Manufacturing Industries. And in Secondary schools: The Renaissance; World War II.

Consulting a Datafile

A datafile which has already been completed has the advantage of offering to pupils a large quantity of information which can be manipulated, interrogated and correlated, according to the needs of the moment. For that reason the teachers constructed datafiles whose central element is the historical happening, chronologically indexed.

The creation of the datafile structure, the insertion of the data, and its classification in all records was a slow task, especially so as the teachers' groups involved did not always agree. Therefore, after being tested in a class situation, it was (and will be again) reformulated, in order to facilitate the research work, and to be more appropriate to the age of the pupils. The following datafiles were, therefore, created by the teachers: The Foundation of Portugal (from 1090 to 1385); The Portuguese Discoveries (from 1415 to 1580); Liberalism in Portugal; The French

Invasion; The Reign of King Lu's; Portugal from 1090 to 1990. The utilisation of these datafiles enabled rapid access to a greater variety of data, the selection of historical facts under conditions suggested by pupils themselves, the examination of similarities and differences, and an easier apprehension of the essential elements, the relationships between facts far distant from one another, both in time and in space, and the relationships between historical causes and consequences.

We think it is much more important that the datafiles have an uncomplicated structure, enabling adequate searches to be performed. With database software, in contrast to other applications, with which the pupils become familiarised within a short period, and can then easily operate them, the teachers must devote some time to explaining to pupils which are the datafile fields, the way the datafile is organised, why and how to do a search operation, and how to follow up to accomplish it. Only in this manner will we enable the pupils to become independent in their researches. The achievement of this independence is indispensable since, in our opinion, one of the more positive and significant educational uses of consulting datafiles lies in the process of conceptualising which relates to the logical thinking exercise the pupil must perform in order to build up the catalysing procedure with the conditions necessary to obtain the desired results.

Completing a Previously Constructed Datafile Structure

During the process of teaching and learning history, pupils frequently analyse historical documents to answer questions and obtain conclusions. We have constructed datafiles we called "open grid", that is to say, datafiles which have a structure already set up by teachers, but where the allocation of data to the appropriate fields is processed (totally or partially) by pupils, referring to the external text field, or through bibliographical research.

An example is the "Concession" datafile, relating to the Middle Ages, which is intended for the study of donation documents, charters to the clergy and nobility, and Fair privileges to the people. We tried to ensure that the datafile structure would include every question usually connected with these documents. The pupil will be able to manipulate a greater quantity of historical documents of the same kind, grasp more easily the essential matters, identify similar divergent ones, establish connecting lines, and try to find the causes and the results of certain events.

Graphics Software in the History Classroom

We used graphics software, whenever we thought it advisable, to accompany a quantitative analysis of data. We chose *Gem Graph*, which has been incorporated into the following plan:

1. Identification of a problem. (whole class)
2. Research and information collection, using manuals, datafiles, etc. (small groups)
3. Processing of data and choice of graphics type. (small groups)
4. Analysis of the graph, discussion and registering of conclusions. (whole class)
5. Identification of new investigation. (whole class)

The pupils prepared, for example, after searching the "Portugal" datafile, graphs relating to mediæval fairs, grouped by reign, which help them to understand the relationship between the development of fairs during the reign of King Afonso III and the end of the Wars of the Christian Reconquest. They also prepared graphs of the products traded by the Portuguese during the period of the Discoveries (the 15th and 16th centuries).

Word Processing in the History Classroom

Word processing software is one of the software types most utilised by every computer user, since it replaces the typewriter, with innumerable advantages. We chose *First Word Plus*, and our pupils utilised it whenever they were asked for written work — descriptions, reports, syntheses, etc. This package was also utilised for the analysis of historical documents, in the following activities:

1. Emphasise aspects of the document, changing fonts and styles, or using the underlining, emboldening and italic script to change the presentation of phrases.
2. Move or copy document blocks.

Desktop Publishing in the History Classroom

We chose *Publish It*, which was mainly used as an integrator of materials produced by pupils using the word processing, graphics and drawing software whenever, during their project work, there emerged the need or the intention to produce posters, small newspapers, or even small brochures or books.

As an example, we will discuss one of the projects beginning in the classroom and developed further during club activities, "Let us know our region — Oeiras". This project was developed in the Preparatory School of Oeiras, by teachers Dina de Sousa and Madalena Pinto, with pupils between 11 and 13 years old. The project was carried out in several phases, which included field work, research and data organisation. It was concluded with the preparation by the pupils of a book, from which many copies were made and distributed both in the school itself and to the other schools in the Minerva Project. The pupils, belonging to two Portuguese History classes, organised research in libraries and local museums, walked around the streets and squares of the historic parts of the village, visited churches, chapels, palaces, noble houses, farms, and lighthouses, and carried out some interviews at the Town Hall and with local associations. Based on this research, they organised a large amount of data about the history of the locality, from the past up to the present, which was processed (word processor), illustrated (drawing) and graphically processed (graphics). They also set up a datafile of the municipal monuments. Finally, using desktop publishing, the whole work was collected and organised into a book, which was then available for anyone to consult.

Teaching Strategies and Classroom Organisation

In the classroom there are no computers. In order to use them, the teachers move, with their classes, to the Minerva Project Room in the school, where they have 5 or 6 computers at their disposal. It is also there that they carry out the curriculum extending activities already referred to. Usually the pupils only visit the computer room if the timetable offers 2-hour classes, which were expressly requested for this work by the Minerva Project from the Ministry of Education — normally classes would last only 50 minutes. Since the classes have between 24 and 30 pupils, the number of computers is not large enough. Because of the methodologies and strategies chosen (we did not consider a situation of one pupil for each computer would be advisable), we arrived at the conclusion that more than three pupils for each computer is not feasible, and does not favour the activities we propose for the pupils. We therefore normally divided the classes into two groups, one operating with the computers while the others are carrying out activities with other types of resource. The activities of both groups are complementary; sometimes they may deal with other matters, but they have never been identical. The groups exchange places and activities when the first hour has elapsed or at the following lesson.

To carry forward the work of the pupils, we took advantage of user-guides prepared by the teachers which dealt with the activities they would have to do with the computer, including relevant technical information. In addition, there are in the classrooms posters or laminated instruction cards with the basic technical instructions: how to turn the computer on and off, insert and remove disks, load, save and print files, etc. When the pupils had become familiar with the technical procedures of the applications they were using, and had at the same time learned the group work rules, the activities and the projects began to be less directed by the teacher, and the groups became more responsible and independent concerning the projects they were developing. This was, however, a long process, and it was easier with some classes than with others.

Teacher Training Issues

We started from the assumption that teachers should not be viewed as software developers, but as curriculum developers, which requires the ability and the creativity to make appropriate use of existing software. We also started with the assumption that, more important than to think of how to use the computer to serve the curriculum, is to imagine how the computer can help the curriculum to change. The process of teacher training was a continuous activity which could not be achieved in a year, but extended over a much longer period of time.

During the training I naturally utilised the tool-based software which could normally be found on the market (utility software applications). Since the computers we used were Amstrad PC1512 or 1640, we decided on the *Gem* operating environment, because it is easier for children to use. The teachers began to attend courses focusing on a single application such as word processing, drawing, graphics, databases and desktop publishing, always with an emphasis on discussing and evaluating its possible educational uses in history. Later, only for about 20 teachers who had already worked with children in the classroom, who had already gained considerable practice in the use of computers, and whose motivation and enthusiasm was great, a longer course (of three intensive weeks) was offered, which included the development of a curriculum project. In addition to the technical knowledge about the use of utility programs, the following matters were discussed: society and technology; perspectives for the introduction of computers into the process of teaching and learning; curriculum management and the use of computers; the use of tool-based software in history didactics; project work; techniques of managing groups; educational use of video.

Besides the intensive period of training, these teachers also continued to meet, one day each week, to plan the units of work, organise and develop materials, and analyse results. The monitor for the Minerva Project took an active part in this work. He became an integral part of several groups, sat in on the planning, development and evaluation of the projects, promoted the exchange of experiences and results, observed classes and, many times, made video recordings of the different phases of the activity.

Conclusions and Evaluation

The experiments have not been easy to carry out. All the participants found their work exacting and intensive, often under less than desirable conditions. In the context of the present Portuguese school structure, such activities face several difficulties: lack of adequate rooms; lack of human resources and materials; too many pupils both at the school and in the classroom; and the difficulty in finding time for teachers to meet.

Concerning the curriculum, it is extremely tight and rigid regarding timetables; there are too many subjects working in isolation; the programmes are too long; and the concern with the development of capacities, aptitudes and values, which would recommend a more active mode of learning, are finally absorbed by the enormous lists of content-matter which, to be accomplished, requires a traditional teaching method to be followed.

Following the evaluation with the teachers throughout the whole process, and my personal observations, I will list some issues I consider important:

1. The introduction of the computer into the classroom is charged with pedagogical implications.
2. The computer has been a powerful motivating tool which led to better results at school — however we think this result is essentially caused by its novelty and will disappear unless the tasks suggested are, themselves, attractive.
3. The computer has spread its influence over the learning process as it has facilitated the projects pupils are involved in, namely:
   - It made possible activities leading to learning methods which, without its utilisation, would be difficult if not impossible to achieve, e.g. by consulting datafiles which, besides favouring the understanding of the concept of time, also makes possible the establishment of connections between historical events, different in time and in space, and the apprehension of the concept of change.
   - It made easier the organisation and processing of data, e.g. the creating of datafile structures by pupils.
   - It assisted the apprehension of the space where historical events take place, e.g. by means of the activities carried out with maps using drawing software.
   - It made possible a better presentation of materials produced by pupils, either for their personal use or for transmission to schoolfellows, e.g. with word processing or desktop publishing software.

- It made quickly possible and graphically accessible the treatment and analysis of quantitative information, e.g. using graphics software.
4. The computer contributes to the destruction of affective barriers, between teacher and pupil and pupil and teacher; we could notice an attitude of accomplice solidarity becoming increasingly evident.
5. The computer contributed to decentralising knowledge from the teacher, and moving closer to a personal relationship between teacher and pupil.
6. The computer made easier the integration of pupils with learning difficulties.
7. We noticed that pupils became more autonomous, responsible, persistent, and cooperative, and developed a critical sense, a capacity to evaluate self and others, which was, for instance, demonstrated during the group projects in which they were involved.

We must point out that many facts we were referring to are a consequence not only of using computers, but also of the methodologies employed and the pedagogical environment created. I also observed certain characteristics of attitudes revealed by teachers which led me to conclude that the computer provides an opportunity for change if it offers to the teacher the possibility of reflection about the nature of the learning activities which should be offered to pupils.

Regarding the relationship between teachers and pupils:
1. There was a strong affective relationship between teachers and pupils involved in the work.
2. The teacher's role was to be a facilitator, a counsellor, a provider, an assessor, and in some cases a partner in the learning environment. I believe that this role, its effective practice, and the pedagogical environment created were essential for the learning success achieved.

Regarding the professional preparation of teachers:
1. The activities and the projects suggested to pupils have increasingly taken on a greater dynamic nature.
2. The involvement of teachers in their own projects led them to make a careful scientific study of the tasks involved (as a result of creating datafiles for pupil management).
3. Most teachers gained greater profit from using local history as a starting point to begin the study of certain elements of the programmes.
4. They have shown an attitude of continuing interest and involvement in searching and studying new information.
5. We were able to attest to a more coherent management of, and growing autonomy in the use of information technologies and, at the same time, a greater consciousness of their role as educators.
6. Throughout the duration of the work, there was a growing atmosphere or state of mind favouring the sharing of materials, activities and experiences.
7. Everybody became fully involved in the ongoing reflection, both on their own and on group activities, considering the reformulation and improvement of the materials used as well as the teaching practices adopted.
8. We sensed a progressively greater feeling of security, professionalism, and independence, both in individual and group activities.

9. Throughout the duration of the work, they showed a willingness to divulge their work, in order to involve and attract other teachers.

10. Above all I must emphasise a genuinely open attitude to change.

A comprehensive programme of educational reform is now under way in Portugal. In the existing curriculum the use of computers or other technologies is not specifically required or even suggested. The Group for Human Sciences of the Minerva Project of the University of Lisbon has published a document reflecting the specific role for information technologies in the history curriculum. This document was discussed with the commission in charge of Educational Reform at the Ministry of Education, in January 1990. The experimental history curriculum for the 5th and 6th years of schooling, published in July 1990, only contains the following phrases relevant to all the proposals we have made:

Objectives: "The pupils must be familiar with new information technologies to be able to develop capacities of communication."

Methodology: "The organisation of thematic archives about concepts or bibliographical references should be made using computers."

"Whenever the materials and human resources permit it, pupils must be encouraged to use new information technologies, namely Informatic and Telematic media. The use of computers by teachers and learners is possible for:

- graphic information processing.
- information processing and communicating ideas.
- search, interpretation, organisation and evaluation of information; for example, in chronological series.

The experimental history curriculum for the 7th, 8th and 9th year of schooling, also published in July 1990, makes the following relevant proposals:

Objectives: "To realise the importance of scientific and technological development to human evolution, having in mind to extend and consolidate the notions of conditionalism and causality."

"The pupils must be familiar with new information technologies to be able to develop capacities of communication.

Methodology: "To use the widest possible variety of didactic resources, including new information technologies."

"Despite the motivational effects on pupils, as learning reinforcement, it must not be the only reason for the adoption of new information technologies."

"As any other resources, new information technologies must be included in a process of learning appropriate to the proposed objectives."

In spite of the fact that some of our proposals have not been included in the experimental history curriculum, we were gratified, as we feel that our work was not in vain. At this moment in Portugal a door has been opened to the general idea of using information technologies in the history curriculum.

Chapter 5

Computing in French Secondary Schools

Daniel Letouzey

Introduction

Computing has been used in France since the early 1970s. This chapter is not intended to give an academic account of what has been done since then, one reason being that the author does not have access to official information on these matters. Instead the author shows, from a personal approach, how computing has been introduced and received by the ordinary teacher, how teachers have managed to use it with pupils and how he sees the present situation. Faced with so many changes to come (including mass teaching and new technologies) teachers must concentrate on the specific role of computers in their classroom.

Working Conditions

History and geography are linked in French secondary schools, so computing can be used for one subject or the other. Teachers have between three and four hours per week for history and geography. In the lycée emphasis is put on contemporary history, the French Revolution in 'seconde' (5th form) and France since 1945 or world affairs in 'terminale' (upper 6th form). With a final examination there seems to be little or no time to work with computers. The average class size is 36 pupils and a standard computing room is equipped with eight IBM machines. All this is a big challenge to colleagues who want to use computers for tutorial purposes.

Computing is an optional subject for a limited number of pupils, in particular for those who will take it for the baccalaureat and those who are studying accounting or commerce. The history teacher may initiate all pupils into using the computer as a tool, but schools and teachers have very little money to buy specific software. A cheap package would cost approximately £50. If eight copies are needed this means a total cost of £400 which schools cannot afford as they must buy maps, slides and other resources. Teachers who want to use software may teach themselves, but they can also go to training sessions (3 to 6 days each year).

Computing in Secondary Schools: Some Landmarks

Computing was introduced as an experiment in the early 1970s. In 1982 10,000 CPM-based French computers were bought for the lycées. The good side of this initiative included the opportunity for schools to use a new technology sponsored by the Ministry of Education, and a compulsory 100 hours training for teachers. On the other hand these French machines had poor graphics capacities and most of the software was rather simple-minded. Moreover, in order to avoid the learning of BASIC, a special programming language was imposed. LSE (langage symbolique pour l'enseignement) proved to be a cul-de-sac, even if in some ways it prepared the user for programming in Pascal. As a result, of the 32 teachers in my lycée being trained to use computers, fewer than five tried to find their way to developing computer assisted learning.

In 1985 Prime Minister L. Fabius launched a plan ('Informatique pour tous') to equip most schools, both elementary and secondary. Once again teachers were given a week of training. The technical choice suited tutorial computing very well: a network which was IBM compatible, with monochrome monitors and up to 32 individual workstations. In fact what was provided was six Thomson MO5 for a class of 24 pupils, with colour TV or monitors. Several programs had been prepared for each subject and were delivered with a 'Nanoreseau' (for instance a spreadsheet, *Colorcalc*; a drawing package, *Colorpeint*; and electronic mail software, *Praxitele*). Trouble came from several points, principally the need to launch this plan before the 1986 elections, the very high price of the screen and the floppy disk for a single MO5, and the quality of the software. For history it was difficult to see the teaching interest of a game called *Le Moyen-Age*. However, improvements came with simulations on planning cities (for instance, *La Ville Ideal*) and understanding the third world (*La Planete Bleue*); progress was also made in word processing and desktop publishing, but using always 40 columns.

After 1988, changes were both political and technical. Lycées could afford to buy XT compatibles with monochrome monitor and two disk drives for a start, with hard disk and colour screen later on. And quite often, now, ATs are bought. Thus it is possible to work with greater efficiency, not least during training sessions for teachers. On the political side, the state ruled CNDP was put aside, and private publishers asked to work for education. To avoid piracy, 'licences mixtes' were signed between the Ministry of Education and the publishers. The right to use a piece of software was agreed and paid for on a national level; as a result each lycée had only to pay £50 for a word-processing (e.g. *Word* junior) or spreadsheet program (e.g. *Multiplan* junior). This was a good way to ensure that general software was made more widely available, but there were few if any history programs available for use.

Comparing French and British experience, it can be said that computing policy in France was led on a national scale, with resources raised by the Ministry of Education. As in Britain, we had a nationalist approach, trying to subsidise French companies (for instance, Leanord which was based near Lille of which M. Mauroy was the Mayor, and the nationalised Thomson). IBM and its clones were preferred to Apple Macintosh. Furthermore, computing became a political issue, with both left and right wanting to profit from a modern and technical image.

France has lived for a long time with two Utopias. The first is that software may help pupils to overcome their difficulties with traditional teaching. That was partly achieved with Foucambert's software on fast reading (*Elmo*), but in most cases the best pupils also excelled with computers. The second Utopia was that teachers were supposed to program the software they needed, with the result that some programs were in fact too personal or too simple and in some cases lacked professional finishing. It also became clear that such work was too demanding for a single person.

Several approaches have been used to try to convince teachers that they should use computers. One approach was a Paris decision that every school should be equipped with computers (with a national target of 10,000 computers in 1981, and of 100,000 in 1985). Another approach has been to rely on individual decisions, on the influence of parents who want to help their children to keep pace with technology or simply with school work, and teachers who have come to appreciate that they need a word processor to help them prepare their work. I myself foresee decentralisation with some fear. The government wants to allow as much as 80% of a generation to go to lycées, to build new universities and to encourage regional bodies to equip the lycées.

Our Objectives

Our responsibility is first to the teaching and learning of history and geography, not computing, so we have to think about developing simple case studies. In these studies, we focus on skills more than on knowledge. Pupils will have had some computing experience between the ages of 11 and 15, but in order to use general software they must be initiated into the appropriate basics including MS-DOS and the main characteristics of each kind of software. Sessions with a computer are always linked with practical work, either at school or at home, as this is the best way for pupils to see what computing can achieve. We have no large scale enquiry on computer assisted learning efficiency but only a few pupils refuse to cooperate, perhaps because you need to have a real personal investment in this type of work.

Having five or six sessions for each pupil in a school year, we prefer tutorial sessions with the computer. All pupils should be confident enough to use the computers available in CDI (the school library) either for their own work or to seek information from CD-ROMS or from a library files (*Memelog*). We try to prepare all pupils to be at least computer literate.

Teaching Examples

Graphs

A very simple but impressive package has been made available to schools. *Graph In The Box* can capture any number on a screen and show them in eleven different types of graphs. For history, interest is in choosing the right types, in analysing a graph, or in comparing several graphs together. Computers allow pupils to go faster, to get a perfect quality print, to make tries and mistakes and to learn from their mistakes. For a start we may draw a simple graph, for instance of coal production in 19th century England. Then, comparing the population of each country since 1750, we can compare production in different countries and at chronological intervals using bar graphs and pie charts. Pupils prefer pie charts but it is often more difficult to read them and most software provides a fixed diameter. Another possibility is that with a simple count and list from parish books pupils can meet the effect of the republican calendar, discover missing data (1793–96) or see the French getting married to avoid conscription in 1809 or 1813. None of this software was developed specifically for history, so pupils have to discover tricky solutions to cope with what they are asked to do.

Statistics

For history or geography we use simple statistics, related to teachers and pupils' levels in mathematics. This can be done effectively using spreadsheets, *Multiplan* being the leader in France. With climate figures we can work on totals and averages. This can also be done using a pocket calculator but the computer allows teachers and pupils to work with a wider range of data, and may also aid the use of decimals. Also in geography, age pyramids can be used to explain how to calculate percentages and how to use repetition orders. More specifically for history it is possible to use the computer to find out the percentage of foreign people living in France in 1881. The results can be captured by a graphic package and printed. A spreadsheet is very effective for sorting important data and by this means it is possible to obtain a classified list, make a graph and study some of the rules of statistics.

Another case study is to calculate the index from different units. For instance, we know from a school book the daily wages, annual benefits, number of miners and annual production in a coal mine in Carmaux (South of France). We can compare all these facts by choosing index and making graphs from them, but we get a better result selecting two series. For instance, we can see productivity by putting together number of miners and total production. Even more interesting is to show the effect of the reference date. Comparing 1860 to 1913 reveals that wages have multiplied by 2.8 and profits by 5, but choosing 1913 as a reference can lead to the impression that wages were always above profits. A reasonable practice can be achieved by elaborating from one table with raw figures two derived tables, one with percentages and the other with index.

Map-making

We have to face some difficulties here. For history, boundaries have changed in Europe, and particularly in France during the nineteenth century. The same remark applies to administrative limits. For geography it can be difficult to get suitable and exact data for each region. In *Eurostat*, we may find facts for 90 separate French departments, but English counties may be grouped together, for instance Suffolk, Norfolk and Cambridgeshire are sometimes grouped as East Anglia. For both subjects, we must check and use the data with care. For instance, some people are sceptical about official figures for unemployment. Studying actual matters allows pupils to check the figures concerning their living places (for example, British owners in Normandy villages).

French history and geography books contain a large variety of maps — often in colour — so why use a computer for this purpose? One reason is that we want to explain how statistical maps are made, and this can be done best by practising with true samples. A second reason is to make use of local data. For instance, poll results can suggest differences between places and several explanations can then be tested (religious belief, social structure, kind of economy, wages, history). Moreover, with a map-making package, *Logicarte*, we can emphasise both the effect of various statistical methods and the result of changing the kind of shading.

Teacher Training

In France every "academy" (L.E.A) has a "Mafpen" or a "Cafpen" to deliver training for teachers. Each individual can take advantage of local sessions, practising computing for all subjects. Most academies have computing sessions for either history or for social sciences. These sessions may last from three to six days, with two or more days devoted to learning to use software and prepare work for the pupils' benefit. One day or more is necessary to evaluate work done and, when possible, to go deeper. The teachers volunteer for the training and the trainers are often faced with dealing with really different levels (from discovering the keyboard to programming). We now avoid the mistake of showing too much software and prefer that each teacher becomes more confident with simple software. In particular, we always begin with a word processing program (*Works or Word*) to help in discovering the computer and motivating the teachers.

Other New Technologies

In what has been described here use has not been made of datasheets. This is because it takes too much time to train pupils. However, the Ministry of Education has spent a lot of money sponsoring new technologies. Regarding electronic mail, for instance, the French *Minitel* is used by several schools to communicate with others or with parents. Pupils may learn how to run a small "service". Many examples were created for 1989 to help commemorate the French Revolution and others will be prepared for 1992 to mark the enlarging of Europe. Regarding satellite images and support for Spot (the French satellite), 100 lycées have been equipped with computers and can study images of their region. There have also been developments with the Videodisk or Numeric images, and with CD-ROM. A special effort was made in 1989 but so far nothing has been produced specifically for history teachers, though *Le Monde* does now sell a package mixing texts, graphs, images and sound on history since 1945.

Conclusion

The reader may think that computing is common in history classrooms in France. In fact only a few convinced teachers study their way through history by computing. It is now time to use these new technologies to a greater extent. Computers are now much easier to use, and new screen environments such as *Windows* may help too. Furthermore, with a personal computer it is now possible to undertake fieldwork in demography or the economy which was only possible for advanced students years ago.

Of course, computing is still expensive. Officials expect us to use computers for appropriate purposes, and parents are worried when they see so much money going for dust (as we say in French)!

In France I see two reasons for hope. The first arises from the fact that a significant number of history teachers have found that they need a word processor, and so they seek a computer rather than a typewriter. The second reason is that the teachers of the future are at present students, many of whom are using datasheets in their historical training and research. They may understand better the importance of a computer in the history classroom.

Perhaps the time has come to leave Utopia and to concentrate on convincing other teachers through obvious and concrete advantages.

Chapter 6
The Use of IT in the Danish History Curriculum
Sten Larsen and Lars Bluhme

The Curriculum in Danish Schools

In Denmark pupils leave basic (compulsory) schooling at the age of 15–16 years. At that point their school careers have lasted 9 or 10 years. They may proceed to upper secondary school (33% did so in 1992). They may choose among a wide range of vocational training programmes. Or they may go elsewhere. The subjects taught in primary and lower secondary school — the Folkeskole as we call it — are shown in Figure 6.1. The diagram shows the distribution of subjects, which is a mixture of compulsory and non-compulsory subjects.

With regard to the upper-secondary school, pupils have to choose between a languages line and a mathematics line. The dark areas in the subject diagram for the languages line (shown in Figure 6.2) indicate the overlap with the mathematics line. And here again, one of the optional subjects can be Computer Science, with 4 lessons per week.

IT Possibilities in Schools

What possibilities do we see in general terms?

IT-Possibilities in primary and lower secondary school (6–16 years):

- IT as a compulsory topic in the lower classes (in line with other compulsory topics as traffic safety, sex education etc.);
- IT as a non-compulsory option in 8th, 9th and 10th — form Computer Science.
- IT as an integrated part of the ordinary instruction in all subjects.

IT-Possibilities in upper secondary school (16–19 years):

- IT as a short introductory user course.
- IT as an optional subject — Computer Science.
- IT as an integrated part of the ordinary instruction in all subjects.

There is no doubt that the investments in hardware in the schools have not been large enough. But it is only a question of time — the development is in full swing. We have another and real problem: we are short of certain types of software simply because there is not much Danish software on the market. This is primarily because Denmark is a very small country, which means that the production of certain types of software is very limited.

	1	2	3	4	5	6	7	8	9	After the reform	Before the reform
Danish	9	8	7	6	6	6	6	6	6	60	60
English				2	3	3	3	3	3	17	15
Christian studies	2	1	1	1	1	2		1	1	10	10
Social studies									5	5	
History			1	1	1	2	2	2		9	11
PE and sport	1	2	2	3	3	2	2	2	2	19	19
Music	1	2	2	2	1	1				9	8
Art	1	2	2	2	1					8	8
Needlework, wood/metal-work, home economics				2	4	4	3			13	13
Mathematics	4	4	4	4	4	4	4	4	4	36	36
Science	1	1	2	2	2	3				11	
Geography							2	2		4	7
Biology							2	2		4	7
Physics/chemistry							2	2	2	6	6
German							3	4	4	11	11
Optional subjects								2	2	4	4
Class time*	1	1	1	1	1	1	1	1	1	9	9

* Added to class teacher's subject.

Figure 6.1 Recommended weekly distribution of lessons in 1st to 9th form levels

3rd year	PE and Sport	Danish	History	Religious Education	Visual Art	Classical Studies	Option	Option	Option
	2	4	3	3	2	3	4 or 5	5	5

2nd year	PE and Sport	Danish	History	Foreign Language (cont.)	Geography	Foreign Language (beginners)	English	Natural science	Option
	2	3	3	4	3	4	4	4	4 or 5

1st year	PE and Sport	Danish	History	Foreign Language (cont.)	Biology	Music	Foreign Language (beginners)	English	Natural science	Latin
	2	3	3	4	3	4	4	4	3	3

Figure 6.2 Language Line: Number of Lessons per Week per Subject

The target is, nonetheless, fully integrated IT in each subject taught — at primary and lower secondary level, and at upper secondary level. The point of integration, indeed, is taken very seriously, and is not just fine words in the IT policy of the Ministry of Education. In the late 1980s the question was asked in the Ministry: how will the teachers be able to integrate IT in practice into everyday teaching? For example, in geography or Danish or needlework. To get an answer to this question, a systematic review was undertaken of all school subjects as seen from an IT point of view. And for each subject a supplement, published as a booklet, was added to the existing curriculum. These supplementary curricula thus give the answers to the questions: why to integrate IT into everyday teaching; and how to integrate IT into everyday teaching.

We have just (in spring 1993) in the Ministry of Education put the final touch to such a booklet about IT in history teaching. The NIT (New Information Technology) supplement includes the following sections: The Status of the Teaching of History in Denmark; NIT and the Collection of Materials; NIT and Information Retrieval; NIT and Pupil Presentations; NIT and Empathy; A Teaching Example. This discussion will focus on those parts of the supplement that are, from a Danish point of view, the most innovative, i.e. the sections dealing with information retrieval and with empathy.

NIT and Information Retrieval

By inserting a diskette, or perhaps more likely a CD-ROM disc, into a computer, or by making contact over the telephone with a so-called external database, it is now possible to leaf around in thousands of pages of historical material. It may be original texts, or texts specifically designed for teaching. And by means of keywords, it is now possible to swiftly move around in these pages and find what one is looking for. This, of course, opens up new prospects with regard to the subject of history, but also new problems.

In actual history teaching, a distinction can be made between two main types of electronic, historical databases.

The first type may give access to large quantities of original material — or rather source texts — about the topic in question. Such material may be available in a quite unprocessed form, for instance as an entire volume of a newspaper or as a number of photos of items from the archives of the National Museum; or it may have been selected and adapted to a teaching situation. The pupils may explore all this and retrieve the required information, thus experiencing an authenticity and getting an impression of a time period in the past, something that would have required a great deal of reading otherwise. It may even be possible for pupils and teacher to make a reconstruction of a time period on the basis of the material, thereby rendering the historical presentation superfluous in some cases.

In order to be in a position to make use of the information so retrieved, the pupils must be enabled to select and sort; and this is perhaps the greatest challenge facing the educator. As regards methods, the work with this type of databases is comparable to work with source collections and makes the same demands on the teaching. It is essential to have discussions about the authorship and inclination of the texts, and the range of available texts must be evaluated — all of this, however, supplementing what is already now being asked of texts in everyday teaching.

In order to be able to ask sensible questions and set up useful criteria for retrieval, it is also necessary to create a frame of reference for the information. The teaching should therefore aim at setting up such a framework of overview and understanding. On the other hand, knowledge of historical details can be down-graded, in the assurance that knowledge, in the sense of a fund of information, can fairly easily be established via the new media.

The second main type is comparable to a historical presentation, while often also including a certain amount of original material. One is, as reader, presented with extracts of texts, explanations, interpretations, pictures, video sequences, sounds and music. A presentation of this type can be motivating and will allow pupils to see events and contexts, which they would not otherwise see when read-ing traditional presentations used for teaching purposes. At the same time the interactive element provides the pupils with the opportunity to do some explora-tion on their own as is the case, likewise, with the purely text-based bases. In order for the pupils to be able to work with these bases — and not just use them as entertainment — it is also here necessary to offer them some overall knowledge of the period or the topic dealt with. This will allow the pupils to see the individual sequences in a larger context and to constantly question and assess the contents. In view of the many possibilities of presentation, it is essential also to discuss the techniques and manipulation possibilities involved in the production of multime-dia systems — questions which are, incidentally, equally relevant as far as video productions are concerned. This will create a consciousness, in the pupils, about the strengths and weaknesses of the new medium — a consciousness which is also useful outside school life.

NIT and Empathy

The aspect of empathy as a teaching method is making its way into Danish history teaching. There are many possibilities such as role-playing, historical reconstructions, drama-documentarism and use of historical fiction. These techniques are applicable whether NIT is involved or not, but the introduction of NIT in the teaching will open up new and better possibilities.

First and foremost, a large number of computer games are available which take their point of departure in a historical period or event. But we are also beginning to see simulation programmes, in which the pupils are required to take the place of various decision-makers, both past and present. Finally, mention should be made of the real models — e.g. politico-economic cycles — in which the pupils may change preconditions and decisions, arriving thus at different outcomes. All these types of programmes have that in common that they attempt to make the pupils/users act in a historical or contemporary reality.

In order to be useful in the teaching, the programmes must be reliable from a historical point of view. The historical background, which forms the basis of the games or simulations, should be historically justifiable. If the contents, for instance, are placed in the European Middle Ages, the historical scene should not be populated by beautiful princesses and dragons like in "Dungeons and Dragons" but could perhaps depict life at the court of the German emperor or situations from wars or peasant rebellions. The beautiful princesses could be used in the subject Danish in the work with fairy tales. But in history it is essential that the stage and scene arrangements should be historically credible.

Another requirement must be that of transparent rules of the games. Behind each model, which forms the basis of a game or simulation, there are considerations about cause and effect. What is it that causes the game to develop in different ways depending on the decisions and acts of the player? These considerations are a very essential part of the historical contents. The characters may be fictitious for the sake of the dramatic element, but their acts and fates must be rooted in an understanding of a given historical period. In order to make it possible to assess and to form an opinion of this understanding, it is necessary both to elucidate the model behind the games and simulations, and to make it the object of analysis and discussion.

It may be an advantage if the characters in games and simulations are historically anonymous. Where a well-described historical event is involved, in which the decisions made and their implications are known, these may seem as answers already provided and thus restrict the range of choices. Hindsight may affect the decision-making of the players, whereby part of the empathy aspect in the present situation will be lost. Must a player repeat the errors of a decision-maker, knowing quite well the implications were disastrous? If such questions can be asked, the issue will soon lose credibility and become useless. However, if the range of characters consists of people — who represent a group, a trend or some ideas — the empathy of the player will become more realistic. A short example will illustrate this. If a game or a simulation takes place during the French Revolution in 1789, the pupils have a better chance of identifying themselves with, and understanding the efforts of an anonymous Parisian citizen to escape unhurt through the upheavals rather than having to go through with the already well-known decisions of Louis XVI in the first years of the Revolution that led to his execution.

As mentioned previously the action game does not assume historical correctness. It may be claimed that games of this character relate to historical presentations like fiction. Like in the historical novel, events and situations are described as they could have taken place, without laying claim to being true in a traditional scientific sense. Like literature, the games contain a problem or a plot, chosen on the basis of dramatic qualities rather than historical correctness. Precisely that in the games makes for empathy with the pupils. The very process of solving the problem, which is often put together from the model with hero/accomplice/adversary, may perhaps be the important thing for the pupils during the game. But the historical learning, which justifies the use of the games in history teaching, has to take place on the basis of credible assumptions of cause and effect. When work with historical games proves successful, the pupils are given not only an experience, but also a consciousness of their own competence regarding a given historical period.

As far as simulations and models are concerned, the range of programs is very large. At the one end of the spectrum are simple programs, often built up as a spreadsheet, which call for the pupils to change various inputs in order to find out what the implications are for the result. These programs may for instance illustrate economic issues, such as feasibility studies in connection with investments in new technology, or the effects of governmental intervention in political economics etc. At the other end of the spectrum are the more complex programmes, which call for the player to govern a city, a nation or even the entire world. By changing certain parameters, and reading the effects on the development, the pupils may gain insight in issues of e.g. national and international politics and ecology. To this type of programmes apply the same considerations regarding credibility, transparency and overview as to the historical games.

What we have been saying about NIT-aided information retrieval assumed the understanding that this is a societal development, which is bound to affect the subject of history. The programs offering empathy will be a choice on the part of teacher and pupils. They can choose whether or not they want to use these programs in teaching. One important aspect in making this decision is that pupils and teacher, in these programs, depart from the same level of knowledge.

Chapter 7

IT and History: A Whole School Approach

Wayne Birks

Introduction

Given the number of recent publications on IT in history and the interest shown by software publishers, one could be forgiven for thinking that the presence of a computer in the history classroom has almost become commonplace. A survey as long ago as 1987 in Leicestershire schools had shown that pupils were using computers in history and humanities work in half the institutions visited [Baker, 1990:18–19]. Blow and Dickinson [1986] referred to surveys suggesting that the use of computers in history was growing rapidly. Certainly the proliferation of material has been considerable and there are now well over 200 computer programs designed for use with history pupils.

The case for using computers in the history classroom has not evolved without controversy. Comparing the June 1982 and January 1989 editions of *Teaching History*, both of which focused upon Computer Assisted Learning (CAL), clear evidence emerges of the growth in computer literacy amongst history staff. There are still arguments, of course, about "good" and "indifferent" programs and whether one or 30 machines are sufficient to meet lesson objectives. The argument that historical understanding can be assisted by IT has also become more widely accepted. In 1985, HMI commented that, "Although the existence of a computer in the classroom does not guarantee successful learning, its use, either for simulation or for information retrieval, encourages pupils to take the initiative to reflect, discuss and evaluate the evidence available, draw conclusions or make decisions." [*History in the Primary and Secondary Years: an HMI View* DES, 1985:38] In 1988 there were similarly encouraging words: "History is strongly rooted in written and spoken language, but information technology (IT) is a useful tool for the historian. When used, it should be employed as historians need it: to store, retrieve and analyse information." [*History from 5–16* DES, 1988:para. 32] But there have been words of warning too: "Teachers should be on their guard against uses of IT which, posing problems ostensibly set in past times, do not really stimulate pupils to ask historical questions or to think about historical issues." [ibid.]

The experience gained by history teachers in using computers in recent years has led to further interest in the cross curricular use of IT within the National Curriculum. The way in which history departments can contribute to a whole school IT policy depends partly on the extent of IT involvement in the first instance. It may be that a department has no IT components in its current scheme of work and needs to develop an initial strategy. On the other hand, a department may make extensive use of IT and need to amend its approaches in the light of national curriculum and other initiatives. Whatever the situation, it is essential that a department decides upon an appropriate strategy.

Developing an IT Strategy

It is in the Information Technology attainment targets and the History Working Group's Final Report that history teachers may find part of the answer to developing an IT strategy in their own subject area. [Editor's note: the details of the National Curriculum for England and Wales have been revised since the writing of this paper, but the validity of the points made here is not affected] The History Working Group suggests that: "IT can offer powerful facilities in storing, classifying, retrieving, analysing and presenting information which can be of particular use in the study of history, particularly local history." [DES, 1990] There are even examples showing how IT may be used to meet attainment targets. Level 7 of Attainment Target 4 (Organising and communicating the results of historical study) may be achieved, the Working Group suggests, by the "interrogation of a range of IT databases" [ibid.: 142]. There are also other examples for Levels 3, 4, 6, 8, and 9 and for Level 3 of Attainment Target 3 (Acquiring and evaluating historical information).

More significantly, a discussion paper assessing the cross curricular implications of IT and produced for the Parliamentary Under Secretary of State for Education [1989] identified history as one of the subjects able to play a role in contributing to IT programmes of study. Communication, modelling, information handling and assessment of IT's impact on society were areas where history was deemed appropriate. Examples were provided of how historians could utilise IT attainment targets to deliver history in an interesting and exciting way. In their Final Report the History Working Group also supported this view.

As well as contributing to the teaching and learning of history, history in turn can make a significant contribution to the delivery of IT in the curriculum [DES, 1990: para. 9.30]. The Non-Statutory Guidance for IT [NCC, 1990] endorsed the role of history in delivering IT capability. Examples cited included a village study using census data and an East-West study using a newsroom/word processing package. There are also many commercial packages on the market which fit into proposed history programmes of study and meet selected attainment targets. Thus there are many incentives for history departments to develop their awareness and subsequent use of IT in the classroom. But much of the planning needs to be set against the school IT policy, if one exists.

There are a variety of models currently in use which contribute to the delivery of IT skills. Until recently computing facilities have often been seen as the domain of the departments of science or mathematics, and IT capability has been delivered by means of a set course which included word processing and database use. Recently, more cross- curricular courses have been established, partly in response to national curriculum developments, whereby IT is delivered within a number of subjects (e.g. word processing in English, databases in Mathematics and modelling in Design and Technology). Some schools now have an IT policy which requires work by a variety of departments on databases in year 7 (ages 11–12), spreadsheets in year 8 (ages 12–13), and so on. Finally, IT has been developed in some areas by encouraging a range of subjects to contribute to an IT programme of study with involvement in work from different subject areas taking place later.

Whatever the scheme adopted, one way forward is for historians to take the lead in formulating IT policy within their own school. Although it is not my intention to suggest that history departments should take prime responsibility for teaching a wide range of IT programmes of study, a willingness to consider cross-curricular links would make demands for more timetable time and access to equipment more plausible and convincing. In some schools, including my own, the history department is a leading player in the use of IT and has been identified as an area where IT competency will be developed. The strategy adopted for this initiative involved matching IT and History programmes of study. Use of simple databases or word processing packages provides a useful vehicle for meeting both history and IT targets.

History in a Whole School Approach

There are major implications for history departments embarking upon the integration of IT strategies into future schemes of work. For instance, progression in IT and in history is not often concurrent and careful analysis needs to be made so that the IT task is relevant to and complements the historical component of the attainment target. Figure 7.1 shows how tasks in history and IT can be complementary. Of course, history departments using IT in a cross-curricular manner will also need to consider the way in which assessment of IT will be conducted and recorded. Moderation procedures will need to be developed to ensure IT competency as identified in one department is matched in others. Thus assessment procedures in, say, word processing or database use, will need to be carefully monitored and standardised.

HISTORY Attainment Target 4: **Organising and Communicating the Results of Historical Study**	TECHNOLOGY Attainment Target 5: **Information Technology Capability**
Level 5	Level 5
Structure suitable material for different forms of communication from sources dealing with an historical issue.	Use information technology to present information in different forms for specific purposes.
Level 6	Level 6
Provide a sound summary of a relevant historical investigation.	Use information technology to combine and organise different forms of information for a presentation to an audience.

Figure 7.1   History and Technology Attainment Target Comparison

Content demands in History may also make inclusion of cross-curricular IT difficult. The issue of assessment, which remains at the heart of the national curriculum, will have various ramifications. Martin Booth [1990] surely had these points in mind when he commented that making history interesting, exciting and enjoyable — the title of chapter 4 of the History Working Group's Interim Report — may not have much relevance since teachers will be restricted by the demands of the content. In a 1989 article HMIs Baker and Paterson highlighted other inhibitions and constraints limiting the use of IT by history teachers. Lack of information, limited advisory assistance and inappropriate INSET were cited as some of the problems, as also were lack of equipment, lack of knowledge and cost. Problems of resources, training and, above all, time to include IT work still remain.

Another significant factor has caused computing facilities in school to be stretched even further. As staff in a variety of subjects become more aware of the potential of IT and its relevance as a cross-curricular medium, the pressure on school resources has increased. No longer is the computer room the domain of just the mathematics or computer studies department; scientists, environmentalists, economists, geographers, and design technology teachers are now realising the benefits of IT. Increasingly, a wide range of disciplines are competing for resources once utilised by only a handful of staff and the problem of access to computers is thus compounded. While leading part of an INSET session on IT in History recently I heard, to my astonishment, the INSET coordinator inform the assembled history teachers of the new resources that would now be at their disposal. The reality in most schools including my own is that access to resources is becoming more constrained as more teachers see the potential of IT. Furthermore, IT attainment targets need to be met in their own right and thus IT and technology departments may be seen as priority access areas. The effect of this upon history staff, who are coping with the implementation of the national curriculum in their area, is all too obvious — the use of IT in history may be squeezed.

Potential Benefits for History Pupils of a Cross-Curricular IT Approach

It might seem from the above that the implications of using IT in a cross curricular approach will create daunting problems for the history teacher. And yet, whilst not trying to underestimate the potential problems caused by the implementation of a new scheme of work, we should not forget the significant benefits to pupils that initiatives such as IT in history may offer. Despite the proliferation of computers in schools, many pupils still find the use of IT exciting and a source of interest. Pupils who, through cross-curricular approaches, are familiar with word processing packages or databases etc., will require less instruction in the use of such packages when they are used in history lessons; thus there would be a saving of teaching time. Moreover, IT approached through a variety of subjects, including history, would be seen less as a bolt-on instrument and more as a tool to be used as and when necessary.

Specific historical skills would also be enhanced through the use of IT. Pupils would become familiar with storing, selecting and retrieving information, analysing data and presenting work in clear and coherent forms. They would also become more proficient in handling large amounts of data and testing hypotheses hitherto unexplored. The potential for interactive programs suggest that pupils will be able to explore the possible effects of their actions and assess the consequences of their decisions. Thus the national curriculum may in fact have provided the opportunity for history to appear more relevant, exciting and rewarding. It is an opportunity history departments will be ill advised to ignore.

The message therefore is clear, if information technology is to remain a feature of school history then history teachers need to respond not only to the methodological flexibility within history programmes of study but also to consider how IT attainment targets can best be domesticated for historical consumption. History teachers should and can be in the vanguard of IT planning and development.

Chapter 8

History and Computing
with Sixth Formers

Jane Jenkins

Introduction and Background

'A New History for a New World' — Fernand Braudel

The National Curriculum for England and Wales has focused attention on the debate which has continued since 1969 when Braudel made this claim. Skills and concepts are now ranked at least co-equal with knowledge and understanding of what happened in the past. It is no longer considered desirable to send young people out into the adult world with heads crammed only with information. The advent of the microchip, and with it computer technology with its databases and information networks, means that knowledge is now more readily accessible; at the same time it is recognised that knowledge constantly changes. A consequence of these developments is that the emphasis has now changed from information and knowledge themselves to the skills of understanding and of applying knowledge.

From various working papers produced by Her Majesty's Inspectorate (HMI) in the 1970s onwards to the more recent Technical and Vocational Education Initiative (TVEI) guidelines, and National Curriculum Council (NCC) Core Skills document for 16 to 19 year olds, recommendations have been made that the educational system should concern itself with equipping young people to take their place in adult life with the ability to think and act for themselves. The pace of change in society requires new methods of learning which emphasise enquiry, flexibility of mind and adaptability of skills, whilst teaching styles are recommended which encourage participation and where the teacher becomes a listener, a partner, an assessor, a facilitator encouraging and guiding. Passive learning, which has been associated with more traditional methods of teaching, should give way to an active, well directed enquiry where students are given greater opportunities to control their own learning. The emphasis now is on learners 'knowing how' as well as 'knowing what'. They are to be helped to 'learn to learn' because, in a time of rapid technological change, the extent to which particular occupational skills are required also changes.

The challenge facing history teachers in the 16 to 19 age group is to find a way to respond to these new initiatives with their stress on active learning through enquiry, problem solving, investigation, negotiated learning and information technology. Students are now expected to take greater responsibility for their own learning and an environment has to be provided in which problem solving can take place. Teachers have to learn the process of 'easing controls' and providing learning opportunities which make it possible to differentiate between students. Teachers must be clear that they understand what recording and reviewing say about teaching; for they are, in fact, evaluating not only the students, but also themselves.

The aim of this paper is to describe how a history department in a Sixth Form College has addressed the challenge of the 'New History' and the new technology.

Implementation of Strategy

The history department at Itchen College was already committed to a strategy of using IT, particularly producing their own databases and using available software. They are used as part of a student supported self-study programme as two responses to the new initiatives and very much influenced by the potential offered by an expert system being developed at the local university. The Historical Document Expert System (HiDES) Sixth Form Project was launched in September 1989 as an extension of this project. A Sixth Form teacher from Itchen, who led the way in supported self-study, together with an academic from Southampton University specialising in the Weimar and Nazi periods, worked in close partnership to produce a work aimed at developing skills/concepts in students. HiDES offers a new strategy of tutoring which supplements traditional classroom teaching using IT as a tool. It enables students to receive tutorial support while engaged in the study, both in breadth and depth, of primary and secondary sources as part of a historical investigation.

A HiDES package contains a historical investigation of a topic which might be the subject of debate and controversy. The author's packages on the Third Reich, already trialled, and widely demonstrated, is used as an exemplar. The question/answer format involves a close scrutiny of sources whether primary or secondary. It is not historical research in the pure sense of a comprehensive review of everything that may be pertinent to a given investigation: rather, the student learns some of the perceptions and methods of the historian's use of sources. The student is encouraged to develop an understanding and appreciation of the historical process and the method by which historical knowledge is attained. Various approaches are possible to achieve this notion that history is an ongoing activity and to give practical experience of working with evidence.

Each of the Third Reich packages uses a progressive form of argument which involves investigation of a number of possible hypotheses. Each is constructed around a historical question — Why did Hitler become Chancellor in January 1933? — Did Hitler Plan the Second World War? — Did Hitler Achieve a Social Revolution? Beginning with such a single historical event the process of question-framing about cause, course and consequence widens the historical significance of the event until the fullest context is drawn out as the 'tutor' conducts the student through a logical sequence of possible explanations. Students' investigations are seen as a problem-solving exercise often involving quite complex interpretations of evidence which stress concepts, issues and the testing of hypotheses against evidence. Along the way discussion of causation and motivation, change and continuity, similarity and difference and historiographical debate develop out of the study of the event. This process of enquiry, stressing stages rather than just outcome, requires contextual knowledge and chronology. Glossaries of leading events and personalities as well as chronologies are provided in each package as an "open resource" for students to consult if necessary. Students are advised to consult these to increase their understanding of specific issues as part of the dialogue in the tutor response to student replies. Another strategy is to use Commentaries to link the various stages to the enquiry.

The tutor provides a dialogue to encourage the student to discuss the sources in a concise and relevant way by framing questions which direct the investigation and influence its course. A number of possible replies is provided which might be expected from the student. The ensuing conversation gives support to students as they progress through their enquiry and explanation. With thoughtful structuring of the package the issue of progression can be addressed seriously. Thus, the first of the packages, *Hitler's Accession to Power*, is intended as an introductory programme not only to the topic (no previous knowledge being required), but also to the skills and concepts explicit at Advanced level. A critical awareness of the nature and limitations of sources is fostered while students' understanding of the nature of the historical process, and the reasons why historians differ in their opinions and interpretations, is deepened in many ways. The second package on the foreign policy of the regime, *Did Hitler Plan the Second World War?*, is more demanding and intellectually challenging. It presupposes a substantial corpus of historical knowledge and understanding of the Third Reich, and of historical skills and concepts.

The core of the Third Reich packages is contained in the Question File (available on disk and as a workbook). A preamble discusses the aims and objectives of the package with their learning outcomes and outlines the nature of the enquiry. It introduces students to the nature of the historical process, particularly to the notion that historians' interpretations of events are influenced by the current preoccupations of their age. Such interpretations can thus never be completely impartial for they derive from diverse value systems, and historians often disagree with each other for very proper reasons. Through studying the issues raised by the central question posed by each package, students feel involved in a real historical debate. They realise its value in opening up new lines of enquiry, possibly leading to a reworking of old evidence and/or new or revised evidence as in the case of statistics on the German economy. This can lead to a new synthesis. Thus the historical controversy over whether Hitler intended to go to war or whether it was forced upon him by events has made it possible for other historians to combine the best of each hypothesis, so that the argument moves rapidly on. Out of all this the total amount of historical knowledge is often increased.

Wide ranging sources have been selected from diplomatic dispatches, government policy statements, private letters, and the diaries of leading Nazis, diplomats and statesmen. Also used, and rarely found in textbooks, are newspaper articles, election results and statistics on the economy which reflect the most recent research findings, as well as coloured posters. Primary and secondary sources are employed in a variety of ways, both in isolation and as clusters of sources for comparison, contrast and reconstruction. They are used in a detailed context to allow for a full understanding of their meaning and for an assessment of their reliability, value and limitations. Primary sources were chosen for their importance, or for their perceptive observations, or to emphasise the importance of improved and more sophisticated data sampling techniques which have led to revised interpretations. Some editing of sources has occurred in the interests of length or of relevance to the line of enquiry. Students are required to understand and interpret numerical data in a range of forms and, as in the case of the statistics on the German economy which feature in the second package *Did Hitler Plan the Second World War?*, select and apply numerical information to support the intentionalist and structuralist interpretations which have characterised this debate.

A hierarchy of skills is tested using a structured approach to ensure that the requirements of the question are made as clear as possible. Progression and differentiation are achieved through the questioning strategy. Students move on very quickly from comprehension to analysis, evaluation and synthesis requiring them to show historical understanding, to correlate and cross-reference, and to exercise reasoning and judgment. Each question is preceded by a set of instructions which inform students of the documents to access from the separate document file. Initially the instructions provide an opportunity for the student to show ability in terms of the route chosen to answer the question. The "tutor" provides support through the responses which have been constructed as part of the dialogue with the students and which occurs through the Notepad. The traditional omnibus type essay question is broken down into a number of parts to ensure that students are taken through a logical line of enquiry or discussion. This type of question strategy ensures that learning occurs within a framework of support. Each new question assumes that the previous stage in the discussion has been completed. In the dialogue which ensues, students are directed to a close and critical reading of sources and in some cases with their provenance. At the end of the enquiry students sum up the argument, review the documents and consider, and then present, an overview of the central proposition.

HiDES has an authoring software based on a word search facility. Keywords, phrases, and passages are identified which students might be expected to use in discussing a question. These are then linked to specific responses. The "conversation" can range from a fairly limited one based on keywords and/or synonyms to a fairly elaborate dialogue based on close textual analysis involving up to 10 possible key phrases, known as "expect(ation)s", each of which may consist of up to 162 characters and 999 possible responses. In the experience of the author, 6 expects — allowing for 64 combinations of student answer — is a more realistic and "reliable" dialogue which in practice has been conducted successfully in 47 different conversations. There is a feeling of genuine dialogue between tutor and students which motivates the latter as they progress with the enquiry. The system has been programmed to respond to relevant phrases which means that through studying the student notepads the teacher can quickly discover whether main issues have been grasped. But HiDES involves more than the computer redirecting students' reading until they arrive at the anticipated answer. A central tenet of the Third Reich packages is that they open up rather than close down the debate.

A tutor comment is included, where relevant, to broaden the enquiry, while additional references are recommended for follow-up beyond the computer dialogue. Or, as a supplement to the question, students are directed to read new documents.

Evaluation

This is based on the experience of the author, who has run workshops for Hampshire teachers on active/flexible learning, and of thirty 16 to 18 year old sixth-formers studying National Socialist Germany 1933–45. [AEB paper 630 option 09]

The Third Reich package has provided, in a unique medium, a wide and detailed selection of historical sources and data which may be inaccessible or unavailable elsewhere. Students' communication skills are refined as they analyse and evaluate information as part of their investigation. This occurs through several stages, requiring problem solving and decision making either alone or in a small group. Most feel that they are involved in a real historical debate, using a range of interesting, varied and often unfamiliar resources. Within a carefully conceived structure students can work at their own pace. Their self-sufficiency increases and they have the satisfaction of knowing that their answers are immediately assessed through individual tutoring and guidance. In evaluation replies students expressed a preference for responses to their notepads which further developed the historical analysis by offering a supplementary tutor comment. This sharpens their thinking and helps them to phrase answers carefully. Through the testing of historical interpretations against the available evidence, students are compelled to consider the hierarchy of sources. Chronology and glossary files are used as an open resource which students access as they would a book whilst use of a concordance facility allows a rapid search for keywords which would be totally impossible in the classroom and which means that they can thereby develop and test their own hypotheses.

The HiDES packages on the Third Reich have been used as a flexible learning tool, freeing the teacher to give individual attention to particular students. Study of student notepads which record the process and performance of their efforts in the key areas of evidence, enquiry and communication, enables difficulties to be diagnosed and the student helped. This makes it easier to differentiate between students and to profile and set new targets for each individual.

Conclusion

Overall this technique of marrying supported self-study with information technology has been successful and student responses have been most encouraging. (See the Appendix for a sample of student replies.) Such responses show the potential for this new form of learning. However, it is heavily dependent on initial teacher input to produce the packages. In the longer term, when packages are freely available, the methodology can provide more effective teaching and tutoring on an individual basis and make it easier for teachers to face new demands and practices.

APPENDIX:

Sample of Student Responses

(There has been no editing of texts for spelling or grammar.)

1. Do you feel that this programme could be used without any previous detailed knowledge of the period covered by the Introductory package on the Third Reich, *Hitler's Accession to Power : A Study of Enquiry and Explanation*?

   All of the first year students who had not covered the theme said: "Yes, but a basic knowledge is definitely useful" or "Yes, but it helps" whereas second year students replied: "It told me nothing I had not studied before though I found it useful for revision"

2. In what way has this programme widened your understanding of how and why Hitler came to power?

   "Creates better understanding of the period in Germany prior to 1933. It has given me more details about the social psychological environment of Weimar Germany. It has widened my understanding of the differing views of Hitler's rise to power, his popularity and his personality. It deals with the different characters and ideologies in the party during the 20s and 30s."

   "It comprised the views of different historians on aspects of Nazi Germany. Very different interpretations of the same events which gave an extremely useful overview — particularly being able to refer to specific historians incorporating their views into the argument of an essay."

   "Graphs and area/voting regions are excellent as are area dealing in political intrigues and personalities. Also idea that there are a multitude of views that must be shifted (sic) through and that personal bias can often alter a historians perception of why and how."

3. Did you feel that the responses to your answers on the notepad were clear, helpful, related to what you had written and widened your understanding of the questions being asked?

   "Yes, to an extent. Some answers gave too much help."

   "Generally they matched the answers given — correct responses for the answers. For the higher level responses they definitely widened understanding but they were not always helpful for the lower level replies. In general the answers were very clear and helpful."

   "Yes, they helped you think about issues involved and helped me to become better at answering questions accurately"

4. What did you find to be the most useful things about HiDES in learning about this period?

   "The graphical information was useful in visualising Hitler's rise to power and understanding it. The glossary helped me find out about the characters of the Weimar Republic and the Third Reich."

   "Provided a variety of views and data especially about voting trends, personalities and propaganda."

   "Mainly the differing views. Increased awareness of historical argument. Statistics, maps and "pictures" were very useful also. Glossary was excellent."

   "I did not have to fight for teachers attention to get a reply to my answers."

5. Could you suggest ways in which the HiDES programme could be used as a learning tool other that the one you have been using so far, e.g. might there be other ways of using the documents, graphs or maps?

"I would like to study more about propaganda — the posters were interesting — it would be good if HiDES programme could be used for studying this. It would be useful for Communications students."

"It would be useful as an English Language exercise as it teaches how to extract information from sources. Useful for Communications as it teaches use of factual information, especially the propaganda and how bias can be brought out in a source. The posters, graphs and maps could be used in English and Communications to show information transfer."

Chapter 9

A Longitudinal Study of the Provision of Information Technology in Ten Schools: Implications for Computers in the History Classroom

David Yeomans

Introduction

This chapter assumes that use of computers in history classrooms will enhance learning of the subject (although this assumption is questioned in the final section). However, classrooms, teachers and computers exist within institutional contexts, therefore what is possible by way of the use of computers in history classrooms is partly dependent upon the policies and practices for information technology (IT) followed by individual schools. This chapter focuses on the provision of information technology in ten English secondary schools and considers the implications of the description and analysis for history teachers who may wish to use computers in their classrooms.

The Research

The research reported here was part of a larger project investigating the effects of the Technical and Vocational Education Initiative (TVEI) on English and Welsh secondary schools. TVEI began in 1983 and was an attempt to make the curriculum for 14–18 year olds in state schools and colleges more practical and relevant. TVEI had two main phases, a pilot stage involving limited numbers of schools and students, and an extension phase in which all schools catering for 14–18 year olds were involved. The Initiative will continue until 1997 by which time the total cost will be in excess of £1 billion, making it one of the most expensive curriculum innovations ever launched by a United Kingdom government.

It is important to note that in the pilot phase history teachers were rarely involved in TVEI. Indeed, TVEI was often seen as being potentially damaging to history, and the humanities more generally, by placing emphasis on technical and vocational areas of the curriculum. However, in the extension phase, which began in 1987, TVEI became broader and more inclusive, giving greater emphasis to changing teaching and learning styles and consequently opportunities for history teachers to become involved became greater.

Information technology had an important place in TVEI from the beginning. Throughout the life of the Initiative a significant proportion of TVEI funding has been spent on computers. However, the management of TVEI has generally been permissive, laying emphasis on "ownership" of change by those in the schools. In IT, as in other curriculum areas, TVEI has not promoted any particular approach. Thus it has been for individual schools to decide how much money they wished to spend on IT equipment, what type of equipment they wished to buy and how they wished to deploy the equipment within the schools.

This chapter reports upon IT provision in ten schools which were visited in 1985/86 and again in 1991/92. Changes in IT which took place are explored and explanations are offered for emerging patterns of provision. The schools were first visited as part of the National Evaluation of the TVEI Curriculum which was conducted by the School of Education, University of Leeds during 1985/88[1]. They were then revisited in 1991/92 as part of an Economic and Social Research Council (ESRC) funded project[2]. The research thus had a longitudinal element which allowed us to trace developments in the provision of IT in the schools over a six or seven year period.

The TVEI context for the research has implications for the generalisiblity of the findings. Each of the ten schools were among the minority involved in the pilot phase of TVEI and thus received considerably higher levels of funding than schools which entered TVEI during the extension phase. Thus, in general, we would expect these schools to be relatively advantaged in terms of the numbers of computers available (see Table 1), the amount of training received by staff (high levels of INSET were available during the pilot phase) and the length of time during which they have had a significant number of computers available for use. Very crudely, it would be reasonable to expect these schools to be in "advance" of most others in their provision and practice in IT.

Changing Justifications for IT in the Curriculum

When IT began to be strongly promoted as part of the secondary school curriculum at the beginning of the 1980s it was with an overt vocational justification. Significantly it was the Department of Trade and Industry (DTI) through its "Micro's into Schools" scheme which provided the major impetus for the development of IT at that time. In 1981 the Minister of State at the DTI, Kenneth Baker, said, "I want to try and ensure that the kids of today are trained with the skills that gave their fathers and grandfathers jobs.... And that is the reason that we've pushed ahead with computers into schools. I want youngsters, boys and girls leaving school at sixteen, to actually be able to operate a computer." (Quoted in O'Shea & Self, 1983)

Certainly during the first period of research in the ten schools in 1985/86 it was commonplace to be told by 15 and 16 year old students that they had chosen computer courses because the skills and knowledge gained would help them to get and do jobs in the new computer-based industries. However, by 1985/86 the vocational utility of computer courses was being challenged in the schools. Teachers were beginning to argue that the sort of computing taught in schools, using the ubiquitous BBC computer with its BASIC language, was at best irrelevant and at worst counter-productive, in terms of equipping students for entry to computer-based occupations (Peacock, 1989; Wellington, 1989). Analysis of the labour market also revealed that the number of occupations requiring other than basic computer skills, which could easily be taught on-the-job, were actually very small and in any case required graduate level entry (Wellington, 1989). Thus the vocational justifications for the promotion of IT began to look increasingly weak.

As the vocational justifications began to weaken, educational rationales came to the fore, with IT beginning to be characterised as a learning tool. In 1989 the Minister of State in the Department of Education and Science, John Butcher, stated: "The government recognises the tremendous potential of IT as a classroom tool. Our policy is to promote IT in schools and see that it is used to raise educational standards. Our goal is ambitious: it is nothing less than the full integration of IT into all classroom studies. We want to increase the extent and effectiveness of schools' use of IT for the enhancement of teaching and learning for pupils of all ages and abilities right across the curriculum." (Quoted in NCC, 1991) Various policy documents and sets of advice to teachers have further emphasised the message that IT is now to be seen as fundamentally a tool for the learning of other subjects (HMI, 1989; NCC, 1990; SEAC, 1993).

These changing justifications for IT have implications for history teachers. Where the justification was primarily vocational the contribution of history would necessarily be limited, since the aim of IT experience would be to equip students with knowledge, skills and attitudes useful in the workplace. The increasing emphasis on IT as a classroom tool, however, promised much greater scope for involvement by history teachers. Indeed the history national curriculum, while vague in detail, clearly encouraged teachers to incorporate IT into their teaching.

At school level IT was also justified as a learning tool. For example Granton School, one of the ten visited as part of the research reported here, had an IT policy which stated that: "Information Technology is both a support for learning across the whole curriculum and an essential life skill for all pupils." Among the purposes of IT was: "To ensure that pupils can use acquired skills sensibly and with confidence across the whole curriculum."

However, the vocational justification for IT did sometimes linger on. Brigham School had recently concluded a deal with a computer manufacturer for the supply of a computer network. In a document outlining the proposed "Centre of Excellence" which would be created, the scheme was described thus: "The system to be installed would provide industry standard equipment for students' use and would thereby prepare them more effectively for entry into the world of employment. This experience would enhance their prospects of gaining employment in fields where computer experience is essential." Significantly this school had suffered a catastrophic fall in students numbers between 1985 and 1992. The same document stated: "The scheme will produce the best school based IT facility in the North of England. Brigham School *will be a Centre of Excellence* in this important curriculum area. This will enable Brigham School to operate as a magnet school for information technology and should begin to redress the present position with regard to student recruitment." Claims for the vocational significance of IT are here coupled with an image of modernity and excellence as a means of attracting students thus pulling the school out of a spiral of decline.

A Model for Analysing IT in the Curriculum

Wellington (1989:44) has proposed a five stage model to describe the evolution of IT in secondary schools.

From vertical to horizontal: the evolution of IT education in secondary schools

Stage 1   Computer Studies as an examination subject: rapid rise in entries. "Vertical" approach to IT education.

Stage 2   Computer awareness across the board, to all ability ranges and both sexes — e.g. to the whole of the first year, with an element of in-service education for staff as well as pupils.

Stage 3   Introduction of computers across the curriculum in separate subjects to enhance learning in those areas, partly as a result of the 'diffusion' process in stage 2 — i.e. CAL across the curriculum.

Stage 4   Increasing pressure on Computer Studies as a separate school subject, and on the computer room as a resource for the whole school.

Stage 5   Integration of computing, and computing resources, into the whole curriculum and classroom practice. "Horizontal" approach to IT education.

Wellington himself describes the model as "crude". Some of the stages are not clearly differentiated, nor does the model make clear whether Computer Studies will survive as a separate subject. However the general thrust — from vertical to horizontal provision of IT is clear enough and accords in many respects with the changing justifications offered for IT in the curriculum and the aspirations expressed in the schools.

It was, therefore, a reasonable hypothesis to have expected IT in the ten schools in the study to have moved somewhat over the six or seven year period of the research from vertical to horizontal provision. One indicator of such a shift might be a decline in the number of specialist Computer Studies and Information Technology courses being offered. Of course in principle there may be no conflict between vertical and horizontal provision of IT. However, with the current numbers of computers and levels of expertise in the schools there is a trade-off between the two approaches. Where computers are being used for specialist courses they cannot be used across the curriculum and where IT co-ordinators are teaching those courses they cannot be training and supporting other teachers.

IT in the Ten Schools

Table 9.1 below encapsulates some of the main findings of the research. Column 4 of the table confirms that most of these original TVEI pilot schools have a computer/student ratio better than the national average, in some cases significantly better, both Redmond and Lympton having in excess of 100 computers. The research also indicates that a considerable amount of timetabled Computer Studies and Information Technology has been maintained. The only school which had taken a deliberate decision not to maintain specialist courses was Granton School, whose IT policy document stated: "Attitudes towards, and skills in the use of information technology will be developed through existing curriculum areas and

Table 9.1 IT Provision in the Ten Schools in Years 10 and 11 in 1985/86 and 1991/92
(The names of the schools are fictitious)

SCHOOL	Timetable Provision 1985/86	Timetable Provision 1991/92	Computer-student Ratio 1991/92 (National avg 1:13)
Paul Branding	Non-exam core course	Non-exam core course	1:14
Redmond	Computer Studies (GCE/CSE)	Computer Studies (GCSE)	1:8
Greenfield	Core modules within TVEI Course (GCE/CSE)	Information (GCSE)	1:10
Brownstone	Computer Studies (GCE/CSE)	Computer Studies (GCSE)	1:14
St Justin's	Computer Studies (GCE/CSE)	None	1:26
Lympton	Information Technology (GCE/CSE)	Computer Studies (GCSE)	1:8
Kenfield	N/K	Information Technology (GCSE)	1:12
Granton	Non-exam core course	None	1:15
Priory	Information Technology (GCSE)	Information Technology (GCSE) (Year 11 only)	1:10
Brigham	Computer Studies (GCE/CSE)	Information Technology (GCSE)	1:10

The General Certificate of Secondary Education (GCSE) is the main external examination taken by most pupils at the end of compulsory education in England and Wales. Its forerunners were the General Certificate of Education (GCE) and Certificate of Secondary Education(CSE) which it replaced in 1986.

not as a separately taught subject." In Priory School Information Technology was being phased out as an examination subject although there would continue to be a timetabled course in years 7 and 8. At St Justin's the absence of a specialist course was a result of difficulties in appointing a teacher rather than because of a deliberate policy decision. Six of the schools maintained Computer Studies or Information Technology as optional, externally examined courses. The seventh school, Paul Branding, had sustained a compulsory IT course which was not externally examined. The five stage model above thus begins to look somewhat deficient as a description of what is actually happening in the schools. Vertical provision of IT continues to be more widespread and more resilient to the challenge of horizontal provision than might have been expected.

In order to ascertain how far the schools had moved from vertical to horizontal provision it was necessary to reach a judgement about the extent to which IT was used in other subjects. Reliable evidence on the extent of IT use across the curriculum was difficult to obtain. The practice during the research was to ask the IT co-ordinator. History and Technology Attainment Target Comparison where computers were being used across the curriculum, to interview staff where it was claimed that there were significant levels of use and, if possible, to see some lessons where this was taking place. The interviews with IT co-ordinators elicited information on curriculum areas, sometimes including history, which were using IT to a greater or lesser extent.

Opportunities to observe actual use were far more limited. However, the research design required direct observation of business studies and design and technology lessons. A computer was used by at least one student for at least part of a lesson in 11 out of 18 business studies lessons visited. On the same criteria use was noted in 8 of 27 design and technology lessons. Surveys of IT use conducted by the Department for Education revealed that Business Studies and Design and Technology were the subjects in which greatest use was made of computers (DFE, 1993). Thus it would be reasonable to expect use in other subjects to be below the levels discovered in Business Studies and Design and Technology. The evidence from the ten schools appeared to confirm this expectation. The only other occasions during the visits in which use was observed was in a Personal and Social Education lesson (exploring a database of work experience placements) and for word processing in an English lesson. No example of use in history was seen. Evidence from the most recent DFE survey was that, on average, IT was used in two or three history lessons per term, thus it was not surprising that no actual use was observed during the visits to the schools.

It is notoriously difficult to research the extent to which a cross-curricular element is, in fact, occurring across the curriculum. The accounts of teachers who have a stake in claiming that computers are used across the curriculum cannot be considered reliable on their own. The overall impression from the research, with explicit support from some school staff, was that use of IT across the curriculum remained patchy. This was a source of frustration for some in the schools who thought that more could, and should, have been achieved.

The "Wellington model" may well remain valid in the long-term, but in the medium-term covered by this research, the move from vertical to horizontal provision of IT has proved slower than might have been expected.

The Role of the IT Co-ordinator

There were many reasons for the slow progress in moving from vertical to horizontal provision of IT in the schools. Many factors determined the extent to which IT was used in particular subjects, these included: access to computers; availability and suitability of software; provision of INSET; accessibility of the IT co-ordinator; personalities, values and experiences of the teachers involved; characteristics of the syllabuses being followed. The importance of some of these factors has been emphasised in other contributions to this volume. Here consideration will be given to the role of the school IT co-ordinator in promoting IT across the curriculum.

The school co-ordinators had a crucial role in developing policy and practice in IT in the schools. The Non-Statutory Guidance (NSG) for the English national cur-

Table 9.2   IT Co-ordinators in the Ten Schools

School	IT Co-ordinator (Incentive Allowance)	Non-contact Time	Technician
Paul Branding	YES (D)	N/K	NO
Redmond	YES (D)	50%	YES
Greenfield	YES (D)	16%	YES (0.5)
Brownstone	YES (C)	12.5%	NO
St Justin's	NO	NO	NO
Lympton	YES (B)	12.5%	YES (0.5)
Kenfield	YES (D)	18%	YES
Granton	YES (D)	28%	YES (0.5)
Priory	YES (C)	28%	NO
Brigham	YES (D)	21%	YES

N.B.   Incentive allowances are additional payments made to English and Welsh teachers who hold posts of responsibility. They range from A (£1296pa) to E (£7155) and thus give an indication of the seniority of the postholder within schools.

riculum lists an onerous set of responsibilities for co-ordinators covering: coordination, resources, staff development and support, monitoring and review and external liaison. The NSG states that: "Each school should appoint an IT co-ordinator, who commands sufficient respect to influence senior managers and reports direct to them. The co-ordinator should have the skills to work with other teachers, and will ensure that pupils' IT experiences are brought together in a single framework of understanding." (NCC, 1990) How did the role actually being played by the co-ordinators match up to these prescriptions?

Table 9.2 shows that, with the exception of St Justin's, where there had been difficulties in making an appointment, each of the schools had an IT co-ordinator, the majority appointed at a relatively senior level. Column three reveals very considerable variations in the non-contact time available to the co-ordinators. A similarly mixed position was evident concerning the provision of a technician with responsibility for IT. Taken together these two factors were important determinants of the extent to which the co-ordinator could realistically be expected to play a cross-curricular coordinating, training and support role.

At one end of the scale the co-ordinator in Brownstone School had little non-contact time (5 periods in a 40 period week) and no technician support. Under these circumstances the amount of assistance which could be given to teachers (including history teachers) who wished to use IT in their lessons was bound to be extremely limited. In Redmond School, by contrast, the co-ordinator was in a position to give very considerable assistance to teachers. However, in five of the eight schools for which information was available the amount of non-contact time available to the co-ordinators compared unfavourably with the 27% average for non-contact time for secondary school teachers (Source: School Teachers' Review Body, Second Report 1993, HMSO, London). In seven of the eight schools it seems justified to claim that the amount of non-contact time was inadequate for the role which the co-ordinators were expected to fulfil.

Two factors make the issue of non-contact time crucial. The first relates to the training needs of teachers and the form in which these could be met. Teachers were commonly expected to learn about IT through attending formal INSET courses. These might be school-based or held off-site, take place in the evenings or on training days. In addition to these courses many teachers learned about particular pieces of software simply by exploring them in their own time, sometimes assisted by the IT co-ordinator. However teachers had to make an exponential leap from attending courses and exploring software to actually using IT in the classroom. We were frequently told by teachers that it was at classroom level where they most needed help and support. The most effective model of INSET was claimed to be where an IT expert worked alongside the teacher in the classroom. Clearly the more heavily the co-ordinator was timetabled the less opportunity there was for them to work with teachers in this way.

The second factor which made the issue of non-contact time crucial was the decline of local authority support networks. Surveys have revealed that advisory teacher support has waned and those inspectors and advisers who remain are able to give reduced time to advising and supporting schools (TES, 1993). Given the British government policy of stripping local education authorities of responsibilities and funding it seems inevitable that support and advice from those sources will continue to decline. The corollary is that teachers must look inside their schools for support, namely to the IT co-ordinators.

The evidence from the schools was that, with the possible exception of Redmond, a feasible role for IT co-ordinators had not yet evolved. They were being asked to do too much with too few resources. Part of the difficulty was that no model for the role existed in British secondary schools. Co-ordinator, resource manager, staff developer, hardware and software evaluator, technician — the IT co-ordinator must be all of these, as well as being a classroom teacher. Partly this is an issue of resources. A model of INSET which requires the co-ordinator to work alongside the classroom teacher is labour intensive and hence expensive. Few schools have been willing, or able, to commit this level of resources.

The argument so far has cast the IT co-ordinators in the role of victims of unrealistic expectations. This, however, is only part of the story. The co-ordinators themselves had deeply ambivalent feelings about their role. Without exception they saw their most important task as working with other staff to promote a horizontal approach to IT. However, as is evident from Table 9.1, they actually spent much of their time teaching specialist courses in Computer Studies and Information Technology.

The cross-curricular role espoused for and by them left them vulnerable in important respects. Firstly it denied them a power base of specialist expertise within the schools. Taken on full-bloodedly, with the phasing out of specialist courses, it would mean that there would be no courses which they could claim to be uniquely equipped to teach. Several co-ordinators commented half-jokingly that under those circumstances if they performed their cross-curricular role too well they would be out of a job. At a time when teachers jobs are less secure than they once were, when schools are dependent upon attracting pupils for much of their funding, this is a genuine and understandable concern. A perfectly plausible scenario would be that where a school lost pupils, requiring a reduction in the number of staff in order to balance the school budget, the governing body would turn to an IT co-ordinator, who did not have a full teaching load, as someone who could most easily be lost.

A second explanation for the ambivalence of the co-ordinators concerns the difficulties of the role, even if sufficient time and resources were made available and they could be confident that their job was safe. The NSG blandly stated that co-ordinators "should be skilled at working with other teachers". Implementing this exhortation was no easy task, requiring special skills and teacher culture which were not always present. Research evidence has continually shown that trying to persuade teachers to change the ways in which they teach is difficult and time-consuming.

Subject teachers were often lacking in confidence, sceptical or downright hostile when it came to IT. The IT co-ordinators themselves had received little or no training for their INSET and staff development role. They had been appointed to their co-ordinators posts mainly on account of their largely self-taught knowledge of computers. However, in their coordination and training role they required not only technical knowledge but inter-personal skills in dealing with the sensitive issue of persuading their colleagues to teach in new ways through the use of computers. Some co-ordinators thought that senior management had unrealistic notions of what could be achieved. It was clear that success in the role was dependent on being able to persuade their colleagues to use IT. Under these circumstances the co-ordinators stood in danger of being held accountable for failure to achieve outcomes which they saw as being unrealistic, and over which they had limited control. Compared with these difficulties the prospect of teaching a specialist course to a class of youngsters who had chosen the subject, and who were thus probably computer enthusiasts, was appealing. At least the criteria for judging classroom success within teacher sub-cultures are reasonably clear — an orderly but pleasant atmosphere, good exam results — and the co-ordinators could feel that the results by which they were to be judged were to a greater extent in their own hands.

For all these reasons there was a tendency on the part of the co-ordinators to promote and support the maintenance of specialist courses in Computer Studies and IT even though the continued existence of these courses militated against what they saw as their most important aim, the promotion of IT across the curriculum.

Conclusion

The general tenor of this paper has perhaps been rather gloomy, tending to emphasise the constraints and consequent slow progress in implementing horizontal approaches to IT in the curriculum. However, it is also important to stress the enormous progress which has been made in IT in English and Welsh schools. This is evident from the Department for Education (DFE) surveys of information technology in schools conducted at regular intervals since 1984/85 (DFE, 1993). These reveal the enormous expansion of IT equipment in the schools, with micro's increasing from 13.4 per secondary school in 1984/85 to 58 per school in 1991/92. Over the same period the number of pupils per micro declined from 60 in 1984/85 to 13 in 1991/92.

At the same time the surveys give some support to the findings in the ten schools given above. The surveys indicate that the percentage of staff reported as making regular use of computers stayed around the 30–35% range and actually showed a small decrease between 1989/90 and 1991/92. The percentage of staff claiming confidence in IT use rose gradually from 48% in 1987/88 to 53% in 1991/92. The percentage of history departments reporting a "substantial" contribution of IT to teaching and learning was little changed between 1989/90 and 1991/92 (although the figures are not directly comparable). Over the same period there had been some decrease in the percentage of departments making no use of IT. As noted above, the figures for lesson use suggest that on average IT was used in two or three history lessons per term in secondary schools in 1991/92 (slightly down on reported use in 1989/90). The percentage of history staff who felt confident in the use of IT with children declined from 52% in 1989/90 to 47% in 1991/92.

The surveys reveal that there is a cadre of history teachers who make regular use of IT in their lessons. This is a substantial achievement. Clearly the shift from a vocational to an educational justification for IT has been advantageous for history teachers wishing to make use of computers in their classrooms and has been coupled with a considerable expansion of both hardware and software in the schools. However both the research reported here and the DFE surveys suggest that progress in promoting the use of IT as a learning tool across the curriculum has been slower than expected. Comparison of the two most recent surveys suggest that, in some respects, a plateau may have been reached.

In conclusion I wish to make three brief points, partly arising from the research cited above, but going beyond the evidence in some respects.

Firstly, progress may only seem to be slow because those of us who are enthusiasts for IT in history, and education more generally, have had unrealistic expectations of what could be achieved. In contrast to these expectations much of what we know about curricular and pedagogical change in schools stresses its slow, uneven and patchy progress. If progress in the use of IT conforms to this pattern we should not be surprised or disillusioned.

Secondly, I suggest, that in England we have seriously underestimated the amount of training which is required and have inadequately conceptualised the form which that training needs to take if it is to influence teachers classroom practice. The notion that one-shot, or even occasional, INSET courses would persuade more than a minority of teachers to introduce IT into their classrooms was naive. Far more individualised, classroom-based and hence labour intensive and expensive training is required. This has clear implications for the resources which need to be provided if training of the requisite quantity and quality is to be forthcoming.

Thirdly, and finally, I wish to return to the assumption with which I started this paper, that the use of computers in history classrooms will enhance learning of the subject. We should always be ready to question this assumption. In his closing address to the 1993 CHC conference in Lisbon, Allan Martin gave some instructive examples from the not-too-distant past of educational technologies which, it was claimed at the time, were going to revolutionise teaching and learning, but which turned out to be blind-alleys (Martin, 1995). One of the lessons we might learn from those examples is to be cautious and humble in the claims that we make for the contribution which IT can make to teaching and learning history.

Evidence from the ten schools was that amongst staff who were advocates of IT there was a good deal of "classroom utopianism" (Robins and Webster, 1989). This was accompanied by a lack of systematic and evidenced justification for the promotion of IT; such justifications as were offered were at best sketchy and anecdotal.

A major problem with discussing the justification for, and evaluating the outcomes of, the IT provision in the secondary school curriculum is the sheer variety of forms such provision takes. The configurations of hardware, software, teachers, pupils, subjects and syllabuses varies enormously. A single or simple set of justifications for, or educational improvements arising from, IT are implausible. A thorough evaluation of IT is likely to be highly context specific, and, at best, result in conditional statements along the lines of: software X, used on computer Y, with students Z, in manner A, under conditions B, appears to lead to learning C. There was little evidence in any of the ten schools that such systematic evaluation was being undertaken.

It could be argued that systematic evaluation of this kind does not take place in other major educational innovations, or, perhaps even more so, in the case of established pedagogical methods. This does not invalidate the claim that it should for IT. This might be particularly necessary given the large resource implications for schools and the budgetary distortions which can result from significant IT provision. Thus one of the important tasks of any IT training programme should be to equip teachers with evaluatory tools and frameworks which will enable them to make informed decisions about when and where to use computers in their own classrooms in order to enhance the teaching and learning of history and other subjects.

Notes

1. The National Evaluation of the TVEI Curriculum Project was directed by Douglas Barnes and Professor David Layton. The field workers were: George Johnson, Steven Jordan, Peter Medway, Michael Peacock and David Yeomans. I acknowledge my debt to all the members of the team for their part in collecting data on information technology during the pilot phase of TVEI. Particular thanks go to Mike Peacock for many stimulating discussions on the place of IT in education.
2. The support of the Economic and Social Research Council (ESRC) for the later period of research on which this paper is based is gratefully acknowledged. The work was funded by ESRC award number: R00023 2568.
3. I am most grateful to Ralph Williams, my co-researcher on the ESRC-funded project, for his comments on an earlier draft of this paper and for his support and assistance throughout the research. However, responsibility for the contents of this paper remain mine.

Part II

The Practice of Teaching and Learning

The chapters in this section are a fascinating combination of optimism and frustration. Together they give a very perceptive insight into the trials and tribulations of exploring the contribution IT can make to the teaching and learning of history, whatever the age of the pupils/students.

The 'frustrations' are evident throughout and include not enough computers, rooming policies, timetable and syllabus difficulties, lack of technical support, inappropriate software and a constant lack of 'enough' time.

Such an array of difficulties could easily lead to defeatism. And yet, alongside all the problems and difficulties that are identified in the following chapters one finds optimism. This optimism comes through as each writer shares with the reader how this problem or this difficulty was solved or circumvented. Why? All the authors are very successful practitioners in their respective spheres of education and would have been so if they had never used a computer in their teaching. What then are the reasons why they have actively sought to explore using IT in 'their' subject when it is so obviously fraught with difficulties and frustrations?

The following chapters each present answers to this question but there is, despite the different emphases, a high degree of commonality between them. The shared belief is that the use of IT leads to better, that is more effective, teaching and learning in the curriculum area of history. It is this belief that has lead them to tackle, and usually overcome, the difficulties and frustrations that often confronted them.

This is where the optimism comes into play. The following pages contain many examples of the joy (Wright), excitement (Gosling) or quiet satisfaction (Martin) that teachers have experienced through seeing the IT component enable their students to become more actively involved in their historical studies and thus to take their historical understanding further than might otherwise have been possible.

However, if there is a link between the use of IT and the quality of the student's learning experience (Wright, Peek, Dickinson, Gosling, Martin) why are there not more teachers using IT? The chapter by Peek and colleagues is a detailed study which attempts to identify the factors that affect this decision and, importantly begin to move the debate beyond the basic concerns of 'enough computers' and 'appropriate software'. It is clearly much more complicated than this.

There may have been, may still be, a belief that 'it's just a matter of time' and as the 'new' teachers emerge from the faculties of education they will be armed with the necessary skills and understanding of the role and contribution of IT. Drawing on a research project with student teachers Easedown's chapter provides some very perceptive insights into the dangers of such an approach. As with the work of Peek *et al.* it begins to identify some of the more significant, and complicated, factors that affect why the use of IT in teaching history is so sporadic.

From his own involvement in 'promoting' the use of IT in history teaching Smart suggests that it is the 'management of the innovation' that must be addressed. The studies by Peek, Easedown and Smart begin to identify the individual teacher as the key determinant in whether IT is used in the history classroom. The personal agenda and the beliefs about what constitutes 'teaching' and 'learning' are factors of great significance for each individual and cannot be ignored. Wright, Jenkins, Gosling and Peek *et al.* all comment on how the use of IT has an effect on the learning situation in the classroom. It is obvious that for some teachers this changing balance is welcomed and there are several references to 'partnership in learning' (Wright, Jenkins, Martin). For others, however, this may not be considered a desirable development and thus may have a negative effect on the willingness to use IT (Peek *et al.*).

Dickinson's own interest in how children learn and develop an understanding of history predates the use of IT in the history classroom. His chapter details research which is currently exploring how IT might be used to provide insights into the process of children' thinking and their developing understanding in relation to history. Although not yet complete the early signs are most encouraging.

The common thread throughout all the chapters is the shared concern to make the teaching and learning of history ever more effective. All the authors come to IT through this involvement in history and, it must be remembered, not the other way around. They clearly share a belief that IT, used appropriately and with understanding, can contribute to this shared aim. In different ways each chapter makes a contribution to a better understanding of the multiplicity of factors which have affected and will continue to affect the use of IT in the history classroom. In varying degrees, each one also contains important insights into how this use can make a positive contribution to the actual historical learning and understanding that takes place there.

Chapter 10

The History Teacher and the Computer: A Case Study from the Netherlands

A.C.M. Peek, W. Veen, I.V.D. Neut and P. Spoon

Introduction

In history teaching it is the teacher who makes those crucial decisions which affect whether the computer will play a part in the course or not. It is not the manufacturer, the government of even the head teacher or principle. This research project attempts to identify some of the factors which affect these decisions.

The Situation in The Netherlands in the late 1980s

By 1989 each school had, on average, 21 computers (COMPED 1989). The same survey showed that less than 10% of regular teachers ever touched one of these available computers. The percentage for history teachers is not known but there is absolutely no reason to believe that it would exceed this 10%. Even within this active group a great majority were identified as using a computer 'incidentally' or 'rarely'.

The reasons given by this computer-using group for not making greater use of the technology were:

- lack of time.   60%
- lack of hardware.   40%
- difficulties in integrating.
- programs into the curriculum.   20%

The same survey indicates that on the one hand the great majority of teachers are curious and think positively about computers while on the other hand they are *uncertain* about the results in terms of learning. So there exists a mixed situation in Dutch secondary schools: a widespread availability of hardware and an incidental use of the computers by a small minority of teachers.

The hardware is there, but at the end of the 1980s and early 1990s the situation regarding software for secondary history education is far from glorious with a limited range of databases, tutorial packages and some test programs, all of varying quality. Most of these are related or based upon specific yet often marginal topics within the overall history curriculum.

The Case Study

Even without the above survey information it was clear by the late 1980s that very few computers were being used in the teaching of history. Our background as teacher educators at Utrecht University made us concentrate on the role of the teacher in our enquiry into the causes of this situation. Most other research in this area to date has focused on the quality of software and the learning of students.

The Starting Point: Presuppositions

It is our impression that the average history teacher is a hardworking man or woman. They are confident with their own style of teaching, which is mostly teacher talk centred. They are, in short, rather successful, more or less traditional teachers.

Why on earth would such a teacher decide to change his satisfying way of working and leave a substantial part of it to a machine? We tried to visualise the problems and uncertainties facing him after such a decision. He has to invest time and money. He must learn to handle the computer and understand its incomprehensible language and system and be prepared to teach out of his own classroom. There the pupils will stare at screens instead of paying attention to him! He must familiarise himself with general and specific history software. He will be frustrated when the computer room is booked, the computers will not work and the technical assistant is not at hand. And last, but not least, he will feel that he has lost control over the learning process because of a profound change in his teaching method. What can the computer offer to compensate for so much trouble? On the basis of these impressionistic presuppositions, the notion developed that no (history) teacher will integrate the computer into his everyday teaching unless at least three requirements are met:

- the computer fits in with his usual teaching method.
- the content of the course ware is seen by him as an enrichment of the curriculum.
- the whole operation will not cost him more time in the end than he usually spends on his work.

Teaching method, content-enrichment and classroom management seemed to us central factors affecting decisions to attempt to integrate the computer. No government or industrial lobby seems strong enough to realise this objective, unless the teacher is satisfied on these points.

An Outline of the Project

The school we worked with can best be described as 'middle of the road', medium sized with no special IT provision and no record of being particularly innovative in terms of pedagogy.

The first phase aimed at making a profile of each individual teacher, the school itself, the technical staff and school management. During the second and third phase concentration was on the teachers; if, how and why they made use of computers in connection with their work. The fourth phase will be focused on the interaction between the teacher and the school organisation. The history teacher referred to in the following example had the same computer for home use as he had in his classroom. This teacher was more or less 'computer illiterate' so a short course was offered on the basic principles of the educational use of computers.

Data were acquired through various means: questionnaires, regular observations, interviews and a weekly logbook. The basic question was: What happens when a computer is provided for a history teacher both at home and in his classroom? That question was broken down into three more specific ones:

a. Which forms of computer usage occur in the monitored CAL situations?

b. Which skills does the teacher use and develop in preparing, giving and evaluating computer assisted lessons?

c. What factors determine how the teacher uses the computer at home or in his classroom?

First Results: Phase 0

What kind of history teacher are we dealing with? The analysed data from phase 0 provided the following picture: He is a University-trained history and economics teacher, 38 years of age, with experience in business and in the last five years, in education. He teaches history and economics periods to pupils between 13 to 18 years of age. His opinions about teaching in general were measured using an established questionnaire and the results were matched with the national average where he was at one with his national colleagues. On two points he scored significantly below the national average: his willingness to innovate and his opinion about discussions and meetings concerning education. He sees good results at exams as rather important. In his view it must be the teacher who determines the content and direction of of lessons. His actual teaching can be described as traditional and following an established pattern. It is teacher-centred and textbook led with elaboration at points determined by the teacher with him posing questions when he thought appropriate. Blackboard and video are regularly used but other resources only occasionally.

First Results: Phase 1 — Time, Investment and Activities

 What did the history teacher do with the hardware configuration at his disposal? Between September 1989 and January 1990, he gave 270 history lessons (of 45 minutes). During this period, he spent altogether 65 hours with the computer and a distinction was made between a number of different activities and a division between school and home based activity.

1. Viewing, judging and selecting programs for use with the computer, took place at home and took him almost 22 hours, resulting in the choice of only one program for use in two of his classes. 80% of this activity did not lead to any useful

follow-up in his work, He rejected other programs for several reasons, the most important of which was that they did not fit into his curriculum.

2. Planning his computer lessons, took about three hours. This excluded his viewing of the program which he later used in his classes.

3. Executing the computer lessons, cost him a little more than nine hours; some 14% of the total time.

4. Preparing student materials occupied 17 hours, 26% of the time. It consisted mostly of preparing texts, tests, exams, and lists of questions with his word processor and printer. He did this exclusively at home.

5. Classroom management involved him wasting four hours on a program developed by a colleague. It was intended to register the marks of his pupils.

6. Computer-related activities, such as installing hardware devices, programs, reading of literature on the subject etc. All these activities were unequally divided over the weeks due to holidays, exams etc.

In making his selection of a program he chose to use, a database called "Beggars of the Sea" the teacher applied three criteria:

— does it fit into my curriculum?
— can I and my pupils handle the program?
— is it attractive for my pupils?

This program consists of a diskette, a booklet for the pupils and a manual for the teacher. Following the directions in the booklet, which provides technical instructions, questions and textual explanation supported by contemporary written sources, the pupils are expected to work through the program individually or in groups of 2 or 3. The manual directs the teacher to the computer room, explains the method of individual beaming and provides all the right answers.

Having decided to use the program, our history teacher never questioned the proposed teaching method. He did not contemplate adapting the program, changing it, or using only parts of it in a more traditional setting in his own classroom with the help of the LCD-screen. He prepared his lessons by trying to master the program.

He gave each class an introductory lesson in his classroom with the help of the LCD-screen. He accepted the length of the program, although he did not have a clear idea as to how much time it would really take. The manual did not give him any guidance on how to assess the results with the pupils. At the end of the day, he included a question about "Sea-Beggars" in his final test. It was poorly answered. The way he prepared his computer lessons did not vary fundamentally from his normal conduct. It was done in a loose way, improvising, easily influenced/directed by circumstances and the authority of the authors of the teaching manual. He did not put his plans on paper and acted according to his own motto: "Let's trust to luck".

Execution of the Lessons

During the computer lessons, pupils worked in groups of 2 or 3, guided by the program, the booklet, the questions, their own discussions and decisions. The teacher walked around, giving advice when asked. Advice was asked only when there were problems of a more technical nature. The pupils were working quietly; there was of course a certain level of noise, but no disturbances. Sometimes the groups discussed a question with each other, which the teacher permitted. After two such lessons — half way through the scheme of work — he decided to interrupt the proceedings. He returned to his classroom and gave a traditional lesson about the Sea-Beggars and the historical circumstances in which they operated. He felt obliged to do so, because in working with the program he felt the pupils were concentrating too much on technical problems and too little on historical ones. Secondly he did not like the idea of having lost control: "At first I was the focus of attention, now it is the computer." After this break he did not change the procedures. Two lessons followed in which the pupils finished the program and the teacher played his role of technical trouble-shooter.

He finished the series with two and one evaluation lessons respectively. He did not use the computer room, but chose to discuss the results in his classroom again with the help of the LCD-screen which did not function very effectively. He decided not to return to the computer room, but to work with the traditional blackboard and his even more traditional explanation.

Having completed the series he did a unique thing: for the first (and up to now last) time in his teaching career he handed out a questionnaire with questions like:
— "What do you think of the computer lessons?
— Would you like to have more of them?
— Do you learn more about history with such lessons?
— Do you have any remarks or complaints about the computer lessons?

Only the last one was not a multiple choice question. The teacher did not analyse the results; he scanned the forms and saw his own opinion confirmed, His own opinion boiled down to: "computer lessons are fun, but not all the time." In fact, the results of the inquiry showed that the pupils were far more positive. A large majority enjoyed the lessons and only a few thought that the emphasis was too much on the technical aspects instead of the historical content.

During the remainder of phase 1, the teacher no longer used the computer in his lessons.

His views about his lessons with the computer included the opinion that trying to draw attention towards himself when pupils are busy with computers is far more difficult than under normal circumstances: "They sit in front of their computers with fanatical eyes, hammering away at the keys, and when I shout that everybody must pay attention to me, they do not do it," He said he had a clearer picture now of the possibilities and difficulties of history teaching with computers. He felt more informed and said he would certainly continue to use the computer in his work. On the other hand he had doubts about the effects of the computers on his pupils.

"I doubt that the children are happier now or that they know more about history than when I told them in more abstract terms about the subject."

He felt the attractiveness of the computer as a new device would quickly vanish, and on this point he compared the computer to the video. However he also felt that integrating the computer had the potential to make history teaching more attractive and he thought that the pupils responded positively to the computer in his lessons. Talking about didactics, he identified the problems of setting up and monitoring of group work, self-activity and differentiation. He felt all these were already difficult enough in a normal situation, and the computer only added to these problems. A prolonged series of lessons in the computer room must be avoided, he stated, and he thought that a break such as he had improvised could be applied more often.

Conclusions

The teaching skills observed in the preparation, execution and evaluation of the computer lessons were noted, and divided into technical, didactical and organisational skills. They contain a lot of normal teaching skills. The only typical computer-related skills are technical ones such as the handling of the computer itself, its operating system, the other hardware and the software. Related to these were skills such as judging and choosing course ware, and instructing pupils in the use of the computer. No specific non-technical computer-related skills were found.

Factors

Some of the potential factors which made the teacher decide to use (or not to use) the computer at home or at school were as follows. The presence of a computer at home made it possible for the teacher not to change his established working routine. It is a significant fact that 80% of the time spent working at the computer was spent at home. He valued the compatible computer at home as "an irreplaceable thing". Technical hitches, such as experienced with the LCD-screen, provided a clearly negative influence.

Another important factor seems to be the availability of good course ware. The fact that his choice was so limited was a serious obstacle to the integration of computers in history teaching. Apart from this, the screen layout of most programs is such that it limits their use to individual learning. The teacher can hardly contemplate other, more traditional usage, as long as this fact remains. Another factor is the curriculum and the question whether a program fits into it or not. The answer to this question depends to a large extent on the freedom the teacher thinks he has within the curriculum. The greater the freedom, the greater the chance of broader use of computers in the classroom, given the limited supply of course ware.

A more personal factor is the willingness to innovate. We have seen that the teacher did not score very high on this point. The limited way in which he used the computer in school confirms this low score.

The factor most in contention is time. Lack of time to prepare and organise lessons, to get to know what is needed for computers in their educational use; to search for and evaluate software, and above all the limited number of lessons available. In the perception of the teacher, time is very important factor.

The style of teaching seems an important factor as well. His personal preference did not prevent the teacher from trying something different but it hindered him considerably in a flexible execution of his computer lessons. It seems that staying close to an established style of teaching is an important factor in integrating computers into history teaching.

One cause of the teacher's uneasiness during the computer lessons was the profound change in teaching method, and the application of group work. Furthermore, he felt insecure because he doubted his abilities to master all the technical problems. He left his secure classroom for a completely different computer room with pupils facing screens instead of him. He was unpleasantly surprised by the number of lessons he had to spend on what he considered to be a relatively insignificant subject. He was uncertain about what he and his pupils would gain and knew precisely what was going to be lost in these 7–8 lessons. It was clear that he felt very uncomfortable with the situation.

Behind these difficulties was an even greater one: he allowed the course ware to decide what teaching method he would employ. In choosing "Beggars of the Sea" he did not only choose a less prominent role in a different setting — he chose implicitly for a completely different kind of history teaching. "The Beggars of the Sea" program is organised around the principle that the pupil is in a way a researcher, a little historian himself. The pupil must construct, on his own, a picture of the past, of who the Sea Beggars were and what their significance was. The pupil is even in the position to verify his own hypotheses. During phase I the teacher never seemed to be conscious of this fundamental difference. He did not make use of databases during phase 2.

Was that the conclusion of the computer experiment? He did go back to the computer room in phase 2 and organised a short series of computer lessons with a tutorial and with some computer based tests for the final national exams and he still spends many happy hours at home at the computer, The analysis of this latest data however, is not yet complete.

Chapter 11

Teaching Strategy and the Management of IT in the History Classroom

Isobel Jenkins

A History Lesson Somewhere in the UK!

Pupils enter the classroom and find that, as usual, there are computers with word processing facilities on their work tables and two further computers in the room. The class is studying the Industrial Revolution in early 19th century Britain. The students have been involved in collecting information about working conditions in mines and factories, about child labour and about insanitary housing. The teacher organises the class into groups. The pupils are to use their word processors to produce newspapers representing the various political views which might have been held in a 19th century mining community in north eastern Britain. The computer by the teacher's desk springs into life, simulating a teleprinter, and the pupils begin to collect this information as the basis for the newspaper accounts.

Information about a mining disaster at Felling Colliery, Durham, in 1812, is being supplied by the 'teleprinter'. After some time another person comes into the room, taking the role of a workman, and makes a statement on behalf of the miners and their families. The statement proves to be very emotional and blames the mine owners for the loss of life of very young girls and boys and even of whole families in the accident. A news briefing is then held by a mine-owners' representative, who refutes the previous claims. It becomes clear that the pupils have no way of testing the truth of the conflicting statements. However they do have access to a computer data file based on a contemporary list of actual casualties and deaths suffered at Felling in 1812. Using the database, information supplied by the 'teleprinter', copies of contemporary pictures and other written resources, the pupils write their newspaper articles. The students in this classroom are actively involved in developing their knowledge and in understanding and interpreting the past. They are also evaluating and analysing sources, appreciating the nature of bias, testing hypotheses, understanding the nature of causation and motivation and constructing an historical account. This classroom scenario should not be presented to teachers as a realistic model — although it does work well. Few history teachers have access to so many computers on a regular basis and it would be unwise to attempt to achieve all of the listed historical outcomes in one exercise. If the computer data file alone were to be used, only one computer would be needed, and the pupils could still test their own hypotheses, as well as text book generalisations about the Industrial Revolution. Moreover they would also be becoming familiar with some primary source material made accessible through technology.

Teachers' Worries

Despite the advantages, history teachers understandably remain very wary of using computers in their lessons. Computers are unfamiliar to many teachers and can, and do, go wrong. There are rarely enough machines for whole class use and to use them involves radical reorganisation of teaching and learning styles. Even if the teacher is convinced that computers can help to teach history, the pupil-based methods seem time-consuming in contrast to the familiar didactic approach. Worst of all — how can the busy teacher become familiar with software? Books and paper resources can be taken home in a bag but a computer cannot always be borrowed and taken home for the weekend.

Planning and Classroom Management

The computer and its programs are a valuable resource to be used to benefit the teaching and learning of history and the secret of effective use is, as in maximising the use of many other resources used, simply careful and conscious planning.

Identifying Outcomes

When planning any lesson, not necessarily involving a computer, the teacher would normally identify the knowledge and historical ideas to be learned and decide on the teaching methods to be used. So, for example, in a simplified version of the lesson described above, the teacher decides to use the Felling computer data file so that the pupils can learn more about working conditions in 19th century Britain and at the same time evaluate source material.

Preparation

The next stage would involve preparing the pupils to use the resources available. The class is already studying the Industrial Revolution and so little new historical knowledge is likely to be needed to make good use of the program. (This data file could, however, be used very effectively by classes with no previous knowledge to provide an introduction to study of the Industrial Revolution.) The pupils may then need to be shown how to use the data file and the computer. This may require the teacher and the whole class to look at some of the records on the file so that field headings, etc., are clear, and the menu system and graphing facilities of the program understood. Another approach would be to structure worksheets so that familiarity with the data file is built into the historical search.

Classroom Organisation

The effective teacher will have been considering the classroom organisation of the computer work from the start. Both the expectation of outcomes to be achieved and of preparation needed are likely to have been shaped by the appreciation of how many computers are available for the history lesson. The ideal lesson organisation for most history teachers is to have 'enough' computers — either by means of a network or maybe 7 or 8 'stand-alone' machines — so that the whole class divided into groups of three or four can work on the program at the same time. Few of us are lucky enough to have access to such facilities, and some sort of 'carousel' arrangement is most likely, with 1, 2, or 3 computers in or near the classroom. Groups take turns to use the data file while the rest of the class is involved in work which supports or follows from the computer investigation. Much valuable work can be done with only one computer in a classroom. The information or data contained in a program can be used as one more helpful resource (along with books, maps, videos etc.) to be referred to when needed. Examples include data files, teleprinter simulations, and programs which allow the searching of collections of written sources. Some simulation programs have been deliberately written for use with only one computer.

Pupil Involvement

We would now expect to find a well organised history lesson with pupils involved in active discussion and investigation using the computer program. However, careful management is still needed if purposeful discussion is to take place. The strategies to be employed are those which would normally encourage serious study in any classroom. The students should have a very clear idea about how their computer investigations fit into the work they are doing. A brief careful record of the results of the investigation should be kept so that each group can report its findings verbally to the whole class and, if required, complete a written account. Each pupil should also be actively involved in the computer work so that the success of the group's work depends on the activity of everyone. Groups of no less than 3 pupils — mixed according to ability and gender — generally work well and encourage lively discussion.

Conclusion

Computer programs can provide versatile and almost limitless resources to enhance the teaching and learning of history. Carefully organised work with computers can allow pupils of all ages and abilities to manage their own learning in an active way. The teacher can become a facilitator of learning experiences rather than a provider of all information. Teachers can be freer to observe the learning process as pupils are using the computer and both informal and formal assessments of pupils' knowledge can be made. Above all, in my experience, the relationship between pupil and teacher becomes one of partnership in history education.

Chapter 12

Progression in Children's Thinking and Understanding in History

Alaric Dickinson

Searching for a Workable Basis for Progression in School History

Attempts to find a workable basis for progression in school history in chronology and knowledge have run into trouble. In particular, it is hard to distinguish chronological structure from aggregation, and does progression in terms of knowledge mean 'knows one fact, knows ten facts … knows almost all facts', or 'knows some simple facts … knows some difficult facts', or what? Finding a workable basis for progression in substantive concepts has also proved problematic. Concepts such as *factory, treaty, king, peasant* or even *revolution* seem as much economic, political or sociological as historical; also such concepts are not equivalent to *volume, density* and *mass* in physics. Notions like *renaissance* or *restoration* or *industrial revolution* offer another possibility; but they are historical particulars as well as concepts. Eventually it may be possible to specify progression in terms of the development of children's frameworks of the past, but attempts so far to clarify progression in terms of substantive conceptual development have proved relatively unsuccessful.

Another possibility is to seek to define progression in terms of structural or second-order concepts, and of skills or understandings. Recent searches for a workable basis for progression have been developing at a time of growing concern among teachers that history in the classroom should amount to more than accumulating historical facts and memorising accounts, and when new models of school history have been evolving. For instance, there has been widespread interest in what has been termed 'new history', with Denis Shemilt (1980) advocating that school history should introduce pupils to the historian's methods and extend pupils' appreciation of the nature of history and of fundamental second-order concepts such as *evidence, explanation, change* and *continuity*.

These developments have led to a contested redefinition of school history in which second-order concepts organise substantive knowledge and understanding, and in so doing provide the key to progression (both by defining the terms in which it is taking place, and setting limits upon it). The higher order referred to is a meta-level, in terms of which the discipline is given epistemological shape. These second-order concepts typically have included *evidence, change, cause, empathy* and *time*; others would have to be added to any complete list.

Progression and the CHATA Project

In England and Wales the introduction of the National Curriculum has made progression a central concern, and the Economic and Social Research Council (ESRC) has funded a major research programme entitled 'Innovation and Change in Education: The Quality of Teaching and Learning'. The overall aim of this programme (1991–96) is to increase understanding of teaching and learning in the context of radical change within the educational system. (Hughes, 1995) Three of the projects in this programme are concerned with progression — in mathematics, science and history respectively.

Project CHATA (Concepts of History and Teaching Approaches) is the one concerned with progression in children's ideas in history. Here progression is taken to be a shorthand for curriculum and assessment design in terms of structured ideas and abilities, such that progression in ideas is elucidated in terms of increasing power and scope of those ideas, and progression in abilities is elucidated in terms of increasing complexity of the abilities themselves, and/or increasing extension over more complex material, or across a wider range of activities.

The research is divided into four phases:

Phase 1   Investigation of the progression of children's ideas about history between the ages of 7 and 14.

Phase 2   Development of instruments for investigating teaching approaches in history and for categorising the way in which history is seen in relation to the wider curriculum.

Phase 3   Exploration of the relationship between pupils' concepts of historical enquiry and historical explanation on the one hand and curriculum contexts and differences in teaching approach on the other.

Phase 4   Longitudinal work at a case study level, the main aim of which is to develop an understanding of the progression paths followed by children.

Investigating Progression in Children's Ideas About History

CHATA has sought to test and refine provisional models of children's understandings, and to develop new models where no adequate models are available. Several possible sub-strands in the concepts of enquiry and explanation have been investigated, in particular *evidence, accounts, rational understanding, cause* and *explanatory adequacy*. In Phase 1 pencil-and-paper responses were collected from over 300 children between the ages of seven and fourteen, across three sets of tasks (on three separate occasions). More than 120 of this main sample were interviewed on all three task sets, including 53 seven-year-olds. In addition video data was collected on 96 children working in groups of three, each group using one set of tasks. Each set of tasks sought to elicit children's ideas in a number of different ways, enabling internal triangulation as well as triangulation across the three tasks sets. In Phase 3 a further 96 children (24 each from Years 3, 6, 7 and 9) were given sets of tasks and interviewed about their answers at the beginning of the Spring term and then again at the end of the Summer term.

Analysis of this data is now in progress. The CHATA team hope eventually to arrive at a model which identifies consistent strategies pursued by children, suggests relatively stable sets of ideas, and allows the characterisation of progression in these ideas in terms of their increasing power and scope. We realise that future changes in teaching and learning may substantially modify the way in which children's ideas develop; it is also possible that the basis for understanding progression may lie not in any particular set of levels but in a multiplicity of alternative routes in the relevant concepts. But any moves towards the project's goals should help to provide a clearer sense of what is at issue in addressing children's ideas in history, aid the development of useful diagnostic tools and offer a more coherent basis for assessment.

As yet it is too early to talk of findings, but initial analysis does suggest a high degree of consistency in strategies adopted by children across the three sets of tasks, despite differences in historical content. It seems likely that the models of *rational understanding* and *evidence* with which we began (Dickinson and Lee, 1978; Ashby and Lee, 1987a and 1987b) can be substantially refined, and the data on cause suggests a clear progression of ideas. (Lee, Dickinson and Ashby, 1995). Furthermore, both CHATA and the project on progression in mathematics and science have found large variations in children's understanding of key concepts, with some seven-year-olds performing at higher levels than some 13 or 14 year-olds. This raises important questions for theorists (what causes this variation?) and for policy makers (how can a national curriculum take account of it?), but above all for teachers who have to deal with such variations.

The data also suggests various fertile possibilities for using IT to aid further progression in children's thinking and understanding. Limitations of space prohibit any detailed exploration of these possibilities here; what follows, therefore, amounts to some brief speculation linked to a scintilla of project data.

IT and Progression in School History: Some Speculative Thoughts

The CHATA video data in particular provides rich evidence that pupils with low reading ages and writing difficulties are not necessarily poor thinkers in history, where experience of personal and social relations count so heavily. Teachers face the heavy responsibility of having to plan work appropriate to the abilities of each pupil; IT can and should be developed as an aid to the achievement of this goal.

Progression can also be aided by providing pupils with opportunities to make clear (to their peers, teachers or to the computer) what they find problematic, plus access to materials that utilise these problems. The timing, nature and content of any feedback, questions and new material are all important. Computers can be programmed to provide these in immediate response to the moves that each pupil makes. An indication of the value of such a service is offered below by reference to some responses to one of the items used in the CHATA investigation.

In order to elicit children's ideas about cause, CHATA used several different approaches (open questions, cause boxes and conflicting explanations). For each set of tasks logically similar items were devised but with different content.

(Historical material sufficient to enable children to form a judgment was provided each time). In the first set of tasks the opening question took the form of a paradox:

There were lots of Britons in Britain.
The Roman army that went to Britain wasn't very big.
The Britons were fighting for their homes.
So why were the Romans able to take over most of Britain?

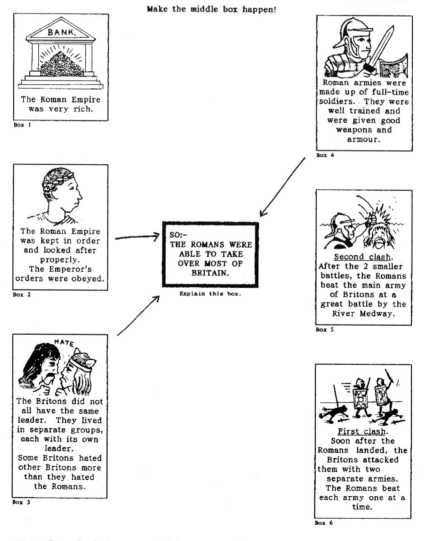

Question 12. Why were the Romans able to take over?

[The boxes on this Chart are not in any special order]
Choose any boxes which help explain why the Romans were able to take over.
Join them up with arrows to show best why the Romans were able to take over.
Make the best explanation you can.
An arrow from one box to another means: the first box helps explain the second box.
Use as many joins as you need. You can have more than one arrow to or from a box.
BUT don't make joins that don't help explain why the Romans were able to take over.

Make the middle box happen!

BANK.
The Roman Empire was very rich.
Box 1

Roman armies were made up of full-time soldiers. They were well trained and were given good weapons and armour.
Box 4

The Roman Empire was kept in order and looked after properly.
The Emperor's orders were obeyed.
Box 2

SO:–
THE ROMANS WERE ABLE TO TAKE OVER MOST OF BRITAIN.
Explain this box.

Second clash.
After the 2 smaller battles, the Romans beat the main army of Britons at a great battle by the River Medway.
Box 5

The Britons did not all have the same leader. They lived in separate groups, each with its own leader.
Some Britons hated other Britons more than they hated the Romans.
Box 3

First clash.
Soon after the Romans landed, the Britons attacked them with two separate armies. The Romans beat each army one at a time.
Box 6

Figure 12.1 Causal relations: an additive response by a year six pupil

This was asked first in the form of an open question, for which children had to write a few lines in answer. In a later question children were asked to draw arrows linking boxes in order to give the best explanation they could. Children were told that an arrow from one box to another meant that the first box helped explain the second, and that they could have as many or as few arrows as they needed. They were also told that more than one arrow could go into or out of a box. (Figure 12.1)

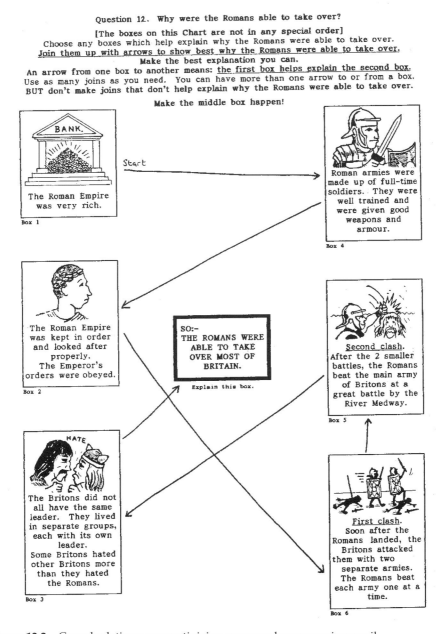

Figure 12.2 Causal relations: a narrativizing response by a year nine pupil

One part of the rationale behind these and the other questions used but not reported here is an attempt to discover whether there is any kind of depth-structure in children's handling of causal explanation. Some children simply give haphazard lists of causal factors in answer to the open question, and then in the box questions make a few simple joins to the centre box which has to be explained.

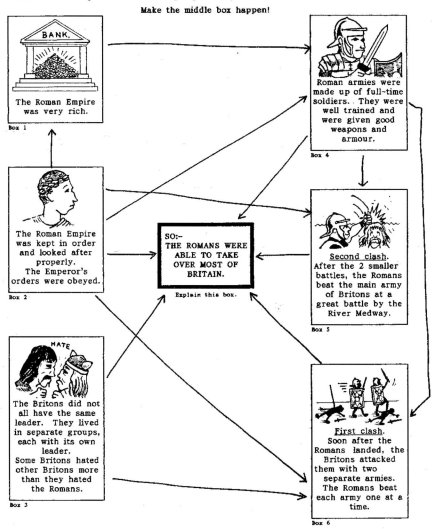

Figure 12.3   Causal relations: an analytical response by a year seven pupil

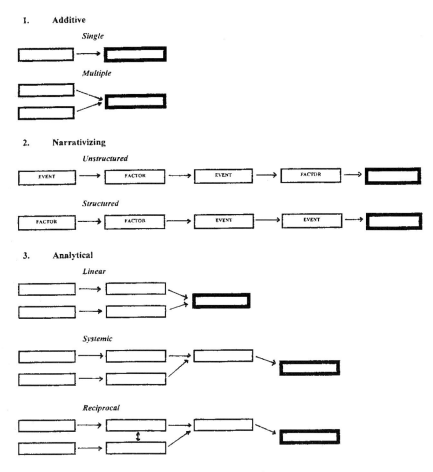

Figure 12.4   Causal relations and casual structure: schematic provisional model

(Figure 12.1) They behave as if causes are discrete and additive. Others give a narrative of events in the open question, and then narrativize the boxes. (Figure 12.2) Typically this consists in producing a linear sequence which may encompass all the cause boxes, or just some of them. There appears to be a range of ideas operating here, with some children treating processes and states of affairs as if they were events, and others showing some awareness of the different status of the connections they make. Finally, some children construct a causal argument in answering the open question, and then use arrows to produce what can only be described as an analytical scheme for the box-question. Background conditions are picked out as separate starting points for different, sometimes separate and sometimes interlinked, causal chains which lead into the events for which they are conditions. (Figure 12.3)

Figures 12.5 to 12.14 show responses by teachers who were asked to use the cause boxes from our second set of tasks to explain why the Roman Empire came to an end. The 28 teachers who kindly agreed to do this were attending a session at CHC 93 in Lisbon and were mainly English or Portuguese; they were not given the background information or the other questions. Most of the teachers' responses showed causal arguments being constructed, and a very high level of valid connections (which suggests that the exercise was taken seriously). In the selection presented here, Figures 12.5, 12.6 and 12.10 show systemic analytical responses,

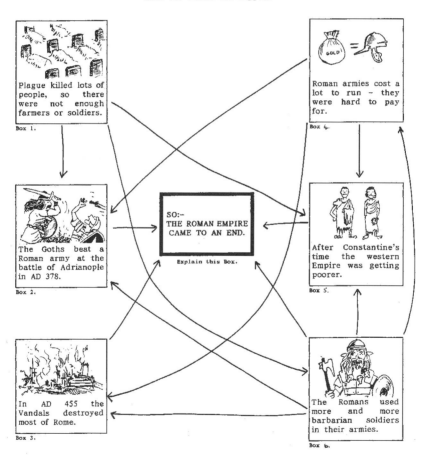

Figure 12.5   Causal relations: a systematic analytical response by a teacher

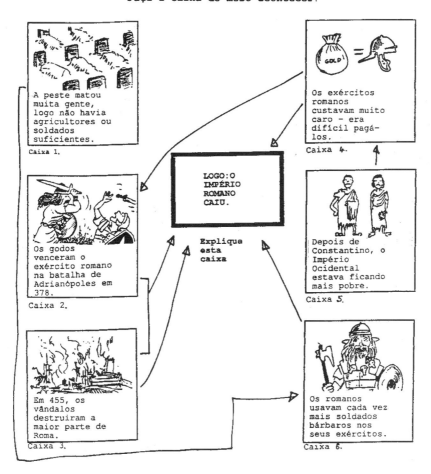

Figure 12.6   Causal relations: a systematic analytical response by a teacher

Figures 12.8 and 12.12 show additive responses and there is an instance of narrativizing (Figure 12.7). Other features present here — and in the project data too — include 'dead-ends' (Figures 12.9, 12.11 and 12.14) and 'reverse-arrows' (Figure 12.8). Figures 12.9 and 12.14 show responses which are analytical with reciprocal links (though without links to the centre box) and Figure 12.11 interestingly contains indications of a change of strategy during the task, and also a mixture of valid and invalid links, two 'dead-ends' and no arrow to the centre. What, one may wonder, would be the effect of providing immediate and targeted feedback (feasible using IT!), including asking some respondents what exactly they were trying to do (this would seem to be particularly applicable here with regard to Figures 12.7, 12.8, 12.11 and 12.14), and also exploring how far instructions have been followed faithfully, the reasons behind the presence of 'dead-ends' and why

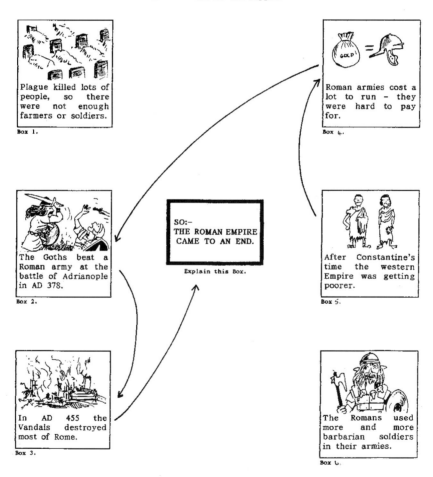

Figure 12.7   Causal relations: a narrativizing response by a teacher

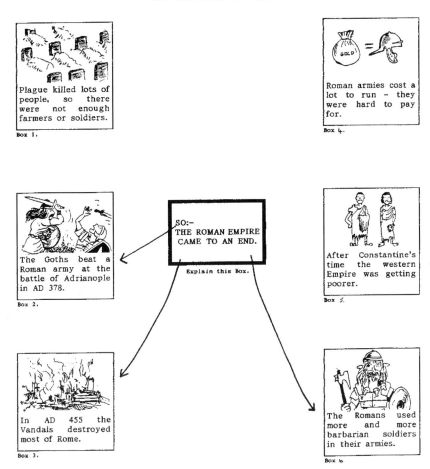

THE END OF THE ROMAN EMPIRE
Question 7.

[The boxes are not in any special order]
Choose any boxes which help explain why the Roman Empire came to an end.
Join them up to show the best way you can why the Empire came to an end.
Draw in arrows to make the joins.
An arrow from one box to another means: the first box helps explain the second box.
Use as many joins as you need. You can have more than one arrow to or from a box.
BUT don't make joins that don't help explain why the Empire came to an end.

Make the middle box happen!

Plague killed lots of people, so there were not enough farmers or soldiers.
Box 1.

Roman armies cost a lot to run – they were hard to pay for.
Box 4.

The Goths beat a Roman army at the battle of Adrianople in AD 378.
Box 2.

SO:-
THE ROMAN EMPIRE CAME TO AN END.
Explain this Box.

After Constantine's time the western Empire was getting poorer.
Box 5.

In AD 455 the Vandals destroyed most of Rome.
Box 3.

The Romans used more and more barbarian soldiers in their armies.
Box 6

Figure 12.8   Causal relations: an additive response by a teacher

some respondents chose not to use all the boxes. With teachers it might prove very constructive to ask them to code some responses using the schematic provisional model set out in Figure 12.4 and also to check the validity of the arguments constructed, and to consider what assumptions and understandings might be inferred from each response and how they might be explored further.

THE END OF THE ROMAN EMPIRE
Question 7.

[The boxes are not in any special order]
Choose any boxes which help explain why the Roman Empire came to an end.
Join them up to show the best way you can why the Empire came to an end.
Draw in arrows to make the joins.
An arrow from one box to another means: the first box helps explain the second box.
Use as many joins as you need. You can have more than one arrow to or from a box.
BUT don't make joins that don't help explain why the Empire came to an end.

Make the middle box happen!

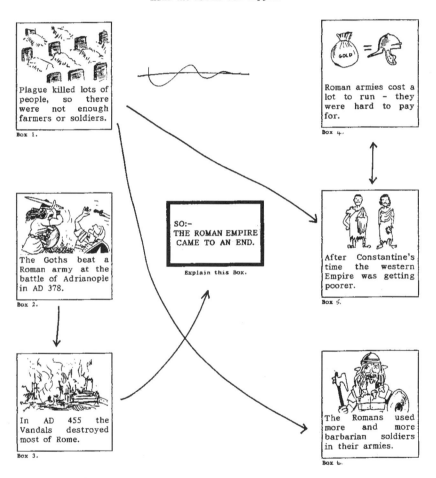

Figure 12.9 Causal relations: a systematic analytical response by a teacher

THE END OF THE ROMAN EMPIRE
Question 7.

[The boxes are not in any special order]
Choose any boxes which help explain why the Roman Empire came to an end.
Join them up to show the best way you can why the Empire came to an end.
Draw in arrows to make the joins.
An arrow from one box to another means: the first box helps explain the second box.
Use as many joins as you need. You can have more than one arrow to or from a box.
BUT don't make joins that don't help explain why the Empire came to an end.

Make the middle box happen!

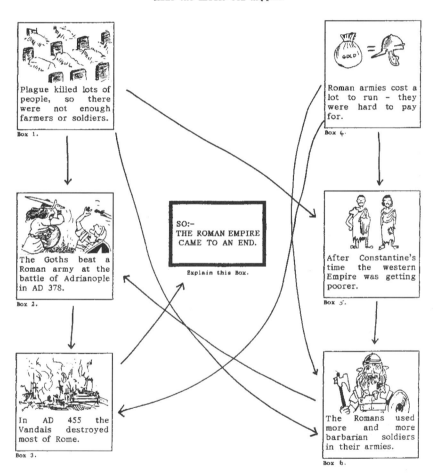

Figure 12.10   Causal relations: a systematic analytical response by a teacher

O FIM DO IMPÉRIO ROMANO

Escolha quaisquer caixas que ajudam a explicar porque o Império caiu.
Combine-as, da melhor maneira que puder, para mostrar porque o Império caiu.

Faça a caixa do meio acontecer!

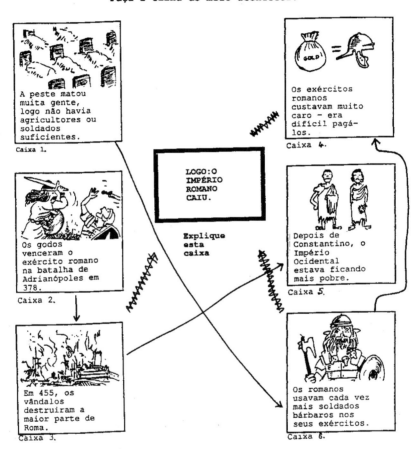

Figure 12.11   Causal relations: a systematic analytical response by a teacher

O FIM DO IMPÉRIO ROMANO

Escolha quaisquer caixas que ajudam a explicar porque o Império caiu.
Combine-as, da melhor maneira que puder, para mostrar porque o Império caiu.

Faça a caixa do meio acontecer!

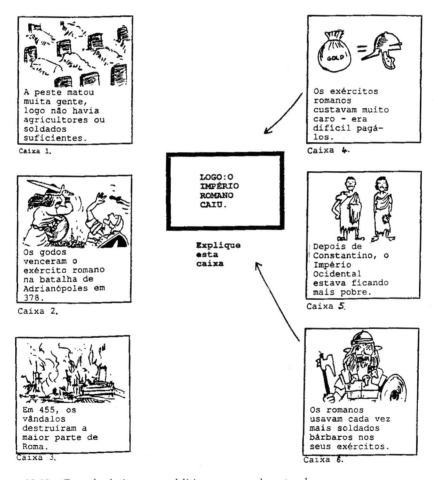

Figure 12.12 Causal relations: an additive response by a teacher

O FIM DO IMPÉRIO ROMANO

Escolha quaisquer caixas que ajudam a explicar porque o Império caiu.
Combine-as, da melhor maneira que puder, para mostrar porque o Império caiu.

Faça a caixa do meio acontecer!

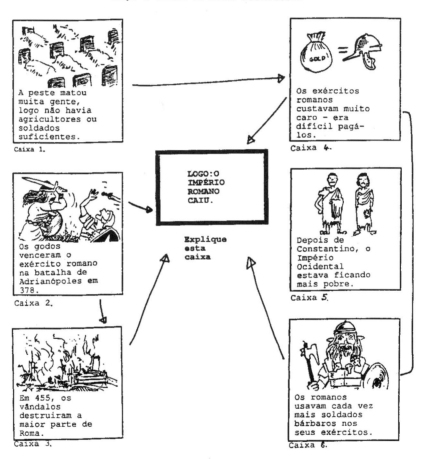

Figure 12.13   Causal relations: a systematic analytical response by a teacher

O FIM DO IMPÉRIO ROMANO

Escolha quaisquer caixas que ajudam a explicar porque o Império caiu.
Combine-as, da melhor maneira que puder, para mostrar porque o Império caiu.

Faça a caixa do meio acontecer!

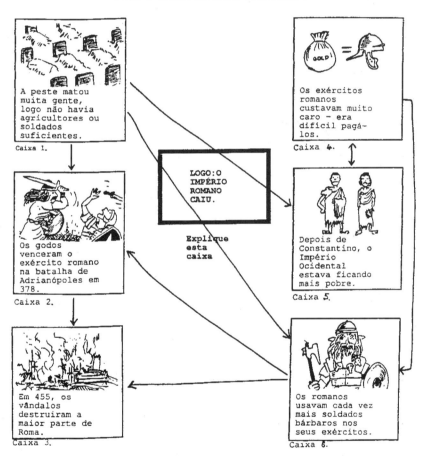

Figura internal text:

A peste matou muita gente, logo não havia agricultores ou soldados suficientes.
Caixa 1.

Os exércitos romanos custavam muito caro – era difícil pagá-los.
Caixa 4.

LOGO: O IMPÉRIO ROMANO CAIU.

Explique esta caixa

Os godos venceram o exército romano na batalha de Adrianópoles em 378.
Caixa 2.

Depois de Constantino, o Império Ocidental estava ficando mais pobre.
Caixa 5.

Em 455, os vândalos destruíram a maior parte de Roma.
Caixa 3.

Os romanos usavam cada vez mais soldados bárbaros nos seus exércitos.
Caixa 6.

Figure 12.14 Causal relations: a systematic analytical response by a teacher

Conclusion

Children's ideas may sometimes seem strange to us, but these ideas are the constructs which make sense of the world, past and present, for the child. The sets of ideas with which children work have greater or lesser explanatory power; they may create or solve problems. One of our fundamental aims as teachers must be to do what we can to help each child to achieve the most powerful explanatory strategies possible for them. In practice this means diagnosing the level they are at and employing teaching approaches that will help them to achieve higher levels as they progress through school. With the dawn of the 21st Century IT can and should be making a truly significant contribution to this noble endeavour.

Chapter 13
Sturt and Pericles: Two Computer-Based Inquiry Units
Lee Wright

Background Information

The observations made in this chapter arise directly from two projects undertaken with students in the 14 to 18 year old range. The focus is on those factors and features that the keen but inexperienced computer user may encounter as they seek to explore the potential of IT in the history they teach.

The computer hardware and software we used was a fairly standard configuration. We used Macs, Microsoft *Works*, *Filemaker Pro*, a modem and a scanner.

I will outline the two units and then attempt to identify some common experiences before drawing together my observations and conclusions, albethey tentative ones.

The Sturt Project

This first unit was a 3 week computer based inquiry for Year 9 students (14/15 years old) investigating the 1829/30 journey of Charles Sturt down the Murrumbidgee and Murray Rivers.

The unit was based on an article by Juhani Tuovinen from the School of Education at Charles Sturt University — Riverina, titled 'Navigating the Murray with Sturt or Using Computer Technologies in History' (*Queensland History Teachers' Association Magazine*, Vol. 30 No. 1, April, 1992), which argues that the skills of research, information organisation and information presentation can be best developed using modern information technology,

The first task was to compile a simulation game, using the *Worldbuilder* program, which then provides the outline for an adventure game in which the players must decide on directions and courses of action. In this I was fortunate that I had in my class one student who was particularly talented and interested in the computer field and we worked together to develop the game. Although we didn't get it completed in time to use it as an introductory lesson, (it took about twelve hours to develop), it did prove successful when it was used at the end of the unit in challenging the students and, I suggest, helping to develop a sense of empathy.

Our original intention was to obtain information about Sturt and the places he visited by setting up computer communications on the Keylink and Nexus networks with schools along the Murrumbidgee and Murray Rivers. Unfortunately, time and a lack of response, meant that information from this source had to be replaced with about seventy extracts that I took directly from Sturt's Journal.

Working in groups of three, students had to enter this data into a Filemaker Pro data base and then make use of the advantages of this program by adding a map and/or a picture to each entry. This required valuable prior discussion about the sorts of information to be collected and how this might most usefully be categorised and a demonstration of how to incorporate and manipulate the maps and pictures. This activity took eight forty minute periods. Throughout this stage I felt that what I was teaching were computer skills, not history skills and that, because of the small, compartmentalised sections of data with which each group was involved, the actual historical aspect was minimal.

However, these feelings changed when we compiled the various parts into a complete data base. After an introduction on manipulating the data base, the students worked enthusiastically in their groups on a worksheet of closed answer type questions for a double period. In the next three periods, I asked the groups to answer the more open-ended question of describing Sturt's relationship with the Aborigines on his journey. This involved reading thirteen Journal extracts, some quite lengthy, and drawing conclusions. Again, I felt that the computer was a very successful motivational tool but that the quality of history work seemed to suffer because students were concentrating more on the computer operations than on the historical material.

Next, I demonstrated the use of *HyperCard* and asked each group to present their sections of data on cards that contained a picture, a date and a very brief summary. This was a very simplistic activity in historical terms but, although the students enjoyed it, and all completed the summarising part, it took three periods for the best group to compile only two complete cards.

While the rest of the class worked on these tasks two of the students used the data, maps and illustrations provided to develop an animated portrayal of Sturt's journey. Again, as with all of the tasks in the unit, the result was very successful, but extremely time consuming.

The students' (anonymous) evaluations of the unit showed that three of the students, out of thirty, would not want to do another unit using computers. Most felt that the best thing about the unit was that they learnt about computers as well as about history, which was indeed one of the aims. However, they also felt the computer work had helped them to learn about Sturt and they were able to explain quite clearly how computers could help in historical investigation. Their main complaints about the unit were insufficient time, computer malfunctions (which may not always have been the computers' "fault"), trying to do too many things and having to wait for the teacher to help.

The City of Athens in the Time of Pericles

This second unit was designed for a Year 11 class that was of below average ability. (Five of the ten students had scored in the bottom 10% in the State in Year 10.) It took five weeks (30 periods).

To begin with, I divided the ten students into three groups and gave each group the task of finding information and pictures on either the Acropolis or the Agora or the rest of the city (Piraeus, the Long Walls, Ceramicus, Houses, Streets, Water Supplies, the Areopagus & the Pnyx, the Theatre District etc.) Each group had to present a disk with scanned pictures and word-processed information. I put the information and pictures into a *HyperCard* stack so that by clicking on any area of the map of Athens they could find the relevant information. In this unit I did the *HyperCard* work for the students. I don't regard this as desirable teaching practice but did it because they had had no previous experience with *HyperCard* and because I knew from the Sturt Project just how slow their initial progress would be. With this unit I was just trying to show students what *HyperCard* could do and how it operates. I intend to cover the City of Rome in a similar manner next year and, with this background behind them, will encourage the students to develop their own *HyperCard* stack at that stage. In the long term, I intend to encourage all students to do some introductory work with *HyperCard* on Family Trees when they first enter the school so that we can build on these basic skills in subsequent years.

To reinforce these skills, the students then took part in 'Pericles' Great Fact Chase', a group competition, where they had to navigate around the stack to find the answer to as many questions as possible in a single period.

Then the groups had to use the information in the stack to organise itineraries for tours of the sites for groups interested in either Government, Religion, Business Life, Entertainment or Art and Architecture in the time of Pericles.

Finally, the groups were asked to use the information in the stack to plan an attack on the city of Athens. Different groups had to report on the methods used in previous attacks on Athens in the Persian and Peloponnesian Wars, the strength and location of Athens' naval and military resources, her financial resources, the location within the city of her political and military leaders, the best options for travelling within the city and the possible timing for an attack.

The students participated in all of these tasks enthusiastically and successfully. The quantity and depth of the work they presented was far greater than in any other unit of work covered during the year. I thought the worksheets on planning an attack on the city of Athens were quite demanding but their analyses were extremely pleasing.

One of the best features of this unit is the way it can be used as a resource by future groups and even expanded. One group will be expected to carry out extension research work on the myths and legends associated with the various buildings in Athens, such as the adventures of Theseus. Since so many of the buildings have religious functions and associations it will also help to have one group enter information about Greek religion. They can research the names, functions and characters of the twelve Olympian Gods and Greek attitudes to the Gods. Information about Greek burial customs could also be included.

It will also help to know something about the system of government and the history of ancient Athens. Students can research such topics as the Peisistratid Tyranny and the Persian invasions of 490 B.C. and 480 B.C. and add the information to the stack as a new card connected to the relevant building. The influence of personalities such as Themistocles, Pericles and Pheidias can be included and so too can a consideration of modern issues such as the Elgin Marbles and the effects of pollution on the buildings of the Acropolis.

After my experience with these two units, I would offer the following advice to teachers contemplating using computers in this way in the History classroom:

1. Quite simply, do it. There is a strong rationale for expanding the contexts in which we teach research, information organisation and information presentation skills to include the modern information technology that our students will use when they enter the workforce. Further, the challenge (and deadlines) provided in programming units of work will provide the necessary stimulus for your own learning about computers.

2. Expect to feel uncomfortable at first. I know my own lack of confidence and competence in a new area meant that I was far from relaxed in class. The students really did have to listen carefully and follow step by step computer instructions or else they would simply be left behind. This was different to what myself and the students were used to but I now think that is simply a normal part of acquiring an important new skill and can be overcome in a short time. I found that I felt far more comfortable when I taught the second unit

3. Make use of the students' interests, abilities and enthusiasm. I feel sure that almost every class now contains at least one computer 'expert' and we can expect that expertise to grow rapidly in the next few years. We can introduce students to the history skills and content but in most cases they can show us the computer skills and, moreover, would love the opportunity to do so. There is a real opportunity here for a true learning partnership.

4. In this context computers are not timesavers, either in class time or in preparation time. I deliberately restricted the first unit to just three weeks, both because that was the amount of time available in the computer room during the Year 12 Exams (an international problem judging the response during the presentation of this paper) and because I regarded that as a reasonable time for a unit of work on just one explorer. Similarly, the second unit took at least a week longer than I would normally expect to spend on such a unit.

   However, the most common complaint about the first unit from the students was that there was insufficient time. In retrospect it would have been better to have divided the separate computer skills into other units through the year rather than combine them all in one unit.

   It would also have been a great advantage if the students had had previous training in the use of computer communications, data bases and particularly in *HyperCard*. I frequently felt that the students were concentrating far more upon the computer skills involved than on the material with which they were working. However, I can see that developments in technology education should mean that in the near future we will be working with students who will be far more computer literate and so much freer to concentrate upon the material with which they are working.

   Of course, in both cases there will be some timesaving in that I now have resources that can be used and built upon by future groups. What I believe is needed is a greater commitment to developing and disseminating these resources by educational authorities otherwise the sheer amount of time involved will mean that the rate at which they can be developed by practising teachers is going to be far too slow for the needs of our students.

5. The use of computers does motivate the students even in such routine tasks as editing and summarising. This was particularly so in the low achievers group.

6. Computers do support learning in history and about the processes of historical investigation. I would have attempted to achieve what I did in terms of my aims for the units but feel I was able to achieve more and a better quality of learning by making use of the computers.

The technological tools to help us investigate and learn in history are available to us right now. I think that some of the failures of my units showed that, in some ways, they are still the tools of the future. But more importantly I think that some of the successes showed that it's a future that is arriving very quickly and it's a future that can improve our teaching of history.

Chapter 14

The Hobbs of Havant: Local History Brought to Life

Nicola Gosling

Introduction

There were many times during the clandestine deliberations of the History Working Group when it looked for all the world as if History would be once again be conceived of as a solid diet of facts, dates — and yet more facts. For those privileged to work with children in the classroom on historical investigations which truly fired their interest and enthusiasm the Report's statement that we "need to reveal to pupils that history is interesting, exciting and enjoyable" (DES, 1990) did however, give some comfort.

A variety of ways of achieving this were identified and these included field trips, museum and site visits, use of archives and artefacts in the classroom, through archaeology, oral history and television and radio. The creation of just one Programme of Study at Key Stage 1 (ages 5–7), introducing pupils to the idea of the past and the dimension of time, by exposing them to local people, places and events seemed to provide ample opportunity to do just this. Turning to Key Stages 2 (ages 7–11), Key Stage 3 (ages 11–14) and Key Stage 4 (ages 14–16), however, we see a quite different structure. Rigidly laid out and obligatory units of study, a chronological emphasis and simply masses, in terms of content, to cover.

For the primary school teacher with an already heavily congested curriculum plan, the task of allocating just a small amount of time to history was a gargantuan one, particularly so in those schools where history had up to then been a low priority area. Even if time and space can be found, how should history be taught? In bite-sized chunks on a weekly basis? Is this the way to excite children's interest in the past and move them towards an understanding of it? All the evidence to date seems to suggest not.A national report of history in schools carried out by Her Majesty's Inspectorate (DES 1989) concluded:

> "Coherence is often best achieved where greater emphasis is given to either History or Geography for a given period of time so as to attain a balance over a term or a year. Such a strategy is usually more successful than tackling both subjects through a weekly timetable".

It was frequently reiterated in the early days of the National Curriculum that although it is described in subject terms, there is no requirement for it to be taught thus. HMI also suggested that historical understanding begins to take shape when it is experienced in a practical way and within a context which makes sense to children. We too often assume children have an inherent curiosity about things past, whereas experience suggests that curiosity is usually aroused when a trigger is present e.g. a significant occasion or event of a local, or even national, nature. It is only then that children begin to ask "How do we know?"; "Why did this happen?"; and "How do I find out more?"

Local History in the Curriculum

It is because of the inspiration which we know local people, places or events can create, that it is pleasing to see the inclusion of at least one, if not two, local history units at Key Stage 2 and the History Working Group's statement that:

> "We support the well-developed tradition of studying local history in school, both in primary and secondary phases"

(DES 1990 para 4.30)

They suggested two distinct roles: first the use of local examples to illustrate national, European and World history — since there are no separate local history units at Key Stage 3 and 4, this presumably is where this role would be most apparent; and second, the use of the locality and its community as a comprehensive field for study, for which there is provision at Key Stages 1 and 2.

There still remains the question, however, of where a local study will be accommodated within the overcrowded curriculum framework.

Local History: A Case Study

The following is an account of how one school developed a local study, giving a clear history focus, but also providing opportunities to "springboard" into other areas of the curriculum. The unit in fact grew out of a larger topic on the theme of 'Travel and Movement', the children having previously been involved in finding out about themselves and their families as travellers e.g. daily travel (to school, leisure pursuits etc.); holiday travel; parents' travel to work, commuting etc.; relocation for job moves etc.

Having plotted on a map of the UK where they had all been born and where their parents had been born, the question was raised: "Have people always moved about as much as we do today?" Researching back to grandparents' childhood was easy enough, but what about one hundred years or more ago, where the people of that time were no longer alive to pass on information?

The following example illustrates one teacher's attempts to tackle this.

Example

A class of 28 eight and nine year old children from a middle school in Havant were sitting in pairs on the 'reading mat'. Each pair had been given copies of a photograph with no other information than that found on the back when it was first found: 'Hobbs, Havant, 1882'. It seems safe to assume that the photo was taken in 1882, that the setting was Havant and that either a person (or persons) in the photograph had the name Hobbs, or the name of the photographer was Hobbs. An unexpected bonus was that a pupil (Louise) in another class in the year below had the surname Hobbs; playtime was eagerly awaited to find out if she was related!

The children are asked what questions they would like to ask of the photograph; these are many and varied:

— Are they Louise's relatives?
— What are the names of the people in the photograph?
— Did the children go to school?
— Where in Havant is it?
— Are the people in the front of the photograph the Hobbs family?
— Why has their house got a "posh" (elaborate) porch?
— Why was the picture taken?
— What time of year was it?

Can we answer any or all of these questions and, if so, how should we go about doing it? One child suggested that

"We could ask someone who knew the family couldn't we?"

Another child pointed out that this wouldn't be easy because the photograph is probably over 100 years old so

"There wouldn't be anyone alive who would remember them".

Calling upon work undertaken the previous year on evidence, it was suggested that something may have been written down somewhere about the Hobbs family; after all we have birth certificates, medical and school records today. At this stage, the teacher introduced the concept of a census and discussed it with the children. Each pair of children was then given a different page from the 1881 Census for Havant. Some time is spent exploring it, working out the different categories, deciphering the letters, abbreviations etc. The children's attention is then focussed on the the Surnames column and they are asked to scan their sheet for the name Hobbs.

Success! A family by that name is found. Copies of this particular sheet were given out to each pairing and the children asked to find out as much as possible about the people who had this name.

The results were impressive:

• there are six members of the family, William, Ann and four children;
• William's brother, James, is a lodger in the house;
• William is a master plumber and painter;
• the middle two children go to school;
• the family live in West Street.

The next stage is to *try* to match up the names on the census with the people shown in the photograph. The two girls *could* be Florence and Olive; they look about eight or nine years old. Alfred could be standing by the doorway. The older brother George doesn't seem to be in the picture, perhaps he is at work (we know he is an apprentice) or "perhaps taking the photo" suggested one child. What about the baby shown in the photo? There is no mention of a baby in the census. Careful rethinking reminds them that there is a year's difference between the two sources — perhaps the child was born after the census was taken! Suggestions now come thick and fast:

> "The 'posh' (elaborate) porch might be because William is a 'master' plumber and painter and therefore more important than his neighbours (one is a pensioner or 'annuitant', the other a blacksmith)."

At this stage, we stopped and returned to our original questions. It is agreed that we had moved a long way forward in finding out about the people in the photograph, but we are not 100% certain. We can conjecture and make reasoned suggestions on the basis of the evidence that we have to hand, but we may never be absolutely sure. It was agreed that we were also unlikely to discover why the photo was taken or the time of day because people do not usually record these things; we could only hazard a guess, or hypothesise on the basis of the available evidence i.e. the clothing the people were wearing.

Feeling well acquainted with the family, the next step was to consider what their daily lives might have been like, how they got to work or school, where they had been born, to compare with our own experiences (our starting point). Looking again at our original photograph, we picked up a number of clues about means of travel: there are no cars; the streets are narrow; a horse and cart can be seen …

When we looked at a map of Havant at this time, we see four main roads, North, South, East and West Streets. What do they look like, and where do they lead? To Portsmouth, Southampton, Chichester and Winchester, all major market towns, perhaps? Further photographs of these streets reveal more clues, certainly no cars and when we compared them with modern day photos, we found we could identify all manner of differences, such as no road signs or yellow lines. It was suggested that travelling any distance must have been very uncomfortable, the carts and carriages did not look very comfortable at all. But, did people need to travel far? Perhaps not for when we looked at the Trade Directories they revealed most provisions and services were available in Havant itself. And what about moving further afield for jobs; did people move as freely as they do today? To attempt to answer these questions the children agreed that we would need to take a good representative sample of people from the census returns.

It is here that IT came into the picture to make a significant contribution. Initial deciphering and wrestling with the census returns is challenging and exciting, but ploughing through 200 names or more is just tedious. Construction of a database would seem to offer a potential solution to handling this amount of data.

Use of the Computer

To speed up the process the census details were transferred onto proformas in the children's own hand. The children decided that names, addresses, jobs, gender and place of birth are all required so each lunchtime for the next week, two volunteers rapidly enter the information on the proformas onto the database (we used GRASS). With almost 200 entries installed, all manner of revelations started to appear. These included: most people were born only a short distance from Havant; it is mostly the people with "important" jobs who have come to Havant from further afield; fewer women had travelled from their place of birth than men. When compared with the original location map showing where the children's families had come from, a great difference was revealed. So the children began to conclude that lifestyles had changed considerably in the last 100 years and importantly it was evident that different people living at the same time had different experiences of travel.

Evaluation

Without identifying it as such, we had been studying the lives of a group of Victorians and the unit could dovetail beautifully with the core history unit on Victorians, giving scope to move on to look at different aspects of their lives, e.g. work, education, religion. Often when we study the past, we move in the abstract, referring to 'The Victorians' as a single whole without ever revealing them as individuals who lived, played and worked in some of the streets and houses in which we do today. Finding a way in through a real family is a powerful motivator (especially if the family is still in existence as in this case) as the children were truly curious about the people captured in the original photograph. If the family name or the location are local, so much the better as the children have something very real to which to relate.

The photograph itself is a very attractive medium: it is immediate; it is familiar (most of us have taken photos or are featured in them) and provides lots of clues without depending on the written word which can so often put children off. It is also frustrating as it seems to tell us so much, but which cannot necessarily be confirmed. Yet this is a powerful and important message: history is not always clear cut; there are always things which remain uncertain and tentative until new evidence comes to light to support or refute them.

The use of IT in this context was appropriate to the needs. It did not replace the other classroom resources, but acted alongside them to enable searching to take place more rapidly and accurately than would have been possible by hand. Decision-making on the format and content of the database was a critical stage with the children selecting only the categories of information which they felt to be relevant to the line of enquiry. Once constructed, the database could be used to test out a whole range of hypotheses e.g. "Women travelled less far for work then men 100 years ago" and we could rest assured that the conclusions reached would be firmly rooted in evidence rather than in hasty guesswork. How the children chose to present the data was also important: Was a pie chart the most effective and meaningful medium of expression? …

As a pilot project, this class of children had the rare commodity of two adults in the classroom who undoubtedly helped in the organisation, always a difficulty in work of this nature. Since then, however, the unit has been amended and enhanced to make it as self-supporting as possible, and is currently being used successfully by a number of schools in Hampshire. One particularly useful addition has been the use of the Concept Keyboard with overlays made up from the original photograph, census return and map extracts. This has meant that children are now able to work independently on the unit, following their own lines of enquiry or using the unit as just one of a number of different options available.

Cross-Curricular Links

Although the intention was that this topic should be a history based one it quickly became apparent how often and relevantly other areas of the curriculum were being drawn upon. These included:
- English: throughout, there was discussion, exchange of ideas, use of documents.
- Geography: map reading and interpretation, mapping skills.
- Technology: investigations into different forms of carts and carriages, model making.
- I.T.: construction and use of a database.
- Maths: use of database graphic facilities.

Resources Required

- Hobbs Family Photograph (1882) from the Hampshire Record Office; often a parent, library, or local newspaper can come up with a suitable photograph.
- Census Data (1881) available from the Record Office.
- 25 inch Ordnance Survey Map of Havant (1890).
- 6 inch Ordnance Survey Map of South Hampshire (1890).
- Kelly's Directory (1880).
- Havant Street Photographs — possibly available from the Record Office or another local source.
- Miscellaneous frustrations and photos of horses and carts.
- GRASS database.
- Map of the U.K.

Thanks to Bidbury Middle School, Havant, for working with me on this project.

Chapter 15
Spanish Armada: The Classroom Use of a Database
David Martin

Setting Up the Database: The Choice of Software

At the school that this project was first developed in all students were familiar with the database programme KEY (One of a range of databases used in U.K. schools). It therefore made sense for the History department to build upon this familiarity as developed in other curriculum areas by the students. Whilst there might be 'better' databases, adopting KEY meant that little time needed to be spent teaching students how to use the programme. Also the programme was suffi- ciently powerful to meet our requirements.

Historical Sources

The database that we developed consists of two files, SPANISH ARMADA and ENGLISH FLEET. The information within them is taken from a variety of sources but they are largely based upon the appendix by Sydney Wignall in *Full Fathom Five* (Martin, 1975) and the information within *Spanish Armada* (Parker & Martin, 1988). These in turn are based upon the primary sources and this explains why there is more information on the Spanish ships, the records of Philip II's Spain being more complete than those of Elizabeth's England. It makes sense for teachers to use the information available from the researches of others, with their permis- sion of course, in order to limit the amount of time needed to set up a database.

Database Structure: The Spanish Fleet

As can be seen from Figure 15.1 there are 16 fields for each ship.

These can be divided into 5 types which utilise some of the possibilities of KEY. *Ship Name* is a 'words' field which has to be long enough to accommodate some of the longer ship names. *Squadron, Fate* and *Port of Return* are 'tokenised' fields so that once the token (Figure 15.2) has been set up it need not be typed in full again.

This obviously speeds up the entry of records and makes searches easier. *Frontline* and *Missing* list are 'logical' fields, i.e. true or false, which again speeds up entry and also makes searching the database easier. All the other fields are 'number' fields with the exception of *Details*. This is a 'free text' field which allows up to 500 characters to be typed in. This flexibility is obviously invaluable when

```
Record no : 1

Ship name      :  San Martin

Squadron       :  Portugal
Frontline      :  True
Missing list   :  False
Fate           :
Port of return :  Santander
Tonnage        :  1000
Soldiers       :  300
Mariners       :  177
Rowers         :  0
Guns           :  48
Roundshot      :  2400
Powder         :  140
Lead           :  23
Match          :  18
Details        :  Flagship of Medina Sidonia. Reached
                  Santander 21st September.
```

Figure 15.1   Spanish Flagship: San Martin

Squadron	*Fate*	*Port of Return*
Portugal	Ireland	Santander
Biscay	Blown up	Galicia
Castile	Captured	Guipuzcoa
Andalusia	Foundered	San Sebastian
Levant	Lost at sea	Lisbon
Hulks	Scuttled	Le Havre
Pataches	Stranded	
Galleasses	Sunk	
Galleys	Took no part	
	Wrecked	
	Unknown	

Figure 15.2   Tokenised Fields

considering the amount of information which is available for some ships. It should be noted that there have been various changes to this database since it was first set up. Improvements have been made in the light of classroom use and it is a feature of KEY that such alterations can be made quite easily. As an example the original version did not have tokenised fields for the field *Fate*. This made, for example the producing a pie diagram to examine the data very difficult whereas with this modification it is now quite straightforward. It would, therefore, be more accurate to describe this database as evolving rather than being set up.

Database Structure: The English Fleet

This database was set up much later than Spanish Armada when it became apparent that some useful comparison exercises could be carried out. As Figure 15.3 shows it contains much less information.

```
Record no : 1

Ship name  :  Ark
Captain    :  The Lord Admiral
Tonnage    :  800
Soldiers   :  126
Mariners   :  270
Gunners    :  34
Home port  :
```

Figure 15.3   English Flagship: Ark

Ship Name, Captain and *Home Port* are 'words' fields, all the rest are 'numbers' fields. Once again this has altered from its original form. The Home Port field has been added to accommodate the addition of those ships provided by the Dorset ports of Weymouth and Lyme Regis. Also it is worth noting that this database is as yet incomplete, most of the 197 ships of the English Fleet not having been entered.

Classroom Management

Preparation of Students

Before using the database students in Years 9 (14 year olds) and 13 (17/18 year olds) were already familiar with the historical context of the events of 1588. They had used a variety of sources both primary and secondary, written and visual. They had experience of working in groups. They were also familiar with the database programme itself. As with any classroom strategy careful preparation is essential for the successful use of computers.

Organisation of the Class

Since the History department had access to a computer room with 12 BBC microcomputers Year 9 classes could all tackle the exercise at the same time. They were divided up into groups of ideally 3 or 4. This ensured sufficient numbers for discussion whilst making it difficult for individuals to sit back and do nothing. This also allowed one machine to be left in reserve in case of technical problems. It should also be noted that virtually every machine had its own printer. A very important factor as students quickly become frustrated if they have to wait for print outs!

Class and Group Activities

Once in the computer room for the first time each group was asked to search for and print out details of the two flagships, see Figures 15.1 and 15.3.

These then formed the basis for a discussion of the database, how it was organised and what type of information it contained. Each group was then allocated a squadron of the Armada and told to find out its fate and to print out their findings. It is essential to have print outs as these allow students to leave the computer and think about what they have found and what they want to ask next. The historical thinking takes place away from the computer. These initial searches posed more questions than they answered each group was then allowed to explore the fate of this squadron more fully. This exercise was then brought together in a class discussion so that each group could report back. From this discussion further enquiries were devised for the next session in the computer room. Throughout the exercise the atmosphere was purposeful as students responded to the motivating influence of the computer and more importantly to the stimulus of taking responsibility for their own learning. The role of the teacher was to consult, lead and refine the students own ideas. Most important was the final classroom discussion where the teacher's role was to draw out and clarify what the class had learnt.

Learning Outcomes

The Events of 1588

One of the more obvious enquiries was to decide why some squadrons suffered such heavy casualties whilst other suffered relatively few. For example the Squadron of the Levant lost 8 out of 11 ships whilst the Squadron of Portugal only lost 4 out of 12 ships. This led students to devise various hypotheses to explain the losses for the entire Armada, such as a connection between the size of a ship and its fate. (Figure 15.4).

Half the ships below 200 tons were missing and they formed over 40% of the total losses. How far can this conclusion be taken? Similarly students tested the connection between the role of a ship and its fate (Figure 15.5).

Over half of the frontline ships were missing. Was this because they took the brunt of the fighting? Once again in answering one question the database posed

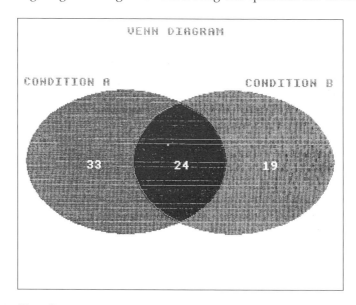

Figure 15.4   Venn diagram comparing tonnage and fate

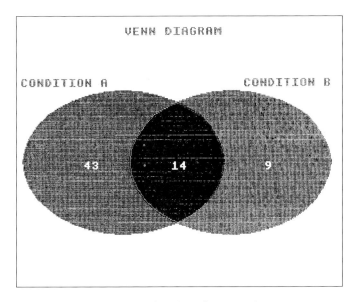

Figure 15.5 Venn diagram to compare frontline ships and fate

another. Depending upon the ability of students a range of other enquiries were tried, the bar graph showing ports of return (Figure 15.6) could be used to argue that the Duke of Medina Sidonia made a considerable achievement in bringing such a large part of his fleet intact to the port of Santander.

At a less sophisticated level the simple discovery that 73 of the original 130 ships returned safely to Spain could be used to argue the same point.

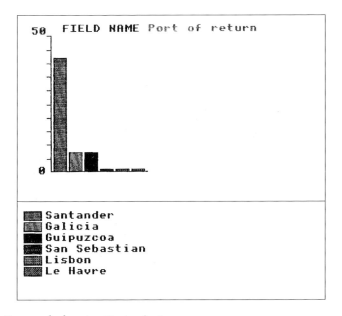

Figure 15.6 Bar graph showing Ports of return

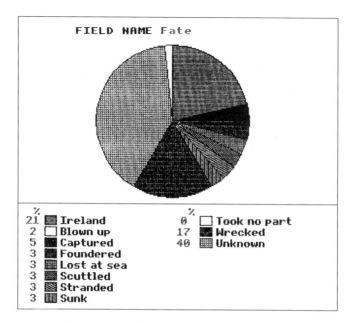

Figure 15.7   Pie chart showing fate of missing ships

Stereotype History

Year 13 students used the database in a similar way to Year 9 but took their enquiries further. They set out to examine some of the stereotype views of the events of 1588. For example were all the Spanish ships large whilst the English were small? A reexamination of the data in the first two sets of figures above illustrates how the database immediately allows the students to examine the data in an accessible way.

Was the Armada as completely destroyed by the English as some textbooks imply with some 57 out of original 130 missing? In response to this last question one group produced a pie diagram of the fate of the missing ships (Figure 15.7)

This clearly shows that the loss of few can be directly attributed to enemy action. Again it poses more questions. Why were so many ships lost in Ireland? What happened to the men who were captured, shipwrecked and so on?

The Methodology of Historians

Year 13 students studying the Advanced Level Syllabus used the database for two purposes. They compared the information in the database with other sources such as Hakluyt's voyages and the list published in Spain (much to the horror of Philip II) before the Armada sailed. This formed part of a source evaluation exercise comparing the varying numbers of ships, soldiers, mariners, etc. This then led them on to examine the value of quantification or cliometrics to historians. They were able to identify some of the obvious advantages as already outlined in the context of their period study. But they were also able to identify some of the problems. First and foremost the value of the database is dependent upon the quality of information put into it and the way in which this is arranged. Secondly, the database cannot stand on its own. Other sources are needed to answer the questions it raises or cannot answer. The answers to these broader questions need to be looked for elsewhere. Thirdly there are technical limitations to a simple database in terms of what sort of questions it can handle. These students did, however, conclude that a database was a valuable research tool for the historian.

Conclusion

A relatively small database ("Spanish Armada" contains 130 records) has great potential for classroom use. Like all historical sources it can be used with different age and ability groups and at different levels. It is not necessary to have huge databases with hundreds of records to utilise the power of the computer. It is, therefore, quite possible for teachers to produce their own small, specialised databases.

A small database should never be regarded as finished. It should change and grow in response to its use in the classroom, and in response to the researches of teachers and students alike.

My experience suggests that the effective use of a historical database ideally requires groups of 3 or 4 students per micro, a printer to each micro, and a database programme with the technical capability to do more than just search and sort.

Using such a database will pose more questions than it answers, thus it must be used in conjunction with other historical sources. It will help to interest and motivate students and allow them to learn about IT by actually using it. Being small it should also help to take students beyond straight forward search and sort enquiries. In this context the graphics facilities of KEY are invaluable.

Finally, it makes it possible for students to explore a range of hypotheses which they can quickly test, it encourages them to frame valid historical questions and it makes possible a variety of learning outcomes.

Addendum

The Spanish Armada Database Pack (ISBN 1 898369 02 X) was published by Tressell Publications in 1993.

For publication a number of changes were made in the light of further classroom experience. Firstly the English ships, 207 in total, were completed so that both sides of the campaign could be examined. Secondly, pictures of each ship, related to its type and size, were added to make the information more visually accessible. Thirdly, a Database Activity Book was prepared to accompany the Database. This Book contains instructions; additional source material, maps, illustrations, written sources; and activities to enable pupils to interact with the database. These materials clearly relate the computer database to other types of historical source material. Finally the whole Pack, in terms of the language used and the level of historical thinking required, has been targeted at pupils in Key Stage 2 (7–11 year olds) in response to the content requirements of the National Curriculum. The whole is intended to form part of the 'Life in Tudor times' History Study Unit where the Armada is specified.

Chapter 16
Facilitate and Enhance
Lez Smart

Introduction

During the first two and a half days of the 3rd International Conference on Computers in the History Classroom held in Lisbon in 1993 a range of speakers from countries ranging across at least three continents outlined where they were in relation to the use of IT in the teaching of history. The audiences heard details of national policies from government ministers, of the creation of regional networks from regional co-ordinators, of college programmes to promote IT literacy among trainee teachers from those involved in teacher education and of school initiatives from classroom teachers.

The crucial importance of the availability of appropriate and sufficient hardware and software was central to all the above and it was encouraging to see the ratios of pupils to machines being reduced in the two years since the last C.H.C. in Leeds. However it was very significant that all those speakers involved in developing the use of IT in the classroom acknowledged that this, in itself, was not a sufficient condition for the desired development. A development which would lead to the use of IT in the teaching of history that it was believed would lead to a positive impact on both the teaching and learning of history whatever the age of the students involved.

Teacher 'education' (used deliberately here rather than 'training') was also high on all the agendas referred to above and different strategies were being evolved and implemented in different countries. Two speakers, Jose Manuel Morales Vaquero of Spain and Jose Thomas Patrocinio of Portugal both drew attention to the need to 'persuade' or 'convince' teachers and sometimes, to 'overcome resistance'. They were not alone in making this point.

These are aspects of what has become known as 'the management of innovation'. There is now a greater awareness that the success or not of any innovation can be seriously affected by the way it is introduced and developed.

The proceedings of the first ever C.H.C. (Leeds 1988) contain a very interesting paper by Almond and Tomlinson (1990) which addresses this very issue. The paper explores in some detail research into successful and unsuccessful innovation and identifies the factors which most affect this. For those interested in this field in its own right, or in relation to their own institutions present position, this paper is worth consulting.

The point I wish to make here is that the findings and conclusions of this paper continue to apply today and will continue to apply in the future. Almond and

Tomlinson use the findings of Rogers and Shoemaker (1971) to identify the key components for successful innovation. Briefly these are:

- relative advantage: that is that the innovation offers some form of advantage over existing practice. It has some benefit to offer.
- compatibility: with existing values and philosophy so that it is not seen as threatening.
- complexity: if perceived as too complex negative attitudes develop very quickly.
- trialability and observability: the opportunity to trial, and further, to observe an innovation in practice in another classroom/institution is likely to increase the chances of a positive response.

As Almond and Tomlinson conclude:

> This approach considers teachers, the users of the innovation, as key determinants of its likelihood of success. Their perceptions of the innovation are more important than the nature of the innovation itself.

I can readily identify myself and many of my present trainee teachers with the above. As a classroom teacher in Britain in the early 1980's I remember being very sceptical about 'this computer thing'. I had to be convinced that it had 'something to offer' to my existing agenda. Fundamentally, this meant offering me some benefit in relation to my aims for the children I was working with: to offer me a benefit that enabled me to achieve these aims more effectively.

This would be not just in terms of knowledge, skills and understanding but also in relation to my pedagogical objectives. The transition from sceptic to convert is detailed elsewhere (Smart, 1988). I suggest that there was nothing unique about my own experience and that something very similar was likely to have been experienced by most of the delegates at C.H.C. '93 and by colleagues in schools and colleges across the continents who now use IT in their teaching.

It is the contention here that this is a process each individual teacher has or will have to go through in relation to the use of IT. This belief lead to my involvement in the project which is explored below. It is the intention of the publication that arose from the project (Smart & Parker 1992) that it should make a contribution to the ongoing process of demonstrating, illustrating or *convincing* individual teachers (albeit often operating in team i.e. a school staff) that the use of IT can *facilitate and enhance what they would be doing anyway.*

Therefore an attempt was made to conduct and present the findings of this project that took into account the 4 key areas that affect the success of innovation as identified by Rogers and Shoemaker (above).

The Project: "Making Links"

Setting the Scene

The National Council for Educational Technology's Primary Officer convened a small working group in 1989 which consisted mainly of advisory teachers and a lecturer from a teacher education institution. They all had a responsibility for history and geography and it was significant that this was their first responsibility, as opposed to it being IT. They also shared a strong belief that IT could make a very real contribution to children's studies in these areas of the curriculum. Each Advisory teacher identified a school (or schools) in his/her Local Education Authority where they felt they could work alongside a classroom teacher who would be interested in exploring and developing IT within his/her planned history or geography studies for the term. The schools that were worked with ranged from small rural schools in Derbyshire and the Lake District to large city schools in central and suburban London. They were all primary schools with children in the 7–11 age range.

The intention was to work with individual teachers throughout the length of their topic from the planning stage through to completion. During and after completion the teacher would be invited and encouraged to reflect upon the contribution that IT had, or had not, made to his/her own aims and intentions.

Calling upon their own experience in the classroom and in their present roles the working group identified that the best use of IT in history/geography work occurred when it was considered at the planning stage of the topic that would be undertaken rather than being 'bolted on' afterwards. This was a strongly held belief that the results of the study further confirmed.

At the early stage it meant that a planning model, or models, needed to be agreed through which this could be explored. As is always the way with any project it was not being conducted in a vacuum. The National Curriculum was in its infancy but it was now established that the 'approaches' to the teaching and learning of these two subjects were similar in one very significant feature. They were to be 'investigative/enquiry based'.

The planning model that was agreed upon therefore had to be one that created an enquiry or investigative approach and which allowed IT to be planned for and to contribute to this process.

Through discussion and negotiation it was agreed that the *key question* approach to planning was adopted by all those involved in the project.

Each teacher used the Key Questions of

What?
Why?
When?
Where?
How?
Who?

as the basis of his/her planning. Once the questions had been determined the teacher then sought to set up activities to enable the children to address the question(s). The planning diagram (Figure 16.1) is taken from the 'Ships and Seafarers' case study and demonstrates how these aspects were brought together.

Working with the teachers involved we identified that there were six areas that particularly affected the effectiveness and success of a topic as it moved form the planning to the implementation stage.

These were classroom management, differentiation and access, progression, resources, cross-curricular issues and opportunities for assessment.

Key Questions	Activities (based on PoS)
1 **SETTLERS 1** Who were the Vikings? Why did they come here? Where did they come from?	Mapping Viking voyages Hypothesising – reference books Atlas work
2 How did they get here? When did they come? How do we know?	Find out type of boat – look at floating and sinking and moving shape through water experiments Looking at local place names; looking at local river systems
3 **TRADE 1** Why do people trade? Who trades with whom?	Looking at 'early' trade routes Map these What was traded, and how do we know?
4 Why were ships used? What type of boats were used? How were they different?	Types of boats used, cobs, galleys, etc. (focus on technology of these, and attempt to identify development); draw and make models to explore these developments; begin timeline of ships Start database on ships
5 **EXPLORATION** Who? Why? Where? What was it like to be an explorer?	Focus on Portuguese, Dutch and Elizabethans Hypothesising, linked to studies above Discuss ideas about shape of the world Write diaries or ships' logs of a voyage studied Start making Discovery Board games
6 What type of ships were used? How did they find their way?	Were these different from the trading ships? How? Why? Navigation (the need to replicate the voyage) work on angles, coordinates, magnets, compasses; use Roamer
7 **TRADE 2** Why was Liverpool important in trading? What type of trade?	Focus on Liverpool as a trading port Mapwork Slave trade. Slave triangle – use data from records Look at ages, number arriving, origin, destination, safety etc. Look at music of slave era, legacy today
8 What was it like on board? How do we know? What type of ship was used?	Visit to Maritime Museum Use literature related to this period – is it a valid source? – discuss
9 **SETTLERS 2** Why did people want to leave? What kind of people left? How did they travel?	Focus on the New World – Liverpool–America links Reference work, literature Use of dramatic reconstructions and dance The change in types of ships
10 What was it like on board? Why did the type of ships change? How did the reasons for travelling change?	How this changed over the years Changing technology Emigration through to luxury cruises; life on board Liverpool's Cunard connection

Figure 16.1
Key Questions and
Activities

In light of the Rogers and Shoemaker (*op. cit.*) conclusion that "the user of the innovation is the key determinant in its success" referred to above it was very important that these were identified and addressed in advance and related to the desired innovation.

Indeed we suspected that the participants response to the IT component was as likely to be influenced by its impact in these areas as in any more tangible sphere such as knowledge and skills development in the specific curriculum areas. Discussions and the areas the teachers focused on in their evaluations at a later stage confirmed this.

The Role and Contribution of IT

During the topic the teachers involved were asked to try to identify where they felt IT had made a contribution to something that they would:

a. have undertaken anyway.

or

b. would not have been possible/would have been very difficult without the use of IT.

After the completion of the topic they were again encouraged to reflect upon these aspects. Each of the case studies in 'Making Links' contains two or three examples (we called them 'snapshots') where the teachers felt that IT had either facilitated or enhanced the educational aims of the topic they had been involved with.

Across the seven case studies included in the final publication these obviously varied but the ones referred to below are representative. They are taken from the 'Ships and Seafarers' topic featured in Figure 16.1 (above).

Snapshot 1

This activity arises from Key Question 5 of the planning sheet (Figure 16.1). The intention was for the children to devise a board game based upon one of the voyages they had been studying in order to create a context in which the children could apply their knowledge and understanding of the events and period they were studying. The game therefore had to be historically authentic, routes, hazards etc. In other words it had to be able to stand up to scrutiny! The further development of collaborative learning skills and the opportunity for the teacher to differentiate by task rather than by outcome were also very much part of the overall agenda.

The teacher writes that

> … there was a great deal of discussion before and during the devising of the games. The children called upon the knowledge they had already acquired … and frequently referred back to reference materials. It became obvious that the drawing up of the rules was one of the most challenging aspects of the whole activity… Without the ability to use the word processing facilities the rules would not have been modified as much, or as closely. The IT factor relieved the drudgery of rewriting and freed the children to concentrate on really getting the words to say what they wanted in a very precise way. The task could have been undertaken without access to IT facilities but reservations must be expressed as to whether both the process and the product would have been as successful.

This, I would suggest is a case of IT both facilitating and enhancing what this teacher would have undertaken with her class anyway.

Snapshot 2

The Key Questions for Week 4 (Figure 16.1) involve the children starting to explore the similarities and differences in ships over the longer period of time. A mass of information was likely to be uncovered and a database was suggested as a means of managing this. As with the setting up of any information storage system the time spent sorting out classifications under which to store is very much part of the process. So it proved with this class as they grappled with appropriate units of measurement and a common notation for power for example. Once set up data was entered by groups of children in relation to ships from different eras.

There was general agreement within the classroom that the information collected was made more manageable by the computer but it was when the interrogation of the data started that the real benefits were seen. There had been a growing and shared perception in the classroom that ships had gradually been getting 'bigger' (here meaning 'longer') over the centuries. Graphs were printed out in different formats to attempt to test this hypothesis. These showed that this seemed to be the case but some children expressed reservations about whether we had enough data…. and there were still lots of small boats to be seen daily on the River Mersey nearby…. What other factors were involved then? Function? Location? More questions than answers seemed the order of the day and these were duly taken along to the Maritime Museum which was the focus for Week 8.

It would seem that the IT component made a significant contribution to enabling the children to collect, collate and interrogate their data and through doing so 'freed' them to develop higher level thinking skills i.e. posing hypotheses. One thing anyone, of any age and experience working in the field of history must be able to do is ask appropriate questions. The presence of IT made a significant contribution here although it should be noted that other resources like the museum had then to be consulted. I suggest that this example is another one that demonstrates how IT both facilitated and enhanced what this teacher would have been attempting anyway.

Concluding Thoughts

The examples above are specific ones relating to one teacher and one topic. What is significant I feel is that no teacher in the project found it difficult to identify situations where IT had made a contribution. Perhaps of the greatest significance were the comments made by all the teachers involved that related to the wider impact the IT presence was perceived to have had. An impact that was much wider than the contribution to the actual subject area. These were comments that related to the impact that IT had upon the overall learning environment.

The concluding paragraph from the Ships and Seafarers section referred to throughout this paper is indicative of all the teachers' comments:

> The contribution of IT over the whole topic was greater than the specific examples detailed here (see above). It permeated most of the work undertaken and the children came to regard it as a tool, either to see if it had any information on their current line of enquiry or to prepare a draft for a piece of writing. It also became the focal point around which many valuable discussions took place and certainly made a contribution to the children's ability to work collaboratively and to exercise more control over their own learning

The intention of the 'Making Links' project was to explore and, if possible, demonstrate how IT could make a contribution to studies being undertaken with children anyway. It sought to show that the systematic planning of IT into the programme could both facilitate the teachers aims and in many cases actually enhance them.

The intended audience for 'Making Links' is individual teachers or schools who wish to explore the possible contribution IT might make to their existing agenda. It is being widely used by those who organise and implement professional development courses (INSET) for teachers.

The ability to relate any innovation to one's own existing practice in a way that is not threatening remains crucial to the take up of the innovation itself. The key factor in the equation of IT in the teaching of history at whatever age range and in whichever country is the teacher. This was the case when all the delegates at C.H.C. '93 first came to use IT in their own teaching but will, I suggest always be the case. The frustrations aired by some of the speakers about 'the need to persuade' some of their colleagues is, in fact, a very healthy sign and what one would expect to find in those involved in education.

What is changing is the number of teachers/educators who have been 'persuaded'. These are now automatically involved in providing the necessary examples of IT making a significant contribution to the teaching and learning of history in schools and colleges.

As the numbers involved slowly but surely continue to increase they both spread and also, importantly, consolidate the use of IT in the teaching of history.

However, the process that each of us went through in coming to appreciate the contribution IT could make to our own teaching and the learning of our pupils/students remains the same for our colleagues who have yet to come to this stage. This should be forgotten.

Chapter 17

Initial Teacher Education and Student Understanding of IT in the History Classroom

Graeme Easdown

Introduction

In 1988 HM Inspectors (HMI) published a report on 'A survey of Information Technology within Initial Teacher Training.' This report concluded that whilst there was evidence of much good practice, overall the quality of provision of Information Technology in initial teacher training institutions was patchy. One area in which they expressed concern related to the apparent lack of consideration given to the curricular implications and classroom potential of new technology. This report thus highlighted an area that was considered to be particularly significant and high on the political agenda. The recommendations of the subsequent Expert Group (Trotter 1989) were then incorporated into the criteria used by CATE (Council for the Accreditation of Teacher Education) to approve all initial teacher education courses (DES 1989b).

Project INTENT (Somekh 1992) was set up to offer support in this development and it is significant that it reported:

> "It is only through trying out their new knowledge and skills in a classroom that student teachers can be adequately prepared for using IT in their first teaching post. There are problems of organising satisfactory experience of this kind because of current patterns of use and lack of expertise among the broad range of teachers in schools and ITE tutors … With the move to closer partnership arrangements with school, this aspect of work with IT will need to be given very close consideration". (Somekh 1992)

This chapter explores a pilot study for a research project investigating the ways in which an established school based teacher education course, the Oxford Internship Scheme, is trying to address the issues raised by the Project INTENT report.

To establish the context in which the pilot study took place the paper will briefly describe the organisational framework and identify the principles of the Internship Scheme. Then, by taking the development of the Information Technology unit in the History curriculum programme as an example, it will show

how those principles are put into practice and how the research project developed. The pilot study will be outlined and then the methodological and substantive issues raised by the research will be discussed.

Organisational Framework of the Internship Scheme

The Internship Scheme is a partnership between the Oxford University Department of Educational Studies (OUDES), Oxfordshire LEA and all Oxfordshire secondary schools who wish to be involved in initial teacher education.

Each school in the Internship scheme accepts an average of ten postgraduate students, who are called interns, in curriculum pairs for an attachment which lasts from October to the middle of June. The curriculum areas covered by the scheme are History, Geography, Modern Languages, Mathematics, Science and English. The schools themselves decide what combination of curriculum areas they wish to accept for any given year.

The Internship course has two main parts:

a. a curriculum programme, concerned with all aspects of classroom teaching.
b. a general programme concerned with wider aspects of schooling.

The History curriculum programme has been developed on the basis of a close partnership between the university tutors and school teachers, in which there is a recognition of the respective contributions which the partners are best able to make. Regular meetings between the curriculum tutors and the mentors are an essential part of this process and are used to discuss general issues that have been raised about the curriculum programme, to review the effectiveness of the programme and as a vehicle for the professional development of the members of the partnership. Interns receive a detailed work unit which shows how the issues raised at OUDES (Oxford University Department of Educational Studies) will be investigated in their school context and how ideas generated in school will be explored back in the University department.

The Structure of the History and IT Unit

Mentors' responsibilities in the current IT programme relate to the use of IT in the classroom. They are asked to discuss their own views on the educational value of IT with interns, ensure that interns become familiar with departmental and school procedures for IT, and that they gain practical experience in planning, managing and evaluating IT within an appropriate unit of the history curriculum. The curriculum tutor is given responsibility for helping interns identify ways in which IT can be used in the classroom, encouraging them to critically evaluate a range of software etc. and further, encouraging them to assess the educational value of IT in terms of learning outcomes and student motivation. A timetable of actions which mentors and curriculum tutors follow in order to discharge their responsibilities and maintain the coherence and continuity of the overall programme is agreed. Mentors are expected to initiate work on the curriculum unit by discussing with their interns the role that IT plays in the work of their department. The interns also have to complete a written assignment which takes the form of an evaluation of a piece of software or IT application that they have employed in the classroom.

A Case Study — Challenges for IT in the History Curriculum

The need for the study was initially identified by a curriculum tutor who felt that interns were not being encouraged to look critically at the role of IT in history or to develop the use of information technology in their own teaching. This concern was based on a range of anecdotal evidence obtained informally from interns. The issue was subsequently discussed at one of the regular mentor meetings. It became clear during these discussions that there were widespread concerns about the current provision for IT in history.

It emerged that mentors were critical of the responsibilities that were placed on them by the course unit on IT. Many felt ill equipped to discharge those responsibilities because of their own uncertainty and inexperience with subject specific uses of IT, while others expressed concerns about the practical difficulties they encountered when trying to provide interns with opportunities to use IT in their teaching. The strength of feeling was such that it was agreed that this area of the programme had to be investigated in a systematic and rigorous way. Consequently a development group was established and was asked to recommend ways in which the course unit on History and IT could be revised.

Given the lack of detailed evidence about existing practice the group recommended that a research project should be undertaken. It was agreed that the study should focus on the assumptions that were inherent in the course unit for IT in history and on the development of an understanding of how individual mentors discharged the responsibilities, devolved to them through the curriculum programme, for this aspect of the course.

The project was structured to address the following questions:

1. how can the curriculum programme's plans for the development of interns' understanding of the use of IT in history take account of the diversity of mentors' knowledge, understanding and expertise in this aspect of practice.
2. how can individual mentors' actions and plans take account of the responsibilities inherent in the role of mentor.
3. how can the actions and plans of individual mentors, relating to the development of interns' use of IT in history, take account of the knowledge and experience that interns bring with them.

Methodology

As the project was essentially concerned with understanding how the inherent factors within a situation relate to each other, a case study approach was adopted. The following methods were used to collect the data:

- semi structured interview.
- documentary evidence in the form of the IT course unit assignments.

- written responses from the whole group of history interns to statements probing their attitudes towards, and opinions about, the use of IT in history.

The study was carried out during the 1992–93 internship year.

Procedures for Analysis

The following procedure was used to analyse both the interview data and the data from the curriculum session. The first step was to become familiar with the data, this was achieved by reading and re-reading the transcripts and notes. Next a list was made of what were felt to be significant phrases. These phrases were then examined in an attempt to identify any patterns or themes.

The rationale for adopting this approach rested on the assumption that what case study attempts to reveal is people's constructs of reality, and that the validity of such case study therefore rests upon how adequately the investigator has represented people's multiple mental constructions (Lincoln and Guba 1985). The research can therefore only report and interpret peoples' words. The analysis aimed to make explicit any attitudes or opinions that were common to individual cases; any that were common to the sample group; and any differences there might be between members of any particular intern partnership. It also aimed to develop an understanding of the ways in which the factors, identified as significant by the members of the sample group, interacted within and between the individual cases.

Given the assumptions underlying the qualitative research cited above, the reliability of the research findings is difficult to establish. However, Lincoln and Guba (*op. cit*) suggest that instead of reliability, the researcher should seek 'dependability' or 'consistency' ie. that outsiders should recognise that given the data collected, the results obtained make sense, they are consistent and reliable. By reporting the results of the interviews with quotations the reader can judge the researcher's interpretations and therefore the reliability of the conclusions or inferences drawn from the data.

Key Findings

The analysis of the data suggested that the use of IT in history was a significant issue for mentors and interns. Mentors were most concerned about:

1. The implications for history departments of the National Curriculum Orders for both History and Technology. There were concerns that they were being expected to deliver aspects of the technology orders that had nothing to do with history, and that this would detract from their function as history teachers. Mentors were very conscious of time being a significant factor given the constraints under which history departments were working to deliver the National Curriculum. Mentors reported that when IT was discussed within their department recurring questions were 'is this an effective use of our time?'.

2. Subject integrity and ideology. Mentors talked about using IT if it conformed to their conception of 'what historians have to do'. Subject ideology was a significant influence in this mentor's views about the sorts of IT applications that were appropriate for use with pupils. Databases seemed to conform to the mentor's

conception of what it meant to be an historian and to do history. However, other sorts of IT applications and pieces of software were perceived to be inappropriate. Simulations, for example, were rejected because they didn't do 'the sorts of tasks that historians would have to do…', and because it was felt that they presented pupils with very simplistic models of historical issues and events, and rather limited opportunities to develop their understanding.

3. How they could contribute to the interns' learning in this area. Mentors recognised that interns had to have the opportunity to gain experience using IT in history but were concerned about the practicalities of creating these opportunities. Mentors talked about the potential effects of an unsuccessful IT lesson on Interns learning.

The dominant issues for interns related to:

1. The 'costs' (ie. time) that would be incurred by having to become familiar with both the computer systems and software that was available to them in school. Familiarity with both the computer system and the software was seen as a necessary prerequisite for effective use of IT in history. This theme ran through the data from the curriculum sessions and the interviews. It was felt that IT could only be used effectively if the teacher had a sufficient grasp of the technology. There was a real anxiety about using the technology and it was obvious that this lack of confidence here was a serious constraint. When interns were asked to reflect on how their anxieties might be addressed they emphasised the importance of having opportunities to observe teachers and pupils using IT and to participate in lessons where IT was being used.

2. Issues of classroom management, associated with the perception that the maintenance of effective classroom control depended on their level of technical competence. These issues were a consistent theme in the data from the curriculum session with interns and in the interview data. Interns in the curriculum session expressed a high level of anxiety about their ability to maintain control of a class of pupils if the system or programme they were using 'crashed' and they didn't have the technical knowledge to solve the problem.

Turning to the questions posed earlier, the study raised a number of substantive issues for the implementation of this aspect of the history curriculum programme. It became clear that the programme needed to acknowledge more explicitly the diversity of mentors' knowledge and skills by developing procedures which enabled them to implement the school based elements of the programme. As a result the following recommendations were accepted for the 1993–94 course:

1. The development of a university based INSET programme, utilising the experience and expertise of mentors and curriculum tutors, which would enable interns and mentors to collaborate on the development of specific IT applications, pieces of software, schemes of work or materials for use in their school.

2. For those mentors who were unable to participate in the INSET programme curriculum tutors would arrange school based sessions to work with mentors, interns and other members of the history department.

3. A subject specific resource base should be developed in the university department, and both mentors and interns should supply reviews of software and IT applications appropriate to the programmes of study outlined in the history orders.

The questions posed by the study raised complex issues, some of which are the subject of ongoing research. It became clear that experienced teachers had a variety of concerns about assuming responsibility for the development of interns' understanding of the use of IT in history. These centred on the assumptions that were felt to have been made firstly about their own knowledge and experience (as history teachers) of using IT in lessons; secondly about their attitudes (as history teachers) to the use of IT in history; and thirdly about the opportunities that could be provided at an institutional level for interns to gain experience of using IT in their own teaching. Mentors' personal anxieties about the use of IT in history seem to have an effect on the development of interns' competence. They also seem to be an inhibiting factor in mentors' recognition of the skills and knowledge that interns bring with them.

Given that all initial teacher training institutions are currently developing school based programmes which must contain compulsory and clearly identifiable elements which enable students to make use of IT in the classroom, and should provide a sound basis for their subsequent development in this field (CATE, 1992). The role of the mentor is particularly significant. The concerns voiced by the mentors participating in the study raise a number of important questions for the planning and delivery of partnership schemes. These are:

1. What assumptions are made about the knowledge and experience of individuals participating in the partnership programme?
2. How far does the programme take account of that knowledge and experience?
3. How can those instances where there is a negative or ambivalent attitude to the subject specific use of IT, or where there is little or no confidence in the use of IT, be taken into account?
4. Given that the principle focus and highest priority for most student teachers at the beginning of the PGCE year is classroom control and discipline, when is the most appropriate point in the course to introduce IT so that they are able to make any sense of it?
5. What are the most effective strategies to achieve this objective?

The development of effective school focussed teacher education curriculum programmes relating to the subject specific use of IT, must take account of the questions raised by the study outlined above. These questions are being pursued currently in further research in Oxford.

Outcomes of Partnership

There is considerable variation between schools and between departments within schools regarding both the quantity and quality of interns' IT experiences. However, this was also the case before partnership schemes came into being. The opportunity offered by partnership is the possibility of planned, jointly agreed agendas for developing student teachers' understanding and experience of IT in the teaching of their subjects. However, even in a mature scheme such as internship in which joint planning mechanisms and procedures have long been in place, IT is still (as far as subject experience in schools is concerned) an area needing considerable development. The outcomes of the research in history to date emphasise the key role of mentors, and the vital need to consider their beliefs, attitudes, experiences and capabilities. Some ways in which partnership programmes can develop appropriate support have been described in this report.

Concluding Comments

Experience of internship, and of the work in history in particular, leads to the following recommendations for other partnerships:

1. Recognise the key role of subject mentors in the development of students IT capability, and involve all mentors in the planning of an agreed agenda and action plan for implementation.
2. Bring mentors concerns out into the open, and devise practical ways of supporting them so that they can meet the responsibilities inherent in mentorship.
3. Recognise that this will take time.

In addition, internship has shown the value of involving all higher education tutors and school professional tutors in the teaching of IT as a whole school issue, in the context of a professional development programme for student teachers. Issues raised needing further study revolve around recognition of the importance of developing shared understandings and action plans, and finding practical ways of supporting mentors which take account of their beliefs and attitudes, as well as the variation in their knowledge and experience of IT.

Part III

Technologies For Learning

This final part of the book comprises a set of chapters which adopt a somewhat more developmental perspective and provide glimpses over the technological and educational horizon. Futurology is always a hazardous exercise and those who indulge stand in danger of looking very foolish indeed when their predictions prove to be spectacularly wide of the mark. The dangers are particularly prevalent in an area developing as rapidly as information technology. Despite this, some cautious predictions are perhaps in order. We can be confident that hardware and software developments will continue apace. Processor power and hard disk capacity will continue to rise. Multi-media applications will grow more attractive and sophisticated. Portable and notebook computers will become more common and the day when 'class-sets' of computers are more widely available is on the horizon. Developments in artificial intelligence and computer modelling techniques are likely to make possible the ever-increasing sophistication of programs which can more fully represent the complex processes of historical decision-making. Since most of the chapters in this section were written the Internet has grown exponentially. The potentialities of networking for education broadly and history teaching specifically are likely to be widely explored over the next few years. However, it is worth remembering that the majority of the world's children, those attending schools in the Third World, do not have and are not likely to have in the near future, access to computers. We hope that in the exciting times which lie ahead the needs of these children and the ways in which they might be met through the use of computer technology will not be forgotten.

Marie-Elise Bitter-Rijpkema, in the chapter which opens this section, provides an analysis of the development of History CAL in the Netherlands, which has many echoes of developments in other countries. In the second part of the chapter Bitter-Rijpkema suggests ways in which we can go beyond the somewhat 'cottage-industry' character of early developments in History CAL and build systems which will take advantage of software and hardware developments in the 1990s. Using an information systems approach she argues for the development of flexible multi-user knowledge resource bases which will be of use not only to educators but to numerous other groups in society. She also makes a strong plea for international co-operation in the production of such resource bases. These two approaches, she argues, will make possible the economies of scale which will provide a base which will facilitate the production of software for use in a range of national and educational contexts.

163

The two chapters which follow describe the use of multi-media technology in history teaching. In their contribution Cornel Reinhart, Michael Sedore and Isamu Ochiai describe the ways in which multi-media technology was combined with the traditional archival and field work skills of the historian to produce a computer program recording many aspects of 19th century life in Canton village in the St Lawrence County Grasse River region of the USA. The program gives undergraduate students access to a multiplicity of text-based, visual and audio sources. However, as Reinhart, Sedore and Ochiai explain the program is designed in such a way that students are not only consumers of the program but can also contribute to the expansion of the project. The effect of the project on students is described as "electrifying" as it combines the traditional intellectual skills of the historian with the possibilities opened up by the latest software developments.

Robin McLachlan and John Messing describe a CD-ROM project which grew out of the Australian national commemorative programme on the 75th anniversary of the World War I Gallipoli campaign. McLachlan and Messing show how materials produced in computer-readable form for the commemorative programme were recycled and combined with additional materials, to form The Gallipoli Stacks, a CD-ROM project containing primary and secondary source material in textual, pictorial and video forms. The material was subsequently published as part of a larger commercial CD-ROM project. The project shows how a small team, with the appropriate skills, can produce most impressive results through utilising material which is already in computer readable format and off-the-shelf software which is simple, versatile and appropriate.

The remaining chapters focus upon software packages developed for use in history lessons in a variety of contexts. In the 1980s history teachers could legitimately complain that there were few high quality software packages available for the subject. However, this complaint has less and less substance as more history-specific programs are developed. The four chapters which follow give an indication of some of the developments in history software and show how this is becoming more sophisticated and attractive for pupils and students.

Peter Hillis provides an account of *Moving House*, a computer package for analysing migration within 19th century Glasgow. Through the use of Hypercard, *Moving House* incorporates databases giving details of rateable values, post office directories, biographical details of residents and photographs of buildings and localities. The material enables students to test hypotheses about urban migration in 19th century Glasgow and levels of social stratification. The package also provides notes for teachers and students and is related to Scottish National Certificate Modules. As workshop participants at C.H.C. '93 discovered Moving House is a wonderfully easy and attractive package to use and yet it raises fundamental issues about 19th century urban history and allows students opportunities to form and test their own hypotheses within a supportive framework.

Yta Beetsma describes the development and evaluation of three computer-assisted case studies in historical decision-making for use in Dutch secondary schools. The three case studies were concerned with specific events in Dutch and international history and aimed to help pupils to evaluate historical decision-making. The programs were each designed to be completed within a single lesson and allowed the pupils to use a variety of sources within the programs to answer questions. In the concluding part of the chapter Beetsma reports on the ways in which the case studies were evaluated and uses the evaluation results to suggest ways in which they might be improved.

The use of computers in the history classroom can have two main aims which may sometimes be in tension. One aim is to help students learn history, the other to help them attain information technology capability. Mary Webb approaches the use of IT in history through the second aim and describes how students can construct and use their own computer-based models in history (and other subjects). Webb explains and provides some examples of the use of *Expert Builder* as a tool for qualitative modelling in history. In contrast to many historical simulations *Expert Builder* allows students to view and modify the computer model which underlies the simulation. In this way students can achieve higher levels of IT capability as well as learning about history. In the final sections of the chapter Mary Webb raises important questions about the use of rule-based computer models in history and suggests ways in which software developments might enable some limitations to be overcome.

Frank Colson and Neil Thompson provide an overview of the early years of the development of the HiDES Sixth Form Project. HiDES is a British project which is the product of collaboration between academic historians, school and college teachers and computer experts. Colson and Thompson explain the ways in which a program originally designed for undergraduate history students was modified for use with 16–18 year olds. Through its use of historical sources HiDES is designed to enable students to test their own hypotheses and develop a sharper intellectual cutting edge. Above all, perhaps, it demonstrates the ways in which history is an exciting human construct, a product of interpretation from evidence and "an argument without end".

Alain Bideau and Guy Brunet provide yet another perspective on the developmental potential of the use of computers in history. Bideau and Brunet describe the development and characteristics of the *SYGAP* package which was developed jointly in France and Canada as a tool for use in historical demography. *SYGAP* enables a wide range of demographic analyses to be made and has much value in both research and teaching. *SYGAP* was originally developed for use by academic historical demographers but in modified forms has great potential for use at other levels and in other disciplines.

The final wide-ranging chapter by Allan Martin appropriately places the development of information technology in education in the historical context of educational technology. Using examples of educational technology which was much hyped in its time but which ultimately had little impact upon educational practice he cautions against information technology utopianism. And yet he presents a convincing case for the potential of IT in education in general and history teaching in particular. He argues that the use of IT may enable teachers to reconsider how history can be taught and learned and he raises important questions about how far these changes may be taken.

Chapter 18

History CAL at a Turning Point: A Quantum Leap Ahead? New Horizons for History Teaching in the Nineties

Marie-Elise Bitter-Rijpkema

Introduction

At the NIOC, the Dutch national conference on informatics and education, held in Maastricht in May 1990, a 17-year-old schoolboy was awarded an important essay prize for his vision on IT education in the year 2000. The jury was amazed by the outstanding quality of the teenager's science-fiction story. It was the only entry that had prize-winning qualities. And this among all the other entries written by academics and teachers! Was the lack of vision on the role of IT in our future education observed by the jury just a mischance? Or is it an indication of a more serious lack of ideas on the future possibilities of educational technology among educators? To those expecting a straightforward optimistic story about results achieved and positive prospects, this opening story with its possibly gloomy implications will be surprising. However, I believe that there are exciting possibilities ahead and ways in which we can build on what has already been achieved. In this chapter I will analyse the past development of History CAL and suggest ways in which it might develop in the 1990s and beyond.

The central question of this chapter is then: after the pioneering years in the late 1970s/early 1980s and the micro-electronic development-programmes of the mid to late 1980s, what are the prospects for History CAL in the 1990s? I will focus on developments in the Netherlands which are relevant to developments elsewhere.

Reflections on the History of History CAL

In the 1980s the features which stand out in the use of computers for history teaching in the western European countries were the initial enthusiasm, the rapid changes, the involvement of teachers, and strong stimuli from the national governments. Computers attracted the attention of history teachers in the early eighties. Grassroots initiatives from teachers resulted in working groups of history teachers, who organised work-shops, communicated through newsletters, and developed programmes. Thus, in 1984 COMIGO, the Dutch history teachers' working group on History CAL was founded.

The growing importance of IT in society and education also led to governmental activity. In anticipation of the 'information society', governments wanted children to be well prepared. However, some basic problems had to be tackled. The situation was characterised by hardware incompatibility, fragmentary private initiatives, and lack of know-how and funds. Several national governments created impressive development programmes. Through strong financial and organisational stimuli during a short period they tried to create an autonomous educational IT infrastructure. The combination of the enthusiasm of teachers with the financial and organisational backing of the government brought impressive results. Space precludes detailed analysis but the main achievements were:

- Setting of standards for school-computers.
- Wide dissemination of computers to secondary schools.
- Large scale teacher training on IT in education.
- Creation of history software materials.

Later Developments: Continuity or Change?

Let us now consider the main features of the situation going into the 1990s. As we have seen in the historical overview, the grassroots initiatives of the teachers, combined with the governmental development programmes, formed the basis for several positive results. However despite these advances there were still a number of problems:

- Existing software was dedicated software: this was expensive and could only be used in the specific situation for which it was developed. Integrated computer-use on the basis of this type of software will be difficult and likely to remain small scale.
- Government subsidies for the development of software was being cut at the very time when development costs were increasing.
- Governmental priorities overruled intrinsic arguments for the importance of History CAL. Governments have tended to give higher priority to the development of IT in other subjects and educational sectors e.g. vocational education and training, which are perceived to have greater economic benefits that investment in History CAL.
- Publishing houses remained slow to develop educational software. The entrepreneurial risks seemed too great given the high production costs and restricted applicability to a specific theme, age group, etc.
- History CAL projects were organised on an ad-hoc basis. No structure existed to support continuity of software production on a larger scale, and offer teachers assistance and information. Historical software developers worked on an ad hoc basis and often in isolation. There were no clear mechanisms for sharing and preserving expertise.
- The crucial role of a sound implementation structure was underestimated. The development programmes focused so much on creating a flying start for IT in education through emphasis on the provision of machinery, training and software production, that the importance of building a sound implementation structure was underestimated.

There are three elements in the situation which particularly hinder the full exploitation IT, and which must be taken into account in any strategy for the future: first, the rapid changes in the field of IT itself; second, the fact that after the phase of government financial backing we will be confronted with the market environment, and will have to learn to live with the market value of information and applications in our subject area (the economic value of materials designed for history teaching is low compared to the information value of, say, economic information — combine 'low' economic value with high development costs, and there is little chance that a firm base will grow for autonomous production of history software); and third, lack of a firm infrastructure to develop and conserve expertise (including development and dissemination of ideas, information and products) might prove to be a big problem. Our strategy for the future should, I believe, focus on tackling these core problems, and in this way construct a sound basis for the future development of History CAL.

Shaping the Future

As history teachers we want the best tools, not only for today but also for tomorrow. We are now in a situation in which we feel that the computer is a very powerful instrument for our teaching. However we have not yet created a system in which the desired range and quality of software is produced and applied in the classroom. The development programmes have not produced an infrastructure that will ensure that an appropriate range and quality of History CAL material will be developed under changing conditions in the future. In order to achieve the creation of the History CAL tools for tomorrow we have to consider carefully: firstly, the extent to which developments which have already taken place can be extrapolated into the future; secondly, the specific IT tools which we want for history teaching in the future; and thirdly, how we can create a structure that will support continuity and promote quality in the production and implementation good and affordable hardware and software.

Looking ahead towards the year 2000, impressive hard-ware developments are predicted. Among these are new graphical, telecommunication and storage possibilities of next-generation workstations, which may vary from powerful configurations with a variety of components like scanners, optical discs, modems, etc., to small pocket computers or notebooks, and include dedicated hardware such as the 'Dynabook' or 'Knowledge Navigator'. Experts predict an explosive growth of processor and memory capacity, graphical, video and audio capacities, as well as a reduction in size and price.

As a result of the application of IT in many areas of society, exponential growth of information-resources is expected. Against the background of this information explosion, the need for people with basic expertise in automated information handling will grow. The increasingly central role of IT in society will result in information retrieval, manipulation and interpretation becoming vital skills for our students. Aside from specific historical domain-knowledge and skills, generic information processing skills can be acquired extremely well in history lessons. Searching for, questioning, structuring and interpreting primary, secondary and other information resources is one of the essential elements of historical activity.

Due to the central role of these activities in history teaching our subject could function very well as a key area for the training of generic information handling notions and skills.

Thus an examination of the current situation and the expected trends leads to the conclusion that in the future educational IT will have to function in an environment of challenging new technical possibilities, growing importance of information skills for students, and new financial constraints as far as government and publishers are concerned.

In order to benefit optimally from these new possibilities and to exploit them to the maximum for history teaching a new approach is needed. The needs of the teacher in the current setting of classroom teaching is, in my view, too limited to act as the basis for the development of History CAL. The strength of this approach is that it takes teachers seriously and puts them at the centre of its attention. But the limitations of this approach is that we will discover only the possibilities which arise from current ideas and practices. I would like to look at the development of teaching materials, including History CAL, from another perspective. Any approach to developing learning materials must take account of teachers' needs (since educational change depends in the end on what the teachers think and do, and thus must be able to exploit the potential of IT for optimising history teaching). The approach I propose is based on an 'information-processing' view of learning, in which we look at learning primarily as a goal-oriented information processing process. Learning in this view involves the reconstruction, selection, simplification, synthesis of information in order to reach a certain goal. Teachers in this view are not so much men and women of knowledge but intermediaries or facilitators. Two forms of expertise are required in the learning environment, the first is concerned with content knowledge, the second with pedagogical aptitude. The pedagogical expert can interpret their role primarily as an information transmitter but she can also be the promoter of discovery-based and active learning by the students.

Assessing the learning environment of a student from this information-systems approach we can identify two elements: (1) data and (2) information. *Data* are the raw material needed in any learning process. Data which are to be used for learning purposes need to be processed to make sense, they can then serve as *information* in the learning process. The interpretative activity in which data get their meaning within the subject and teaching area, consists of representing the meaning of data in their contexts through classificatory, semantically and logically structured activity. The sources we use for our history teaching are in one way or another data which have been processed to make historical sense and represent a piece of reality. This might be the historical reality of past times as evidenced by documents, account books, treaties, or the reality of the 'historian' as the interpreter of the historical events. The same data, are used again and again in different knowledge representation activities, that is in the interpretative activities of historians. In relation to the teaching goal, and taking account of the constraints, an educator will construct the instructional process. To optimise its effectiveness, the teacher will steer the learning process by planning activities and creating materials which will motivate learners, give information on objectives, check the prerequisite knowledge, stimulate recall of relevant pre-knowledge, present stimuli, provide learner guidance, elicit student performance, provide feedback, assess performance, and enhance retention and transfer. On the basis of expertise in the subject area and in guiding learning processes, the educator designs the best didactic route to the chosen objectives within the conditions set.

The novel element of this vision is the role of the teacher in preparing instructions using data which have been structured to information in one or more ways on the basis of his or another person's domain expertise. A history teacher uses data, consisting of facts, numbers, documents, maps, photographs, video and tape recordings structured by domain experts to represent as clearly as possible the historical reality or its interpretation, for the realisation of his teaching purposes. This could be done in a number of ways, for example a teacher might want a thematic structure for one part of his lesson involving progression from simple to complex learning and a chronological structure for part two of his lesson combined with a set exercise or a case study.

I am inclined to the idea that this information systems approach might open up new perspectives, compared with a viewpoint which focuses on the teaching process, the classroom situation or IT. The important thing is that by seeing data as raw material with the possibility of translating and enriching them so that they become information we can construct modular instructional systems. This concept is much broader than the classroom-oriented approach and, apart from stimulating modularity, can also handle any knowledge domain that can be transferred.

We can look at instruction as the specific use of data. The data and information can be used for a whole range of applications including instruction. In schools knowledge is transferred and disclosed to students by a domain and didactic expert in the single person of the subject-teacher. But aside from this specific instructional setting we might think of a whole range of situations in which, for different purposes and under different conditions, people use the same or similar data and information e.g. journalists, researchers, novelists, documentary writers, laymen, etc. In this vision different people will have different objectives, queries and wishes related to the use of the same or similar information sources. Learners, teachers and a whole range of other users of a certain information source are, from an information point of view, all restructuring the domain-knowledge according to their specific needs.

This way of approaching education fits in very well with new theories in informatics, and new developments in software engineering. In the academic world of informatics research, and in the commercial world of systems-development there is a major trend towards more flexible, multi-purpose information systems with a shift from dedicated tailor-made software to flexible, generic software tools. This shift is accompanied by a growing interest in modular programming and multimedia software development systems.

Thus the starting point of this view is that data and information from a knowledge domain are resources to be used for a whole range of purposes by a variety of people who need it for information transfer. Teachers and designers of teaching materials are often just one user-group of multi-purpose knowledge resource bases. Instead of continuing with the production of dedicated tailor-made 'stand-alone' software, we need the development of History CAL applications which use generic tools that can handle historical data organised in large multi-purpose, data- and knowledge bases. These generic tools include hypertext and authoring systems that handle information-elements according to the needs of the designers and/or users of the system. Sharing the information resources with other users may enable economies of scale to be made in the production of history IT-materials.

The development of tools, materials and ideas for teachers is crucial to the improvement and integration of IT in history teaching. I have argued that we cannot develop the IT tool-box on a national basis using tailor-made dedicated software. However, to seeking co-users of the same resources within individual states, we can look across national boundaries for co-operation. On an international scale there are, of course, differences between educationalists working in different countries in specific objectives, culturally based preferences, language and interpretations of the same historical event. However, there are also many similarities, common approaches, problems and objectives. There are also overlaps in the information and knowledge resources we use.

This sharing of common elements with other professionals and colleagues offers the possibility of co-operation in production. On the basis of the information systems model we can identify elements of the domain-knowledge useful for history-teachers from different countries, and the specifications for educational use (i.e. the precise content and the mode of offering information and guidance) which might differ from one learning situation to another. The acquisition and production of those parts that we have a common interest in, such as interactive visual databases, large textual databases, hypermedia systems, which will remain too expensive to be produced on a national scale, might become cost-effective if we construct and develop them together with international partners. In particular, the construction of multi-purpose/multi-user sets of resource materials could be co-produced leaving nationally based groups to build their own applications. Where there is sufficient commonality parts of the applications might also be developed on an international basis.

The sound development and dissemination of IT tools for history teaching in the future will require a change in the orientation and method of software development. However if we want this to result in IT tools for History CAL which can keep pace with the educational possibilities of history teaching and IT, working towards changes as proposed above will not be enough. The initiatives proposed will only bear fruit if accompanied by the creation of a suitable organisational structure perhaps analogous to that for the production of traditional materials such as textbooks. Software development still lacks such an infrastructure. As a result there are two difficulties: it is difficult to retain the expertise developed by history teachers and educational software developers, and to design the desired range of history applications. We need a professional management structure which is well equipped to instigate the development of the required range of tools and software and is able to keep participants motivated by the prospect of IT-applications for their teaching. In the end History CAL will only succeed if it motivates teachers and students in classrooms. In educational technology we have seen that, at least in the Netherlands, management structures have tended to become over-bureaucratic. We now need a management structure which:

- organises people, resources and processes in order to ensure continuity and the achievement of goals.
- has low overheads while maximising efficiency.
- is accountable for its effectiveness.
- is flexible and adaptable.

Conclusion

What have we learnt from reflecting on the past, present and future possibilities for History CAL in the Netherlands and elsewhere?

We saw that in the early eighties we became aware of the role IT could play in history teaching. We started from scratch in a chaotic situation with a variety of machinery and software tools and no organisational structure at all. Through the combined grassroots initiatives and enthusiasm of the teachers themselves and the government development programmes impressive results were achieved in the creation of dedicated teaching materials, the provision of hardware and the growth of a cadre of informed teachers.

In the 1990s we have been confronted with a changing situation:

- The situation in which History CAL is developed and used has changed with the end of the initial development programmes. Autonomous development of CAL materials is now confronted with problems of funding, organisational support and lack of expertise.
- New trends in hardware and software have opened up interesting educational possibilities for history teaching. However the cost of powerful, sophisticated applications will require new technical, educational and organisational structures. Development on an individual basis is out of the question. Thus the need for co-operation is urgent.
- With the growing importance of information processing skills throughout the curriculum, it may be advantageous for history teachers to stress the role of history in developing these generic IT skills.

If we fail to change our ideas and strategy on the development of History CAL, we will probably see a growing discrepancy between the new possibilities for IT in our subject area, the need for applications in this area and the actual exploitation of these possibilities. To prevent this, a new approach to the development of learning materials is needed.

The model proposed in this chapter takes an information processing perspective. It states that:

- Everyone uses information resources for their information handling in order to retrieve, manipulate and transfer data and information.
- Education is a specific class of activities in which information is transferred and manipulated between persons and/or systems.
- Several groups, including educators (e.g. history teachers), may use the same databases and information resources for different purposes.

A model was offered in which a learning system consists of:
- a database layer.
- a knowledge-representation layer where data are interpreted semantically and/ or logically to represent domain knowledge in one or more semantic networks.
- a transaction and user-interface layer, which trims and manipulates the data and knowledge base for the specific purposes of the user.

The conceptual/modular structure of this approach offers good possibilities for tackling the problems identified in the development of History CAL, and exploiting the new educational possibilities of IT.

Finally suggestions were offered as to ways in which the approach can be put into practice. In combination with the new programming and software tools such as hypertext, object-oriented programming, Artificial Intelligence, etc., it was proposed that educational materials can be built in a modular way, whereby sometimes the same data and knowledge base are developed by different people (teachers and non-teachers, teachers from several countries, etc.) using them for different purposes. By constructing together the common parts of the system and designing on an individual basis the unique/specific parts of the application, using as far as possible existing tools, we can create a system for developing useful, flexible and affordable software.

Chapter 19

Canton, New York: An Interactive Computer Project for the History Classroom

Cornel J. Reinhart, Michael O. Sedore and Isamu Ochiai

Introduction

We have for several years now been persuaded that history as a discipline can utilise computer applications in the classroom to greater advantage than is occurring now at many institutions. The obstacle for their greater use, it seems to us, is simply that faculty, especially, and students alike are not yet familiar with both hardware and software technology and find it difficult to take the time to learn entirely new, and as yet unproved, classroom methods. We share those fears and concerns. Yet, we are increasingly certain that much of value for students and faculty can be found in new computer assisted course work.

The computer as a classroom tool responds to our sense of the active learning strategies already encouraged by most academic institutions and increasingly sought by students. This is more than glamour. It seems to us that we as faculty need to encourage thinking, problem solving, writing (not to mention reading) and analysis. Certainly our traditional lecture and discussion formats do these things and still do them well. Yet the establishment of classroom settings, either in independent courses or as supplements to existing courses, where students can work independently or in networks with other students on common historical problems with faculty direction and support, promises to transform our notions of the classroom and the faculty-student relationship — and we think do so for the better.

With these thoughts in mind and with encouragement from St. Lawrence University's History Department and Academic Dean, we decided to turn our thoughts into a real experiment (perhaps even to fail a few times). We began our work together utilising the project outlined below that we hoped might serve as a useful point of departure and perhaps, in our less cautious moments, as a model project for other history departments.

The Project's Origins and Early Problems

American settlement of the present St. Lawrence river valley region is synonymous with the appearance of water powered industrial sites on the several tributaries to this major waterway. While some sense of this early industrial history has been saved, the full scope of these activities has been largely lost or unexplored. In an effort to understand fully the impact of these enterprises on the region's socio-economic history Dr. Cornel Reinhart and Dr. Jonathan Rossie of the St. Lawrence University History Department received a grant from the St. Lawrence University North Country Research Center to support student efforts relative to site identification, mapping, and related document research for all 19th century industrial sites in the St. Lawrence County Grasse River watershed region. The 19th century Canton village industrial complex rather quickly became the pilot for the remainder of the project.

The work used students, with faculty guidance, to identify sites, catalogue any remains, and create an inventory of records relating to these industries. To accomplish this, extensive archival research was (and is) necessary including examination of early newspaper records, federal and state census data, early atlases, local and county histories, as well as existing federal, state, and local industrial surveys. We also hoped to locate and reproduce relevant visual materials, such as period photographs, prints, maps, and paintings. Known portraits or photographs of individuals or groups associated with these endeavours would be equally valuable. Necessary field work entailed the examination and photographing of physical remains of early industries (as well as present uses). It also included important industrial archaeological investigations where appropriate.

We did not propose to duplicate the efforts of local historical agencies or the university library archives. These institutions serve well as repositories, but they often prove to be difficult for students to access. They are typically remote from the classroom and are ill-equipped to handle the onslaught of a full class of eager young students. Primary materials are fragile and often pose problems for reproduction. Additionally, the sheer difficulty involved in making slides or finding other means of presenting these materials to others is formidable. As a result, students are largely relegated to secondary materials and are thereby cut off from just the kinds of creative endeavours that make history a stimulating scholarly pursuit.

Evolving a Technological Solution

As a solution to these difficulties we set out to collect and organise historical materials in a computer-mediated environment. The environment we envision promises reliable storage, intelligible organisation, and broad accessibility to students in individual or group settings.

Recent advances in computer hardware and software make it possible not only to realise this vision but more importantly to place students, rather than faculty at the centre of the pedagogical historical activity. Falling prices have made large-scale storage a norm for reasonably priced systems. Network connections distribute exact and protected copies of original materials to as many learners as may need access. Sophisticated graphical capabilities and scanning technologies make every kind of visual experience available from magnetic sources; digitised audio and motion video bring the experience of live historical characters and events directly to the student's own senses. Finally, tools for manipulating, editing, and connecting these materials have become sufficiently easy to use that students and faculty alike can work with the materials without onerous technical distractions.

The technical term for the environment we wanted to create is 'Hypermedia', which implies both the multiplicity of source material types and also the rich learner-centred interaction style that characterises the experience. We began by creating a ToolBook that consists of about 35 screens of photographic images, period drawings, academic papers, and sound recordings, all of which consumed about 8 megabytes of disk storage space. The project's boundaries and scope are set out in a digitised image of Canton, New York as depicted in a bird's-eye drawing done in 1885. At the click of a button the drawing is overlaid with 'hot areas' highlighting important districts. The Industrial District and the Opera District are outlined, and a screen direction invites the user to click on any hot area. By clicking on hot areas the user can ultimately arrive at images of individual buildings, street scenes, industrial machines, theatrical productions, and the like. Also available are audio clips describing life in the period and papers, complete with footnotes, on related themes. All of these materials are selectable by the learner and in accordance with the learner's interests and insights. There is no set order in which the materials must or should be experienced. The overall effect is to allow users to explore freely the sights and sounds of 19th century Canton.

What sets The Canton Project apart, however, is not so much the program's content, but rather the opportunities that the project creates for students to create projects of their own that build on its (largely conceptual) basis. The program is designed in such a way that students can build their own projects around the central theme and have them either incorporated in, or linked to, the central program. Our vision is that students should be the major contributors and builders of the project, and not merely consumers of it.

The effect on students has been electrifying. Drawn by the power of the images and enticed by the freedom to explore them, students invariably begin raising questions and making suggestions. Offered the opportunity, students, including some who are not computer users at all, have eagerly accepted the challenge of producing their own books. The results have been outstanding, both as presentable products and also in the learning and growth that have arisen from the process. New projects underway or completed include the fairgrounds, the university section, and neighbourhood census studies. An unexpected outcome has been the growth of real collaboration among students as they confront the technology and its rich set of possibilities. As individuals become expert in various aspects of the subject-matter or the technology they share their insights and skills to the collective benefit of all. The synergy that develops has proven to be very exciting and very productive.

Transforming Instruction with *ToolBook*

ToolBook, described by its publisher as "a software construction kit for *Windows*," seemed most appropriate for our purposes, providing precisely the necessary operating environment. It allows for the collection of various kinds of material: textual, graphical, audio, and video. *ToolBook*'s guiding "book" and "page" metaphor offers a familiar format for organising, connecting, and presenting historical materials. The program enables users to author a new presentation or "book" from an existing data base or to add new subjects or data. (Apple Computer

Corporation's equivalent program, *HyperCard*, is equally useful.) *ToolBook* differs from traditional authoring environments in that it is a complete visual programming environment in which objects and their actions can easily be controlled. In addition to its graphical prowess *ToolBook* imports text easily, and it provides excellent support for textual links ("hot words"), connecting words and phrases to related materials. Further, the program can search all included text for any name or phrase. In these ways the traditional text-and-citation apparatus of scholarship is supported, enriched and extended.

We believe The Canton Project takes advantage of these capabilities in a way that transforms instruction. It involves the student in the creative organisation and presentation of primary materials in all their variety. In doing so it provides unprecedented opportunities to supplement standard secondary textbooks with active learning modes not practical in the past. Nor need these modes be restricted to single groups or classes. The products generated are essentially cumulative and extensible in nature. Research seminars can build on work done by prior classes, each adding insight and clarity to the ongoing project. The project in this way mirrors the long scope of historical research at the student's level, placing students squarely inside the historical process.

This seems important to emphasise. As scholars and teachers our craft involves exposure to a wide array of 'materials' from the past. Our 'tools', especially our teaching 'tools', must include building skills in collecting, organising, documenting, writing, and presenting these 'materials.' These are features common to the work of all historians, and increasingly important aspects of the education of any social scientist. But for most of us, our training did not include, because they did not exist, the electronic tools now available. These new software programs, while very useful for individual research and writing tasks, also must allow for the introduction of many more students to history as we know it: a demanding exercise in patient research and investigation, set in a context of questions and discovery; an intellectual enterprise as much *done*, as received second hand. We are confident that The Canton Project begins to respond to this challenge: to create a useful academic tool for the teaching of history to undergraduates.

Chapter 20

Recycling History: A CD-ROM Project on the Cheap

Robin McLachlan and John Messing

Introduction

This chapter will report on a project to place historical reference and archival material onto CD-ROM in an integrated multi-media format for low-cost public acquisition. Much of the material used was originally developed for other purposes and
has been 'recycled' into a multi-media format for use on the Macintosh with
HyperCard 2.1. The purpose, techniques and processes of the project may be of
interest to historians and archivists concerned with the wider dissemination of
historical materials through multi-media, especially in situations where the commercial market for such software is not viable.

The historical material used in this project concerns the 1915 Gallipoli campaign
of the Australian and New Zealand Army Corps (ANZAC). For Australians, this
military campaign is seen as critical to their development as a nation. Unfortunately, the geography of Australia makes for difficult access to the main archival
source of information, the Australian War Memorial (AWM) in Canberra. While
we do not claim to have found the complete solution to problems of access, we
think that our project shows something of the potential of disseminating historical
material, especially material already in a computer-readable form, via simple
multi-media on CD-ROM.

Background to the Project

The CD-ROM project had its origins in 1990 during the 75th anniversary of the
Gallipoli Campaign. One of the authors of this chapter was commissioned by the
AWM to design and manage a national commemorative programme aimed at
schools and communities. As part of the Gallipoli 75 programme, the AWM funded
a number of commemorative activities. These included a newspaper and radio
series based on soldiers' letters and diaries held in the Memorial's collection as
well as a comprehensive education kit for schools with an accompanying national
project involving schools researching the biographies of local soldiers for entry into
a simple flat file database. Some of the material produced for the commemorative
programme had a life beyond 1990. For example, the database based on the entries
provided by students is still available as a software package as well as via the
NEXUS electronic mail system. (McLachlan and Starick, 1991) However, other elements of the programme, notably the extracts from letters and diaries, appeared

179

only once in 1990 with no arrangements for any future re-publication. This collection of several hundred extracts was destined to remain locked up for evermore as *Microsoft Word* files in the project manager's hard disk drive. Also sitting on the hard disk was a sizeable collection of material from the AWM's archives not developed but utilised in the commemorative programme. This included extracts from unit war diaries, operational orders, etc. As well, in the course of researching the commemorative programme, a miscellany of material had been located and assessed but not developed for various reasons. Given that much research had been done and that much of the archival material was already in a computer-readable format, Gallipoli 75 was a perfect candidate for 're-cycling' into an integrated multi-media package. A 'home' for the package was offered by Apple Computer Australia in the form of space on *Avalanche II*, a CD-ROM of Australian and New Zealand educational *HyperCard* Stacks.

In late 1991, the authors approached the Australian War Memorial to gain their support and permission to 're-cycle' the Gallipoli 75 material, together with additional material, in a *HyperCard* form. The AWM gave their consent to the proposal and, although unable to help financially, provided facilities and material aid for the project. Apple Computer Australia provided technical assistance with the loan of equipment and software to enable film material, for example, to be included. The bulk of the development work, however, was carried out on personal equipment owned by the authors. The entire project was undertaken with no financial assistance. By January 1993, The Gallipoli Stacks, a set of six *HyperCard* stacks, had been developed and provided to Apple Computer for the *Avalanche II* CD-ROM.

A Mini-Archive

The metaphor used to describe our collection of Gallipoli *HyperCard* stacks is that of a 'mini-archive'. Obviously, The Gallipoli Stacks contain only a tiny fraction of what is available in the AWM's collection in Canberra, but there is sufficient breadth and depth to provide a good working collection of material in text, pictorial and video media. Some of the material contained on the stacks has never before been seen outside of the AWM.

The main target group for the stacks is the history classroom, but the quality and quantity of information provided will be of use to academic researchers, journalists and others requiring access to a broad selection of material on the campaign. (Messing and McLachlan, 1993). The minimum target machine is the Macintosh LC with 4 megabytes RAM and colour monitor. The integrated use of the different types of material, such as text and photographs, is provided through a variety of indexes, navigation links and other retrieval tools. These allow the 'mini-archive' to be used in a highly efficient and flexible manner. For example, information can be accessed through alphabetical and/or chronological indexes, as well as through free-text searches and familiar *HyperCard* 'Button Links' (both inter and intra stack).

There are also within the Diary Stack three special types of imbedded hypertext links:

- Some words in the text (indicated by underlining) are linked directly to an additional reference located elsewhere; clicking the text will take you directly to this information.
- Other words have similar links with multiple references elsewhere; clicking will display a list of all of these references for selection by the user. For example, clicking on the word 'Turk' in a diary entry will bring up a list of other references to 'Turks' in text, photographs and film clips.
- Other words have similar links to broader categories of information. For example, the word 'cheese' in a diary entry, when clicked, will link with other 'food'. Ten general categories based on common themes found in the content material have been provided.

This variety of pathways to and from any point in the 'mini-archive' will support a range of different uses and activities, ranging from very specific searches to general browsing. At the simplest level, one can look through a given stack doing nothing more complicated than proceeding in a linear fashion, card by card, by clicking on the arrow button. Or, one can enter the web of connected references provided by the imbedded links, moving not only within stacks but across to other stacks. It must be stressed that these imbedded links and webs are meant to be suggestive of the many combinations that can be made with the resources in the stacks. Those connections that have been provided reflect perhaps the 'neural pathways' of the authors! The usual Macintosh and *HyperCard* editing and printing facilities are also available to transfer material from the host stacks to other stacks, word processing documents, printer, etc. In some respects, therefore, the CD-ROM 'mini-archive' is a more useful research resource than the original 'maxi-archive' in Canberra.

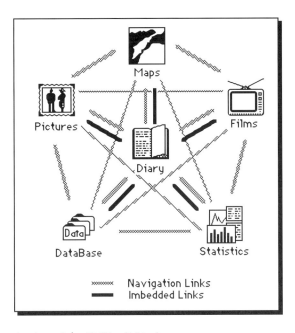

Figure 20.1   Organisation of the Gallipoli Stacks

The Gallipoli Stacks

The material has been organised into six stacks according to the nature of the original material, as shown in Figure 20.1. Each of the stacks will function as an independent data file; navigation links provide pathways from any one stack to any other stack. Each stack has an introductory card providing background information on the sources used as well as the selection and editing rules applied in preparing the material.

The Diary Stack (626k)

As indicated in Figure 20.1, the Diary Stack is the gateway to the system. This stack is organised with daily entries (separate cards) for most days from 1 April to 31 December 1915. A pop-up calendar provides a fast and simple way to locate a specific day. Each day, or card, contains two scrolling panels (fields) of text relating to that particular day. The left-side panel, 'Letters & Diaries', contains extracts from letters and diaries written on Gallipoli. Most of this material was originally developed for the 1990 commemorative programme's weekly newspaper column and radio series, as discussed above. A team of four historians worked on selecting and transcribing the original extracts so that, overall, the collection does reflect a number of perspectives.

The language of the diaries and letters presented an interesting problem for text-based computer searches of archival material. As might be expected, 1915 English uses a vocabulary very often different to that of the 1990s. As well, letters and diaries written on Gallipoli contain military terms and slang unique to that time and place. A dictionary has been provided to assist users. Another problem has to do with the naming of places and events. Battlefield features change name over time and battles tend to be named well after the event and not in letters and diaries written at the time. Various devices have been used to solve this problem, including providing key words in [   ] or intentionally including them in the corresponding 'Daily Accounts' entry so that a search on a key word will locate the relevant card.

The right-side scrolling panel, 'Daily Accounts', contains information on events of that day. Sometimes this panel includes copies of signals, extracts from unit war diaries or operational orders. For the most part though, each day's entry has been especially researched and written for that day.

Collectively, the 'Daily Accounts' panels provide a chronological narrative history of the campaign, giving supporting detail to matters discussed in soldiers' writings and putting daily events into a wider context. Key words have been consciously used in the panels to support free text searching and references are frequently made to material located elsewhere in the stack collection.

A sample page from the Diary Stack (cut to fit the page) is provided below. The underlined words are imbedded hypertext links to additional references. For example, 'weather' will link to a general category on weather (as would the words 'snow', 'rain', etc.). Similarly, 'Anzac Cove' will link to a collection of references (in this case photos and maps) on Anzac Cove (a key location in the campaign). The icons, or buttons, along the bottom are links to the other stacks in the collection.

Figure 20.2   Sample Page from the Diary Stack

The small diagonal crosses are markers to indicate that there is a direct link available to a photograph and a map of specific relevance to this card.

The Picture Stack (218k & 4506k Pict Compressor Docs)

This stack was developed specially for the CD-ROM project and contains 160 black and white photographs scanned from the Australian War Memorial's research collection. The selection provided in this stack is arguably one of the most comprehensive pictorial collections of the subject produced. The photographs were selected to support and reinforce comments about life and duty made by soldiers in their diaries and letters. Each photograph is accompanied by a pop-up text panel which provides information, often very detailed, on the photograph. Initially, photos were scanned using *HyperScan* software but with very disappointing results. The scanning was later redone with the same hardware but now using *AppleScan* and *QuickTime* software, which combined excellent picture compression with high quality reproduction. Within the stack, access to a photograph is via an alphabetical index of short caption-titles or a free text search on a word within a photograph's caption-title or its longer information panel. The panels and titles have been written with this in mind.

The Map Stack (712k)

This stack contains a comprehensive selection of 50 black and white maps, ranging from global to trench in scale, providing a cartographic history of the campaign. The maps are in a chronological order, roughly one for each week of the campaign, and cover events ranging from major battles to minor trench raids. Each map is

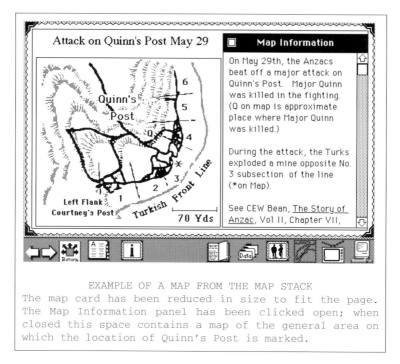

Figure 20.3   Example from the Map Stack

accompanied by an information text panel and a full area map showing the rela-
tional location of the territory covered. The maps serve to locate landmarks and
places referred to elsewhere, to show troop dispositions at key moments, the sites
of key battles and, most importantly, to foster an appreciation of the intimate scale
of the Anzac area. Particular attention has been given to including maps which
support the accounts of soldiers in the Diary Stack. Access within the stack to individual maps is organised as with the Picture Stack.

Most of the maps in the stack are scanned copies (using *HyperScan*) of original
maps in the Memorial's collection or in the Australian official history of the First
World War. (Bean, 1921) The editing features of *HyperScan* were used to modify the
maps, for example to provide labels or to remove unwanted features, so as to enhance their usefulness. While *HyperScan* was inadequate for photographs, it was a
very effective tool for producing the maps in this stack. Figure 20.3 shows an example of a Map from the Map Stack. The map card has been reduced in size to fit
the page. The Map Information panel has been clicked open; when closed this
space contains a map of the general area on which the location of Quinn's Post is
marked.

The Statistics Stack (616k)

While the Map and Picture Stacks were developed specifically for the CD-ROM
project, the Statistics Stack is based almost entirely on material re-cycled from the
original 1990 project, specifically the education kit. The Statistics Stack, named so for

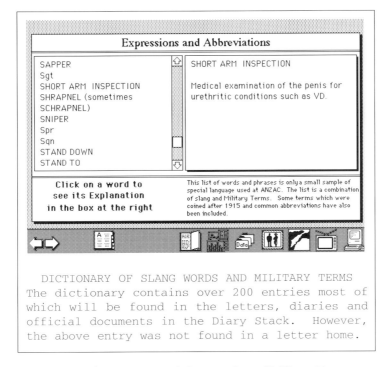

Figure 20.4   Entry from the Dictionary of Slang Works and Military Terms

the lack of anything better, is meant to be a compendium of miscellaneous inform-ation, statistical and otherwise, of possible assistance to users of the collection. The stack consists of eight sections which provide information on such topics as:

- Nations involved in the campaign, with casualties.
- ANZAC units; army rank & unit structures.
- ANZAC enlistment and casualty statistics.
- A dictionary of expressions and abbreviations.
- Biographical information with photos of key persons.

The stack also includes a small collection of soldiers' humorous sketches found, but not used, during the 1990 project. The dictionary contains over 200 entries most of which will be found in the letters, diaries and official documents in the Diary Stack. Figure 20.4 shows an entry; it was not found in a letter home.

Figure 20.5 shows an example of Anzac humour. This is one of several humor-ous drawings provided in the Statistics Stack. The 'swank' general looks not unlike General Hamilton, a British general who was usually nearer the biscuit tin than the front line. The faded hand-written caption on the original has been replaced with an easier to read typed text. In other cases, the original pencil text was enhanced using *HyperScan* editing tools. Some of the drawings in this stack were originally intended for publication in the 1916 Anzac Book but were rejected by the editor, C.E.W. Bean, as inappropriate. Fortunately, they were preserved in the Australian War Memorial's collection and a few at least have now seen publication.

Figure 20.5   Drawing from the Statistics Stack

The Film Stack (144k & 15602k Simple Player Docs)

This stack contains a selection of 18 short film clips taken from both rare footage shot on Gallipoli in 1915 and a popular colour feature film, 'Gallipoli', produced in 1981. Clips from the modern film were selected from those scenes showing carefully researched reconstructions of Anzac. In several cases, it has been possible to link a film scene with the original letter or diary, or photograph, used by the filmmakers in their research for set construction or background action. Each of the film clips is supported by an information text panel. Permission to use clips from the commercial film was obtained from the owner of the film's video rights in exchange for our including information on the availability of the video. This is an approach that might be used elsewhere in dealing with the thorny problem of film copyright.

The video clips, like the photographs, provide an important visual dimension, enhancing particularly the word pictures provided by the soldiers in their letters and diaries. However, the photographs have proven to be the better visual re-

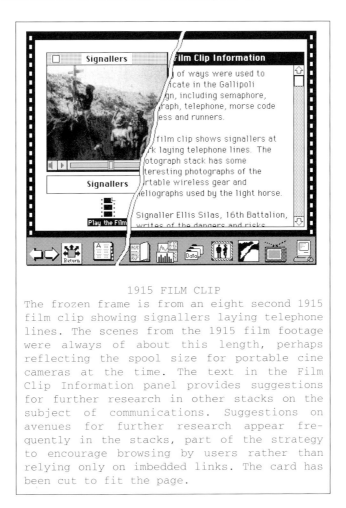

Figure 20.6   Frame from a 1915 Film Clip in the Film Stack

source. The reason for this is mainly due to a combination of imperfect technologies from both periods, 1915 and 1992. 1915 film making was very crude; 1990s computer-based video is less than perfect. In terms of screen size and quality of reproduction, the 1915 photograph is excellent. By comparison, the video clip is limited to a small window on screen and a relatively short run time.

Film clips were digitised using a Video Spigot card and then compressed with *QuickTime*. Apple's *Movie Shop* was used to optimise playback from CD-ROM. The compression capabilities of *QuickTime* allowed for the film to be compressed down to less than one third of its original 60 megabytes size.

Figure 20.6 shows a frozen frame from an eight second 1915 film clip showing signallers laying telephone lines. The scenes from the 1915 film footage were always of about this length, perhaps reflecting the spool size for portable cine cameras at the time. The text in the Film Clip Information panel provides suggestions for further research in other stacks on the subject of communications. Suggestions for further research appear frequently in the stacks, part of the strategy to encourage browsing by users rather than relying only on imbedded links. The card has been cut to fit the page.

The Biography Database Stack (732k)

This is a *HyperCard* version of the AppleWorks database produced in 1990 as part of the Australian War Memorial's commemorative programme. (McLachlan and Starick, 1991) Brief biographies for 558 soldiers and nurses were contributed by students and local historians using information provided from AWM records as well as from locally researched sources. Other than converting the original database to a *HyperCard* stack and providing an enquiry system for searching, little further development took place with this material. Imbedded links have been provided from the Diary Stack to the entries for specific individuals in this stack. Figure 20.7 shows a sample Biography Card. This is one of the more than 500 biography cards in this stack, nearly all of which were contributed by school children in 1990. Information on contributors appears via a pop-up screen on clicking the (C) button, upper-right corner. Information provided by schools was double-checked against official records and editorial comments were added if appropriate, as within the square brackets on this card. Family and community sources were sometimes more reliable than the records kept by the military.

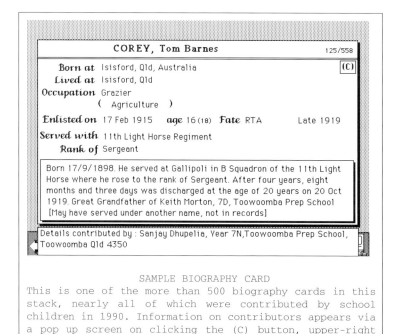

```
                    COREY, Tom Barnes                          125/558

      Born at  Isisford, Qld, Australia                              (C)
      Lived at  Isisford, Qld
   Occupation  Grazier
                ( Agriculture )
   Enlisted on  17 Feb 1915    age 16(18)  Fate RTA      Late 1919
   Served with  11th Light Horse Regiment
      Rank of  Sergeant

      Born 17/9/1898. He served at Gallipoli in B Squadron of the 11th Light
      Horse where he rose to the rank of Sergeant. After four years, eight
      months and three days was discharged at the age of 20 years on 20 Oct
      1919. Great Grandfather of Keith Morton, 7D, Toowoomba Prep School
      [May have served under another name, not in records]

   Details contributed by : Sanjay Dhupelia, Year 7N, Toowoomba Prep School,
   Toowoomba Qld 4350
```

```
                    SAMPLE BIOGRAPHY CARD
   This is one of the more than 500 biography cards in this
   stack, nearly all of which were contributed by school
   children in 1990. Information on contributors appears via
   a pop up screen on clicking the (C) button, upper-right
   corner. Information provided by schools was double-checked
   against official records and editorial comments were added
   if appropriate, as within the square brackets on this
   card. Family and community sources were sometimes more
   reliable than the records kept by the military.
```

Figure 20.7
Sample Card
from the
Biography Stack

Dissemination of the Stacks

Thanks to *QuickTime* compression of photographs and film clips, The Gallipoli Stacks are only about 23 megabytes in size, a size considerably smaller than the authors anticipated when commencing the project in 1991. However, the collection of stacks is of a size too large for dissemination by 3.5' microdisks but too small to justify its own CD-ROM. The dissemination of The Gallipoli Stacks has been done via a cooperative CD-ROM. The Stacks have been placed at no cost on Apple Computer Australia's *Avalanche II*, a CD-ROM of *HyperCard* stacks on education topics developed in, and for, Australia and New Zealand. *Avalanche II* was released in May 1993 and has been sold nationally via an educational software distributor at a very modest price, A$25.00 (about US$15.00), a sum sufficient to cover production and distribution costs. The Avalanche series CD-ROMs have proved to be an excellent dissemination vehicle for *HyperCard* projects too small (or commercially unviable) for an independent CD-ROM. Copyright of material remains with the contributors, which in our case includes the Australian War Memorial. The only restriction placed on our material is that it cannot be used for commercial purposes.

Conclusions

The authors of this chapter are confident that they have provided an effective and low cost educational and research resource on the Gallipoli campaign. Thanks to the power of the computer and the unique opportunities provided by multi-media, The Gallipoli Stacks represent an exciting new approach to assembling and disseminating historical information. We also believe our project may serve as a model for others wishing to create simple, low-cost multi-media packages.

The success of our project rests on a few simple points, which are easily applied to other situations:

- Only a small team is required, but it should be one combining historical and computer expertise. Our team consisted of only two people, an information technology specialist and an historian.

- To minimise your work, try to base the project on material already available in a computer readable format. Given the use of computers over the last couple of decades in preparing computer typeset books as well as word-processed documents, an enormous amount of material is now available for recycling. The material produced for the commemorative programme provided the core of our project, although additional material was developed in support. The work required to develop this additional material, however, should not be underestimated.

- You need to use nothing beyond off-the-shelf software which is simple, versatile and suitable for your purposes. In our case, we used *HyperCard 2.1*, together with *HyperScan, AppleScan, QuickTime, etc.* This combination of readily available software was able to handle all of our requirements and to facilitate the linking and integration of the material in all the formats used.

- If you cannot afford to produce your own CD-ROM, consider disseminating your material via a cooperative CD-ROM.

Multi-media on CD-ROM does not have to become the exclusive domain of corporations responding mainly to market demands. There are opportunities for small-scale projects with limited resources, as demonstrated by our Gallipoli Stacks project.

As the Anzacs would tell you, this is 'dinkum oil' (reliable or trustworthy information).

Chapter 21

Moving House. A Computer Package Analysing Migration within a 19th Century Urban Area: Glasgow

Peter Hillis

Historical Background

A ubiquitous feature of many European city centres is the multi-storey car park. Present day Glasgow is no exception with a plethora of featureless towers built to accommodate the internal combustion engine. In the 19th century Cambridge Street United Presbyterian Church stood on the site of the present day Cambridge Street multi-storey car park. As many members of the congregation benefited from Glasgow's commercial and industrial prosperity they moved house from the city centre to the west end suburbs. Sunday worship then entailed an inconvenient journey into Glasgow which led to demands for a new church in the west end. Consequently, Lansdowne Church was opened in 1863 with the following poem chalked on the door to greet the first worshippers and their minister the Rev. John Eadie:

> *This Church is not built for the poor and needy*
> *But for the rich and Dr. Eadie*
> *The rich may come in and take their seat*
> *But the poor must go to Cambridge Street.*

Situated close to Kelvinbridge, the Church was re-located in the prosperous middle class west end of Glasgow away from its original position, nearer the city centre in Cambridge Street.

Increasing social segregation as witnessed in the movement away from the slums was common in many Victorian Cities. London, Leeds, Sheffield, Cardiff, Nottingham and Manchester could all boast a prosperous west end. Some contemporaries noted with alarm the increasing divisions in urban society which were seen as an important cause of social tensions. Norman Macleod, Minister of Glasgow's Barony Church from 1851 until 1872 reflected these concerns along with a wish to recreate the closer knit pre-industrial communities in an urban environment:

> *"The separation outwardly of society is terrible. Only see the old and new Town of*
> *Edinburgh. What type of British Society! It used not to be so. In the old town and in the*

191

older times families of different grades used to live in the same tenement, and poor and rich were thus mingled together in their habitation and in their joys." (MacLeod, 1876:287)

The deterioration of living conditions in the historic centre of many towns brought on by industrialisation was a more powerful consideration influencing choice of house than the more altruistic desire to preserve communal identity.

Between 1851 and 1871 Glasgow experienced a dramatic growth in population from 375,000 to 568,000, much of this increase resulting from migration into the city. Population increase was shadowed by the growth of slums concentrated in the old city centre and east end. Sally O'Hara, a widow living in a one apartment house off the High Street, was typical of many living nearby. Her only income was earned by gathering rags during the day and then selling them at night, from which she made 1d or 2d. This was supplemented by the wages her children earned at the mill. The apartment was a mere six feet wide, ten feet long and seven feet high with "damp clay" nature's carpet. There was "no table, no chair, no stool, not an article of furniture, but some broken crockery ..." and "the children sleep with her on the wooden bedstead, which is a fixture; not a vestige of blankets, but a little loose straw, not one particle of food in the house ... The hovel in which she lived was unfit to shelter a human being ... and the crowded neighbourhood renders the air that encircles and visits this wretched abode most pestiferous and deadly." (Smith, 1846:16–17)

Although picking up pace as conditions in the old city declined the move west pre-dated industrialisation. Many Tobacco Lords built their mansions in what became the Georgian area of Glasgow. The street names give both location and origin; Jamaica (1764), Miller (1782), Queen (1765), Buchanan (1785), Howard (1769), Maxwell (1772) and Dunlop (1772). As the Glasgow economy expanded business and commerce colonised these streets. In 1840 Andrew Buchanan's house in Virginia Street was demolished to make way for the Union Bank with most of Buchanan Street taken over by shops and warehouses by 1830. Both the more acceptable face of industrialisation, in the form of commercial growth, and the unacceptable conditions in the slums forced the middle classes to re-locate in previously undeveloped areas.

The choice, as Brian Dicks has noted, was not entirely unrestrained. (Dicks, 1985) The availability of housing at an affordable price and the wish to live in a 'good' area influenced decisions. Moreover, the type of building was often carefully controlled by feu charters. Those granted for Kelvinside detailed style and size of building, width and quality of footpaths, nature of shrubbery and type of gas lamp, all designed to maintain an exclusive environment.

With a view to attracting purchasers, property advertisements emphasised architectural features, accessibility, environmental quality, leisure facilities and proximity to institutions. Built on drumlin hills Glasgow's west end met all these criteria. Westerly winds blew unpleasant smells to the east while trees and parks were incorporated into town planning. "Now trees appear scanning terraces, and through them warm lights shine through open doors that mean the west end the world over," wrote one contemporary (Muir, 1901:5). The re-location of the Botanic

Gardens from Sandyford to Kelvinside in 1846 further enhanced environmental attractiveness. Many institutions also moved to the west end, notably Glasgow University which re-opened in Gilmourhill in 1870. Several years earlier it had been forced to cease evening classes in its original College Street home because of the indelicacy of making its respectable young students run the gauntlet of the women of the town arrayed in front of the College entrance. The movement of churches into the west end has already been noted and can still clearly be seen in the present day west end skyline of spires and towers. Private transport companies soon realised the profitable potential of carrying west end inhabitants to and from their workplace in the city centre. In 1894 electric trams replaced horse drawn vehicles; in 1899 the Caledonian Railway Glasgow District Subway opened with 4 stations close to the west end while the Central Railway also served the same area with Botanic Gardens its most famous station.

The growth and character of the west end was epitomised in the Park area on Woodlands Hill. Designed by Charles Wilson the hill top position was used to its best advantage. The top of the hill was covered by two arrangements of buildings, one inward facing, Park Circus, and surrounding a garden, and the other looking outwards, Park Terrace, over the west end park and beyond it the Clyde. Close by was the Free Church College and College Church. The exclusive shops in Byres Road and the Botanic Gardens were in close proximity both adding to the area's appeal.

Nevertheless it would create a misleading impression if it was indicated that social segregation went along rigid lines. J.G. Robb in his analysis of the Gorbals area has shown that it retained a working and middle class mix throughout most of the century (Robb, 1983). Although predominantly residential the west end had an industrial area based in Woodside by the River Kelvin. Many neighbouring streets, such as Kelvin Row, Park Road and South Woodside Road, were working class in social composition as illustrated in census returns and rateable values. These areas were, however, exceptions to the general rule with most working class families condemned to live in slums close to industrial areas further north and east.

Educational Context

The past decade has seen a new emphasis on investigative approaches to the teaching of History in Scotland. In secondary years 3 and 4, Standard Grade History assesses investigative skills as a separate element with pupils required to undertake a historical investigation. National Certificate Modules in secondary 5 and 6, and the Extended Essay in Revised Higher History further develop investigative skills. For example, the National Certificate Module, 'Practical Investigation In The Social Sciences: People and the Past', involves students undertaking a detailed investigation into a wide range of topics relevant to the overall themes within the series of 'People and The Past' modules. The investigation should be completed in approximately a 40 hour period culminating in the production of a 2000 word report. Within certain broad parameters pupils and students are encouraged to choose the issue for investigation. Common to many syllabuses are certain themes including migration, the family, social stratification and mobility, and patterns of employment. *Moving House* provides a resource to aid pupil/student investigations into these and other areas. Running parallel to these developments has been the Technical Vocational Education Initiative (T.V.E.I.), a government sponsored scheme to enhance technical and vocational education in schools. One aspect of this programme has been the increased provision of computer hardware in schools with Apple MacIntosh being the generally favoured system in Strathclyde Region. Despite TVEI there are still History Departments with regular access to only one computer and this is a significant constraint on the use of History software. *Moving House* was therefore designed to supplement a wide range of source materials relevant to investigations.

The *Moving House* Program

Moving House was produced as part of a Scottish project to support and promote information technology in teacher education (SPRITE). It was hoped to encourage the use of information technology in the teaching of History through the production of resource material applicable to student investigations in secondary 5 and 6 with particular reference to a selection of National Certificate modules. This package forms one component of a two part resource for History teaching from primary 6 to secondary 6. A related unit entitled *A Tale of Two Cities: Rich and Poor in Victorian Glasgow* allows pupils from primary 6 to secondary 4 to analyse contrasting lifestyles in 19th century Glasgow. Several features are common to the programs. Both utilise *HyperCard* 2 on Apple MacIntosh, a range of similar primary sources, and contain details of one family who moved house, between 1851 and 1881, from the area examined in *A Tale of Two Cities* to Park Terrace.

Moving House can be used to test the hypothesis that people, as they became more prosperous, moved to middle class suburbs. Various sub-hypotheses can also be checked. For example, claims to social exclusivity by the west end of Glasgow can be checked for accuracy against an analysis of the social composition of selected streets. Alternatively, did a previous residential area of Glasgow, Monteith Row, deteriorate to slum status as a result of westward migration by its wealthier inhabitants? Nevertheless, it is to be hoped that teachers will devise more innovative ways to use the program than those indicated in the accompanying notes.

The program is divided into 5 parts presented as a menu on the title page (Figure 21.1).

The two opening sections comprise student guides to the National Certificate modules which could be used as a framework to an investigation using the program (Figure 21.2). The guides represent details of the modules presented in a 'user-friendly' format.

Teacher and Student notes on the theme of urban migration provide background historical information and advice on how to interpret a range of primary sources.

Two databases take up the largest memory on the program. Park/Woodside contains rateable values for 1881 for a range of streets within the Park and

Figure 21.1   *'Moving House'* Main Menu

Figure 21.2   Module People and the Past

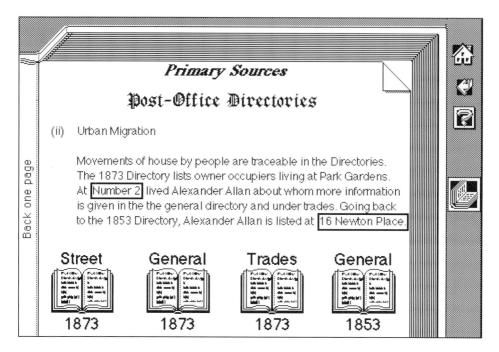

Figure 21.3   Primary Sources Post-Office Directories

1 PARK TERRACE	RATEABLE VALUE 251.00	NO. OF UNITS 1

DETAIL OF OWNER

OWNER CLOUSTON   PETER

OCCUPATION INSURANCE BROKER

ADDRESS 1 PARK TERRACE, GLASGOW

Click ▨ & Hold   **DETAIL OF OCCUPANTS**

SURNAME	FORENAME	OCCUPATION	R/V
CLOUSTON	PETER	INSURANCE BROKER	251.00

Owner and occupier.

Figure 21.4   Park Terrace Detail of Owner

Figure 21.5 No. 1 Park Terrace

1 Park Terrace (1)

RATEABLE
VALUE

NAME and Surname of each Person.	RELATION to Head of Family.	Condition as to Marriage.	AGE Last Birthday Male / Female	Rank, Profession, or OCCUPATION	WHERE BORN	Whether 1. Deaf and Dumb 2. Blind 3. Imbecile or Idiot 4. Lunatic	Rooms with 1 or more Windows
Peter Clouston	*Head*	*Wid*	*73*	*Retired Insurance Broker*	*Greenock*		*24*
Christine do	*Daur*	*Unm*	*45*		*Lanarkshire Glasgow*		
Elizabeth K. do	*do*	*do*	*38*		*do do*		
James Kerr	*Serv*	*do*	*25*	*Butler*	*Ayrshire Ayr*		
Catharine Smith	*do*	*do*	*46*	*Cook*	*Islay, Lall*		
Ann McNeill	*do*	*do*	*28*	*House Maid*	*Nairn*		

NAME and Surname of each Person	RELATION to Head of Family	Condition as to Marriage	AGE (Last B'day) M	AGE (Last B'day) F	Rank, Profession or OCCUPATION	WHERE BORN	Rooms with 1 or more Windows
Peter Clouston	Head	Wid	73		Retired Insurance Broker	Greenock	24
Christine do	Daur	Unm		45		Lanarkshire, Glasgow	
Elizabeth K. do	do	do		38		do do	
James Kerr	Serv	do	25		Butler	Ayrshire, Ayr	
Catherine Smith	do	do		46	Cook	Islay, Lall??	
Ann McNeill	do	do		28	House Maid	Nairn	

Figure 21.6 Census Data: 1 Park Terrace (1)

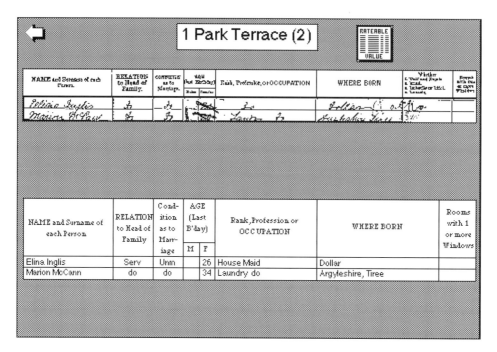

NAME and Surname of each Person	RELATION to Head of Family	Condition as to Marriage	AGE (Last B'day) M	AGE (Last B'day) F	Rank, Profession or OCCUPATION	WHERE BORN	Rooms with 1 or more Windows
Elina Inglis	Serv	Unm		26	House Maid	Dollar	
Marion McCann	do	do		34	Laundry do	Argyleshire, Tiree	

Figure 21.7   Census Data: 1 Park Terrace (2)

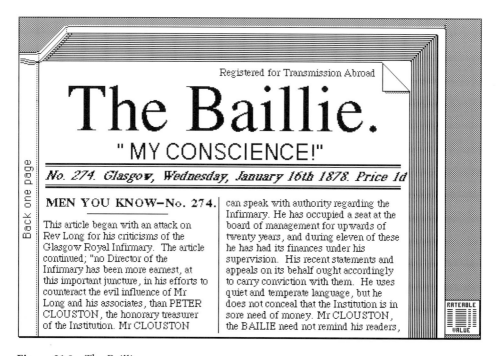

Figure 21.8   The Baillie

Figure 21.9   Mr Peter Clouston

Woodside areas. Rateable valuations provide an insight into the social milieu of house or street. In order to allow an in-depth analysis of two contrasting streets within Park and Woodside, census returns for 1881 have been transcribed for Park Road and Park Terrace (Figures 21.4, 21.6, 21.7). Moreover, biographical notes are provided for the 'Head of Houses' within Park Terrace alongside photographs of both streets (Figures 21.5, 21.8, 21.9).

A single field search was written for the databases which provides scope for a range of investigations. An investigation on immigration could be enhanced by typing in a search for "Ireland" which will display everyone whose country of birth was recorded as Ireland. By tracing someone living in the Park area in 1881 back through the Post Office Directories (Figure 21.3) a picture of moving house/ patterns of urban migration can be compiled.

The Monteith Row database contains background information on the locality and rateable values for every house in 1832, 1861, 1881, 1911 and 1931 (Figures 21.10, 21.11, 21.12). The street or any given house can be compared over this 100 year period. Close to the city centre Monteith Row, was a fashionable area in the early 19th century, therefore, one application of this database could test the hypothesis that westward migration led to more central residential districts declining into slum status.

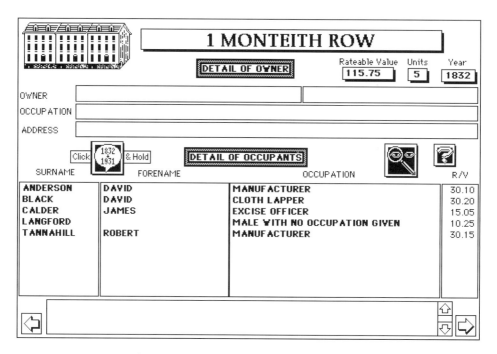

Figure 21.10   1 Monteith Row, 1832

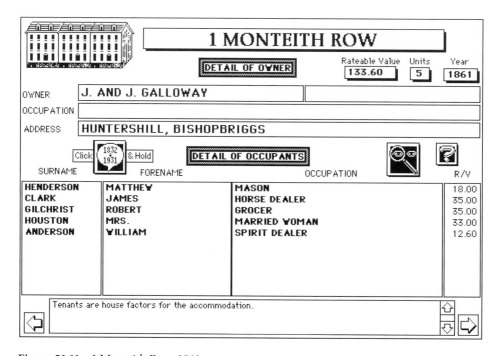

Figure 21.11   1 Monteith Row, 1861

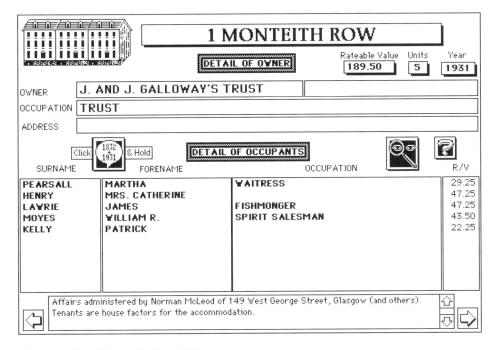

Figure 21.12 1 Monteith Row, 1931

Applications of the Program

History graduates wishing to teach their subject in a Scottish secondary school must complete a one year post graduate course. Within this course the role of computers in the History classroom is discussed, partly through a student evaluation of a range of History computer software including *Moving House* and *A Tale of Two Cities*. It is also hoped to offer *A Tale of Two Cities* as a History elective within the B.Ed. Honours Degree for intending primary teachers. In-service training on *Moving House* has been provided for practising teachers with many Advisers in History purchasing copies for schools in their area. Although an evaluation form is included in the package at this early stage it is not possible to provide a comprehensive review of its application in schools. However, one Principal Teacher of History reported that *Moving House* had been used with her second year class with some pupils visiting the local library to study the primary sources described in the Student Notes. It is to be hoped that this innovative use of the program outwith the intended year groups will not prove an isolated example.

Chapter 22

A Comparison of Three Computer-Assisted Case Studies in Historical Decision-Making

Yta Beetsma

Introduction

The project described here started in 1985 with the goal of exploring the possibilities of computer-assisted learning in history. By August 1990 five computer-assisted case-studies in historical decision-making were ready and four test programs covering topics which appear in the Dutch history syllabuses for secondary schools. The development of these programs (described in Beetsma & Beetsma, 1990) involved four stages, each of which was passed through several times. A close working relationship between a history educator and the technical implementer was important, as was feedback from potential users, students and teachers. During the project an increasing degree of learner control was enabled and tools were developed to aid pupils using the case study. Here we compare the ways in which pupils handled three of the case studies.

Description of the Three Case Studies

Content

The three case-studies are:

- *De Jonge-Snijders* about a conflict between the secretary of war (De Jonge) and the commander-in-chief of the Dutch army (Snijders) in 1918.
- *De Zeven Provincien* concerns a mutiny in the Dutch navy in 1933. The mutineers were discontented with a reduction in wages and took over a navy vessel, De Zeven Provincien.
- *U-2 Affair* about the crash of a US spy plane in the Soviet Union and the implications for the US/USSR summit in 1960.

Basic Structure

The case studies have two goals. The first is to offer information about the specific case, the second is to create a situation in which the user becomes involved in the cases and can evaluate the decisions which were taken.

Each case study is divided into small parts which are presented in chronological order. Each part consists of the presentation of text, followed by one or more multiple choice or open-ended questions. Immediate feedback is given on the answers to the questions. The questions are not meant to test knowledge, but to involve students in the case. Many questions relate to decisions which had been taken in the historical situations. The feedback provides hints about these decisions.

When a 'wrong' answer is given, the pupil has to try again until a maximum allowable number of attempts has been reached. The correct answer is then given. With the multiple choice questions in *De Jonge-Snijders* and *De Zeven Provincien*, pupils must judge after feedback if their answer is right or wrong. This was provided in order to force pupils to read the feedback. In *De Zeven Provincien* and *U-2 Affair* it is possible to interview major characters in the case. Questions appear as a menu. After reading an answer the learner returns to the question menu and can choose the next one. Pupils can decide how many questions they want to ask. In *De Zeven Provincien* an interview was included for the first time. We wanted to know if our questions were relevant, so pupils had to formulate five questions themselves. In all the case studies a summary of events already dealt with can be obtained at any point. In *De Zeven Provincien* and *U-2 Affair* one or more maps can be viewed at any point. One can also move backwards through the program, and end the program at any time.

Specific Structure

De Jonge-Snijders is made up of 2 parts: Part 1 with 18 blocks of text and 23 questions, Part 2 with 17 blocks of text and 25 questions. *De Zeven Provincien* includes 26 blocks of text and 30 questions. *U-2 Affair* includes 18 blocks of text and 37 questions. Questions are open-ended or multiple-choice with between two and four alternatives. Figure 22.1 shows the distribution of questions over the case studies. It is interesting to note that the same basic structure gives a rather different pattern for the three cases. *De Jonge-Snijders* is the most extensive and includes the most open-ended questions. *U-2 Affair* includes the most multiple-choice questions with 2 alternatives.

With all the case studies there is a check for invalid answers to multiple-choice questions. It is not possible to press only the <ENTER> key, to answer outside the valid range or to give a multi-character answer. The pupil gets a message about the

	JS1	JS2	ZP	U2
open-ended questions	5	5	1	2
mc with 3,4 alternatives	12	7	15	7
mc with 2 alternatives	6	13	14	28
Total number of questions	23	25	30	37
Total number of texts	18	17	26	18

JS1 =*Jonge-Snijders part 1*   ZP = *Zeven Provincien*
JS2 = *Jonge-Snijders part 2*   U2 = *U-2 Affair*
mc = multiple-choice

Figure 22.1   Specific Structure of the Case studies

invalid answer and can try again. The tools are available at any time by pressing <ESCAPE>. *De Zeven Provincien* includes one interview with 7 questions, *U-2 Affair* includes 3 interviews each with 10 questions. In *De Zeven Provincien* the interview occurs halfway through the case study, in *U-2 Affair* the interviews can be done after finishing the case study. In *U-2 Affair* it is possible to give points to the USSR or the USA on who caused the failure of the summit (liability-element).

Evaluation

Questions

Questions asked during the trials, allowing us to collect data on the use of the computer-assisted case studies, included:

a] Functioning in the Classroom

 a.1. In what situation is the case study used?

 a.2. How much time is needed to complete it?

 a.3. How difficult is it?

 a.4. Do the pupils like using it?

 a.5. Do the pupils learn from it?

b] Improving the Program

 b.1. Does the program have any bugs?

 b.2. What happens if the user does something unexpected?

 b.3. Do the tools included in the program help the pupil?

 b.4. How do pupils use the interviews and the liability-part?

 b.5. Are the questions formulated correctly?

 b.6. Does the program evaluate the answers given correctly? (especially for open-ended questions)

It should be remembered that the three computer-assisted case studies differ in their structure, in the way tools are used and in the way learner control is enabled.

Collection of Evaluation Data

The case studies were tested in secondary schools. The following data were collected:

• Opinions of pupils and teachers.

• Log-data: at each answer the following data were written to the log file: time (in seconds), answer given, a code if the tools were used, and time spent consulting the tools.

At the end of the programs, 23 multiple-choice and 2 open-ended questions were inserted, asking the pupil for opinions of the program. These questions included:

• Was the program instructive?

• Did you like the program?

• What did you learn from the program?

- In which ways can the program be improved?

To get results it was necessary to condense and transform the data on log-files. The following data were summarised:

- Time taken over each question.
- Time taken over all the questions.
- Number of attempts necessary before the correct answer was given.
- Number of consultations of a tool during one question.
- Time spent consulting the tool.
- Number of invalid answers given during a question.
- Time spent giving invalid answers.

In the case of multiple choice questions the following answer pattern was summarised: the specific answer at the first attempt; the answer on judging an answer wrong or right at the first attempt; the specific answer at the second attempt in cases when the answer at the first attempt was wrong, and so on. The specific answers to the open-ended questions were written to a separate file sorted by question number. Answers to the interviews were also written to a separate file along with the answers at the evaluation.

Results

Situation

In the case of *De Jonge-Snijders*, 63 sessions of Part 1, 40 sessions of Part 2 and 39 sessions of the evaluation were recorded in four schools. For *De Zeven Provincien*, 39 sessions and 26 sessions of the evaluation were recorded in two schools. In the case of *U-2 Affair*, 64 sessions and 47 sessions of the evaluation were recorded in two schools. The lessons took place in the computer rooms in the schools. In some schools there were between 2 and 4 pupils per computer while in others pupils worked alone. The case studies were tested with 3rd — 6th grade pupils. Some teachers used the programs without a lesson of preparation and discussion.

Time Spent

The mean time spent on Part 1 of *De Jonge-Snijders* was 36 minutes; on Part 2 23 minutes; on *De Zeven Provincien* 39 minutes and on *U-2 Affair* 37 minutes. When the time spent from the start of the program to the first question is removed the mean time of the case studies was reduced greatly, except for *De Jonge-Snijders* Part 2 (see Figure 22.2). All the case-studies were completed by the pupils with the exception of *De Zeven Provincien* which was completed by 60% of pupils.

Evaluation Items

One of the evaluation items asked about the difficulty of the programs. 18% of the pupils judged *De Jonge-Snijders* "difficult", 15% *De Zeven Provincien* and 8% *U-2 Affair*. Pupils were asked if they liked the programs. 46% liked doing *De Jonge-Snijders*, 53% *De Zeven Provincien* and 80% *U-2 Affair*. Another item asked if pupils

	JS1	JS2	ZP	U2
time spent (minutes)	36	23	39	37
time before start (minutes)	20	22	34	29
sessions	63	40	39	64
evaluations	39	26	47	
schools	4	4	2	2

JS1 = Jonge-Snijders Part 1   ZP = Zeven Provincien
JS2 = Jonge-Snijders Part 2   U2 = U-2 Affair

Figure 22.2   Time spent on the Case Studies and Number of Sessions and Schools

learned from the programs; 84% said they learned from *De Jonge-Snijders*, 69% learned from *De Zeven Provincien* and 76% learned from *U-2 Affair*. One item asked if pupils could remember the work better through the use of the computer; 38% said "no" with *De Jonge-Snijders*; 58% said "no" with *De Zeven Provincien* and 56% said "no" with *U-2 Affair*. A further item asked if pupils had suggestions for improving the programs: some suggested that the programs were too specific and too slow.

Bugs

The teachers reported that it was not possible to crash the programs, and that no disturbing bugs occurred. There were some problems with the evaluation after finishing the liability part. In some schools problems arose with the maps and the layout of the programs. This was because the computers used were not equipped with the correct graphics card.

Invalid Answers

The percentage of invalid answers to the total number of answers given was 8.9% with *De Jonge-Snijders Part 1*; 9.2% with *De Jonge-Snijders Part 2*; 4.8% with *De Zeven Provincien* and 3.1% with *U-2 Affair*. With *De Jonge-Snijders Part 1* and *De Zeven Provincien*, most invalid answers were given to multiple choice questions with more than two choices. For these questions pupils had to judge their answers after they had given them. In *U-2 Affair* the type of answer was ambiguous, for example 'no' instead of 'don't agree'. In the Dutch language these type of answers consist of one word.

Tools

The percentage of questions answered using the tools was: 3.7% with *De Jonge-Snijders Part 1*; 2.9% with *De Jonge-Snijders Part 2*; 1.1% with *De Zeven Provincien* and 1.7% with *U-2 Affair*. *De Zeven Provincien* and *U-2 Affair* have several types of tools; *De Jonge-Snijders* offers only a summary of events. With *De Zeven Provincien* the tools were consulted as follows: 40% used a summary of events; 10% a map; 5% an interview; 10% moved back in the program and 35 % quit the program. With *U-2 Affair*, 44% used a summary of events; 10% a map, and 19% moved back in the program. Nobody quit halfway through the program.

Interviews

In *De Zeven Provincien* mean time spent on the interview was 6.5 minutes, mean time spent by pupils formulating their own questions was 5.2 minutes and mean time spent on the programmed items of the interview was 1.5 minutes. With *U-2 Affair* mean time spent on the interviews and the liability-part was 5.2 minutes. Pupils became frustrated when they had to formulate their own questions because it took a rather long time and the computer did not comment on their questions. Seven pupils (17%) quit the program after this section. The programmed interview in *De Zeven Provincien* consisted of 7 items and a possibility to quit. Pupils consulted 3.2 items (mean).

Within *U-2 Affair* four sections could be consulted: the liability-part question, and interviews with Khrushchev, Eisenhower and the pilot of the U2. 16% of the pupils did not consult any of these sections; 30% consulted one section; 37% consulted two sections; 8% consulted three sections and 10% consulted all sections. The liability-part was consulted most often (46%), the interview with the pilot next (26%) and the other interviews less often (14%). There was much variation in the number of sections pupils chose, in the sections chosen and in the items chosen within sections.

In the *De Zeven Provincien* pupils may not have had enough time to consult the interview. However, no relationship was found to exist between the time spent before the interview and the number of items which were consulted.

Specific Answers

The evaluation also provided data on pupil responses to questions and interviews which are too specific to report here but are important because they suggest ways in which the case studies can be improved.

Conclusions

The evidence suggested that a complete, or discrete part, of a case study could fit into one lesson of 50 minutes. The division of *De Jonge-Snijders* into two parts was beneficial from this point of view as was *U-2 Affair*. This was particularly the case when the interviews could be done independently of the chronological section of the case study. In the case of *De Zeven Provincien* a division of the chronological section into two parts would improve the program. The interview could be done independently of the chronological order and further interviews added to enlarge this part of the case study. The option of quitting the program at any time and then restarting at the last position before quitting would ease classroom management.

It should be noted that the selection of the schools for this research was unsystematic and decisions about how the programs were used were left with the teachers. The research therefore leaves a number of questions still to be answered. For example: should the case studies be used with or without preparation and with or without discussion after-wards? Should pupils work alone or together? What is the maximum number of pupils who should work together? What age range are the case-studies most suitable for? More research is needed, for example in testing pupil knowledge after working on the case-studies.

From the evaluation it was evident that pupils liked *U-2 Affair* the best and *De Zeven Provincien* least. Perhaps this was due to the inviting character of *U-2 Affair* — it is an international subject which took place in the post-World War II period. It was stated above that one of the goals was to teach pupils about historical decisions by involving them in simulations of the historical incidents. This is a different approach to history, and this goal should be emphasised in the written material.

We now hope to include a test which can be done on a computer after completing each of the case studies. The evaluation of *De Jonge-Snijders* indicated that judging the given answer to multiple choice questions should be removed (Beetsma and Beetsma, 1990). The same conclusion can be drawn from the evaluation of *De Zeven Provincien*. The aim of asking pupils to make these judgements was to force them to read the feedback, but it caused too much confusion and pupils became irritated. In this case the remedy proved worse as than the 'disease'.

The collection and inspection of specific answers is a very useful tool for the authors of the case studies. Pupils however should not be made aware of this collection of answers. The collection of data from interview questions formulated by the pupils in the *De Zeven Provincien* case study was also very useful to the authors. However the collection of this data should be introduced very carefully, because pupils became frustrated by the absence of feedback.

As this project developed, an increasing level of learner control could be seen and tools were implemented to aid pupils in going through the case study. It was a little frustrating to see that the single tool provided with *De Jonge-Snijders* was consulted more often than the tools provided with the other two case studies. One explanation might be that the introduction to *De Jonge-Snijders* included suggestions about using this tool, whereas in the other case studies no such hints were given. This suggests that cues concerning the use of tools, with examples, should be given. It also became clear that the time spent using the interviews was very short, compared with the time spent on the chronological sections of the case studies. Furthermore, pupils tackled these interviews very differently. Some did not work on any of the interviews, others worked through all the interviews and all the questions. More research is needed in order to discover if some pupils were pressed for time. As the programs are developed further a summary of results will prove a useful tool for pupils. With the programs reported on here, pupils did not know which items they had already chosen. A further modification would be the inclusion of exercises which would force pupils to read the interviews.

Our final conclusion is that we have made much progress. We became more and more fascinated by the work, and we hope to produce several more case studies which will offer teachers and pupils fun and satisfaction in their history lessons.

Chapter 23

Computer-Based Modelling
in School History

Mary Webb

Introduction

The Integrated Modelling Project is developing software which will enable children to build models. The software is intended to fulfil the model-building component of the National Curriculum for England and Wales. The software is applicable at Key Stages 2 to 4 (ages 7 to 16), and above. Information technology capability is expected to be achieved through other curriculum areas rather than through a subject called 'Information Technology'. It is possible that in history, children might build computer based models, thereby developing their understanding of history at the same time as acquiring information technology capability.

Expert Builder is a qualitative modelling system which allows users to construct logical models through an interactive graphical interface. The project is now developing an interactive dynamic modelling system. The overall aim is to combine these and other modelling tools into an Integrated Modelling System — Modus.

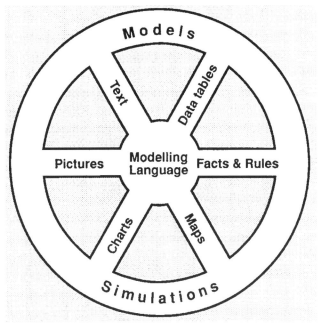

Figure 23.1   Modus — The Integrated Modelling System

211

This paper focuses on ways in which the study of history in school could be a vehicle for developing modelling capability.

Why Build Computer Based Models?

Modelling is a worthwhile activity for children to undertake for two main reasons. First, modelling has become an important tool in business, industry and research and therefore, to be prepared for the world or work, children should understand the nature of modelling and develop the requisite skills. Second, and perhaps more important, there are expectations that the process of modelling will contribute to learning by increasing understanding of the subject matter modelled and by improving thinking skills. The increasing use of modelling is largely due to developments in computer technology which have provided tools for constructing a range of model types and facilities for executing the models to obtain results, rapidly, with different sets of data. The National Curriculum for England and Wales recognises the importance of modelling skills within the programmes of study for information technology capability.

What is Computer Based Modelling?

What causes revolutions? If you lived in England in the 18th century should you consider emigrating to America? What might the outcome of the Arab-Israeli conflict in 1947 have been if…? When considering questions such as these, you need to examine the important factors and how they are related, and to elucidate possible causal relationships. In effect, you are constructing a model of the situation or phenomenon, even if that model only exists inside your head. For most people, a means of expressing all or part of the model externally, e.g. by writing notes or drawing a diagram, is helpful for clarifying their ideas. This is particularly true for a learner who is becoming acquainted with a large number of facts and concepts.

Learners develop understanding by forming mental representations. This is an active process requiring effort and concentration by the learner. The constructivist approach to learning builds on the Piagetian theme of students as active builders of their own intellectual structures (Driver and Easley, 1978: Needham, 1982). Constructivists contend that school children are never empty vessels who can be filled with knowledge, but already have mental constructions based on their everyday experience. These mental constructions have been termed 'mental models' although this term has been given a variety of meanings (see Brewer 1987). In this paper the term is used for any mental representation of an external phenomenon. In order to assist children in improving their mental models so that they are more complete, consistent and accurate, or perhaps closer to accepted theory, teachers must provide a learning environment which will facilitate children in reconstructing their mental models. The conditions needed for this to occur are those in which the inadequacies of a child's mental model become apparent to that child and she/ he is in a supportive environment where she/he can experiment with alternative models. It is possible that computer based modelling software may facilitate this learning process.

Modelling can be defined as the formal representation of some aspect of a problem, process, idea or system. A model might be:

- a physical model, e.g. a castle made out of cardboard.
- a pictorial model, e.g. diagram of the way the heart works.
- a word model, e.g. 'increased supply leads to lower prices'.
- a rule-based logical model e.g. a statement of the conditions likely to lead to a revolution.
- a mathematical model, as in Newton's Laws of Motion.

The tools and materials used for modelling are many and varied. In recent years there has been an increasing use of computers for modelling, not only for investigating three-dimensional structures, but also for modelling systems which can be represented by logical rules or mathematical relationships. A model created on the computer is especially powerful, because it can be made to work, quickly. The computer helps in its design and construction as well as its operation. A computer model can be tested, and modified, and tested again.

The process of modelling assists the modeller in understanding the real world and asking questions of the form: 'What would happen if ...?' Some of the earlier computer based modelling systems gave the impression of much technical complexity but more recently, better user interfaces and more powerful software make it possible for more people to build models without learning a complex programming language. Students can work in groups to discuss their ideas and construct and test their models. Essential stages in modelling can be defined as:

- obtaining relevant information about the subject area under investigation.
- understanding the problem and defining it clearly.
- selecting the important components of the model.
- deciding how to represent each component.
- deducing the relationships between the components.
- expressing these relationships in a modelling language.
- testing the model and comparing it with reality.
- refining the model and then repeating some of the previous steps.

Qualitative Models

A range of different types of models can be identified including *dynamic models* where quantities change over time; *spatial models* where entities are positioned or moving in space; and *data analysis models* which are applied to data in order to identify patterns. These models are all quantitative to some extent. Another group of models can be described as qualitative models. These are distinguished by the fact that their values and relationships are qualitative rather than quantitative. A survey of teachers' views of modelling (Webb and Hassell, 1989) suggested that teachers regard qualitative modelling as being a particularly useful type of modelling for learners.

Tools available for qualitative modelling include knowledge based system shells, including expert system shells. A range of PROLOG-based shells have been developed and have showed some promise for children to use to organise their knowledge (see Nichol *et al.*, 1988). A simple expert system shell, Adex Advisor (Briggs, 1987) has been available to schools. This is a PROLOG-based shell where the knowledge is structured into rules with the structure: 'conclusion *if* premise'. Some classroom research has been done with *Adex Advisor*, where children have used it to build models (Webb, 1988; Hassell, 1988; Galpin, 1989). This work suggested that this type of modelling may benefit learning but that the user interface was inadequate, an interactive graphical user interface being desirable.

Expert Builder — **A New Tool for Qualitative Modelling**

A model in *Expert Builder* consists of a set of relevant knowledge arranged as statements which are either true or false. Statements may depend on other statements in any combination using the logical operators AND, OR and NOT. Dependency diagrams are constructed on the screen using a set of mouse-controlled tools which make it easy and fun to build and alter the diagrams. Figure 23.2 shows the *Expert Builder* screen with a simple model of whether a site is suitable for an ancient settlement.

The model was built by a group of 12–13 year old students following a humanities course. They were considering the factors that influence the choice of a site.

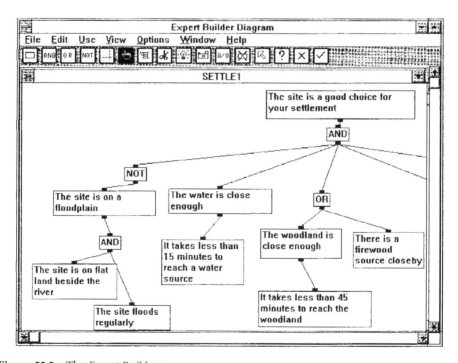

Figure 23.2   The *Expert Builder* program

Later they went on to discuss and evaluate their model by referring to a map and testing the model for a number of different sites. An important feature of *Expert Builder* is that when the model is tested, the reasoning of the system's inference engine can be examined as the boxes on the screen change colour when they are proved to be true or false. When the model is executed, each advice statement is evaluated in turn to see whether it can be proved to be true, and any piece of advice that is proved is given to the user. *Expert Builder* runs under Microsoft Windows (versions 2 and above).

Another important feature of *Expert Builder* is the facility for the model builder to provide a page of explanation, which may be an illustration, for each clause. There is, therefore, opportunity and encouragement for the learner, who is building a model, to explain the terms she/he is using.

Expert Builder in Use

There are about 150 educational institutions ranging from primary schools to universities, exploring the potential of *Expert Builder*. The program has been used in a range of curriculum areas, including the humanities, maths, science, and technology. Most children seem to become adept at manipulating the user interface within a half hour session. Some examples of the range of systems built include: where to site a reservoir; osmosis; who will win a battle; a binary adder; and how to cut down energy use. Most of the models built by schools are quite small, consisting of 10–20 boxes. Teachers have suggested several topics for modelling in history, including analysing the role of women in a particular situation; studying the outcome of conflict situations such as the Arab-Israeli war; planning a voyage of exploration; and designing sentences for offences for a particular time period. However the system provides the facility to construct much larger models with several hundred boxes so that students could undertake a more complex model building task as a project.

When we consider the programmes of study for information technology capability in the National Curriculum for England and Wales, it is clear that students will need to be given opportunities to use IT to complete the whole modelling process from the initial identification of a subject through to testing and evaluation of the model. It is unlikely that many students, at present, will attain the higher levels of IT capability for a variety of reasons, including lack of access to appropriate hardware, software, curriculum time and teacher expertise. At lower levels of IT capability, students are expected to explore computer models and to begin to understand how they work.

This exploration of computer models could be achieved through a simulation where the pupil can gain an understanding of the model and how it works by testing the outcome with various inputs. There are many examples of the use of simulations in history, a few of which are outlined in this book. If the student uses these simulations a number of times, she/he can construct her/his own mental model of the underlying computer model. It is not easily possible, however, with any of these simulation packages, for the student to examine the underlying model itself. The model is buried in programming code and at best a brief description of its structure and underlying assumptions is provided in the documentation. Thus, at higher levels of modelling capability such simulation packages are no longer appropriate. Students need to be able to view and modify the model itself. One example of where *Expert Builder* has been used to support modelling capability comes from work in a primary school (Goodall, 1986), where the class was working on a topic about the Battle of Hastings and constructed a model which would predict whether or not an army was likely to win the battle. The model was constructed jointly by the teacher and the class. They researched the topic and discussed the factors which lead to success in battle, grouping them into three categories, tactics, strategy and equipment. They decided that if one army had the best of two out of these three they would win. The teacher built up this part of the model during the class discussion, so demonstrating the use of the software. The logic of the model was then checked by the students, who took the role of either Duke William or King Harold as they tested the model. Groups of students went on to define parts of the model further; Figure 23.3 shows one part of the model.

Observation of the students during this activity revealed that one or two of the brighter students had a very good grasp of the model and were contributing well to its design and construction and could therefore be said to be working at National Curriculum Level 5 or 6. Other students were working at lower levels and gaining experience of entering knowledge into the system and testing the model. Although this particular exercise was conducted in a primary school, it is relevant to Key Stage 3 of the History National Curriculum (ages 11–14) and certainly provides opportunities for developing modelling capability at Key Stage 3.

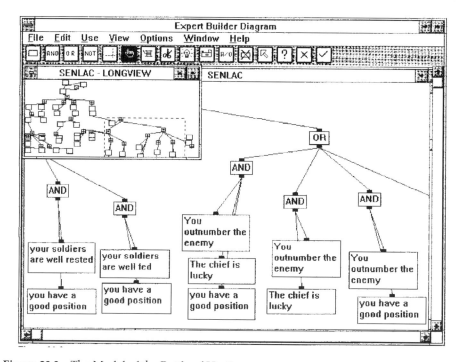

Figure 23.3   The Model of the Battle of Hastings

The Nature of Historical Modelling in Schools

The approach of this chapter has been primarily from an information technology perspective, and has begun to explore whether it is possible for students to use computers to model history. As we have seen, software is beginning to become available which enables some modelling of historical events and situations. There are a number of questions which this raises for history teachers. What is the nature of historical models? Modelling tends to generalise; is it possible to generalise about history or is each event unique and thus requiring to be examined as such? Our own mental models include both general schema and specific models. Some history teachers have questioned whether students can be expected to construct their own models because in order to generalise, they need to have a very broad knowledge. This argument suggests that modelling is of no value unless the end result is a good model. However, the process of modelling may be a valuable learning experience. Models are never perfect, and an important aspect of modelling is to test and evaluate the model. The example from the Battle of Hastings showed where a model was developed for a specific event. Students could go on to test this model in relation to other battles and if necessary modify it to accommodate more battles or develop a unique model for each battle.

Does Computer Based Modelling Help Children to Learn History?

Anecdotal evidence from history teachers whose pupils have modelled with *Expert Builder* suggests that the experience is motivating and encourages children to think on a deeper level. However, there is no doubt that this approach to learning is more time consuming than a more traditional one. In the future it may be less demanding on time, for any one particular exercise, as students become more skilled in the use of software and develop modelling skills from an early age.

Another important question, which is raised by work on the Integrated Modelling project is whether rule-based models are appropriate for modelling history? It has been possible to construct, in *Expert Builder*, a number of simple models of historical situations and to reconstruct, fairly successfully, some of the simulations, which were developed for history. A current limitation of *Expert Builder* is that no variables are possible within a statement so if there are many outcomes depending on the value of one factor, it is necessary to create a separate statement for each value of the factor. This can lead to an unnecessarily large diagram. Another feature, which some history teachers have suggested should be included, is the ability to state that an outcome depends on 2 out of 3 factors being true with-out having to specify all the combinations of those factors. This would simplify the construction of the Battle of Hastings model, but would not have given the children the opportunity of exploring the nature of combining factors in this way. Some history teachers have also expressed a desire to be able to indicate degrees of certainty when answering questions in *Expert Builder* rather than simply stating true or false. To some extent it is possible to express different levels of certainty within the rules by using statements such as 'it is likely that …' or 'it is almost certain that …'. However, there is currently no way of mathematically combining these degrees of certainty together. Such features also make the models harder to understand. One of the difficulties of providing more sophisticated features in software is that of maintaining its ease of use and this is one of the challenges of software development. Currently, *Expert Builder* is technically easy to use because it is basically very simple. There may be a need for a modelling environment which supports the development of reasonably sophisticated simulations so that curriculum developers can produce simulations for students to explore. However it must still use a simple language so that learners can view and modify the model.

Conclusions

There are opportunities for children to develop information technology capability, as required by the National Curriculum for England and Wales, through modelling historical events and situations. Using historical simulation packages provides opportunities for students to attain lower levels of modelling capability but higher levels require them to work on the model itself. In a simulation the model is hidden in the program code. Rule based modelling, using software such as *Expert Builder*, provides one environment for such work. Students find this approach interesting and motivating but further research is needed to determine whether this is an appropriate way to promote the learning of history.

Chapter 24

HiDES in the Sixth Form: Exemplars taken from the HiDES Project, 1990

Frank Colson and Neil Thompson

Southampton University has long cherished its contacts with teachers in the region. By mid-1988 teachers in the local sixth form colleges (catering for students aged 16–19) were alerted to the possibilities offered by the 'packages' being developed by the HiDES Project. Their enthusiasm was charged by the opportunity to take advantage of current technology to teach the traditional skills of document analysis in a way which would well command such resources as were available. It was heightened by the opportunity offered by the History Department at the University of Southampton for a teacher to work in tandem with a member of its staff to develop a 'HiDES package' which would stimulate discussion and debate in the classroom.

The Project, has been generously supported by the Local Education Authority, IBM(UK) and the University of Southampton. In its initial stage a number of teachers were chosen to work with members of the History Department to experiment with the existing HiDES software and produce suitable versions for work with Sixth form students. Appropriate areas of the syllabus were chosen by the teams and support was received from the HiDES Project. IBM PS/2 Model 30 computers were subsequently located in the Colleges which agreed to collaborate, to provide a unique resource for the appropriate teachers. A number of packages have been built, on *The Third Reich*, *Martin Luther*, and *Politics and Parties in England and Wales 1900–1929*.

A second tranche of packages was commissioned, on the *Russian Revolution*, the *Poor Law in England and Wales, 1834 and after*, and the *Reign of Henry VIII*. The original teacher-authors were largely retained, as were their academic advisors, while new authors were also recruited.

Though the software environment of the sixth form HiDES packages bears the hallmark of the university version from which they have been developed, there is a sense in which the various datasets (Questions, HQS files, Documents, HDC and domain files) have acquired an entirely different pedigree. This is hardly surprising since the circumstances in which the packages are being used are very different. One example will suffice, HiDES packages demand a great deal of time from the University Finalist for whom they were designed, but the sixth form student can only spend a limited amount of time at the keyboard. The sequence of questions and responses have therefore had to be redesigned. Needless to say, the need to structure a dialogue which would provide a more 'conversational' approach placed great demands upon the software environment in which the package was developed and called for high levels of ingenuity among the teachers concerned and the technical staff in the laboratory. At the same time documentary sources are constrained and graphical representations are widely used as an integral part of the argument.

For the sixth form, packages are still about argument and interpretation in history, this they have in common with all other versions of HiDES. Though the technology used implies the requirement for a close reading of the sources the sophistication of the dialogue which can be achieved by sensitive and intelligent authoring means that the packages are certainly not about 'drilling' students to respond to 'correct' answers. Three packages developed in the first year explore problems in interpretation, asking traditional questions: accounting for the ascent of Hitler to power in January 1933; for the emergence of a coherent criticism of contemporary doctrine by Martin Luther; or for the decline of the British Liberal Party. In each case the packages do not 'close the argument', but are designed to provide students with the ability to challenge existing interpretations and to be used in conjunction with the traditional resources available to them.

For the sixth form student working on a HiDES package there are a number of obvious attractions. Most feel they are involved in a real historical debate, using a range of interesting, varied and often unfamiliar resources within a carefully conceived structure. There is a feeling of genuine dialogue between author and students, one which motivates and absorbs the students as they participate at their own pace. There is the feeling of satisfaction that the sources have been read, the questions answered, the responses immediately interpreted and useful supplementary explanation offered. Not only do the packages allow for thorough and directed preparation prior to a seminar, tutorial or lesson, they also present opportunities for group work in which students can collaborate to combine their NOTEPAD responses. This sharpens their thinking, helps them articulate their ideas to others and encourages them to phrase their answers more precisely knowing that there will be an immediate response from the computer. It also 'frees' the teacher to give individual attention to particular students who are perhaps not working on a HiDES package at that time.

With thoughtful structuring of the package the author can seriously address the issue of progression. Students' understanding, whether of a historical debate, a particularly significant document or a problematic incident, is deepened in many ways. Obviously there is no substitute for a close reading of the sources (which include coloured posters, maps, and graphs rarely found in textbooks), especially when the package can quickly ascertain whether the students have grasped the main issues. But HiDES is far more than the computer redirecting the students' reading until they come up with the anticipated answer. For one of the central tenets of HiDES is that it should open up, rather than converge, the debate. Students could, for example, decide to challenge some of the author's assumptions by carrying out their own research, perhaps from other sources, but also from within the body of the package. Use of the concordance facility allows the sort of rapid search for keywords which would be totally impossible in the classroom.

Students can thereby develop and test their own hypotheses, bringing a freshness to their studies and arguably a sharper intellectual cutting edge to the discussion with their tutor. They are taking part in a debate that they in a sense have initiated and are thus far more likely to understand what it means to think historically.

The quality of the package depends on skilfully setting up the enquiry, on the judicious selection of sources and on the use of carefully structured, progressively more demanding questions (refer to the Appendix). For the sixth form students, however, even greater store is put by their ability to learn, not only from the experience of the enquiry, but also from having their answers constantly monitored and evaluated. It is this individual attention that is so highly prized and hitherto so difficult to achieve.

Appendix

A copy of selections from the draft HiDES Question file for the prototype "Hitler's accession to power, a study of historical enquiry and explanation" is attached. Space restrictions preclude the inclusion of the complete question file but it is hoped that the selection will provide readers with a flavour of the package.

HITLER'S ACCESSION TO POWER: A STUDY OF HISTORICAL ENQUIRY AND EXPLANATION

General Introduction

This is intended as an introductory programme to Hitler's "Third Reich". You are presented with an historical event, Hitler becoming Chancellor of Germany in January 1933. You are then asked to explain why this happened placing it within its wider historical context.

- You are encouraged to think historically about problems in the past.
- Your historical understanding is promoted by presenting you with four hypotheses put forward by historians to explain the event.
- You are provided with evidence, both visual and written to analyse the historical 'correctness' of each hypothesis. You then report back with your conclusions.
- Through your study of this historical event you are encouraged not only to acquire an understanding of the past, but also an appreciation of the method by which you attain historical knowledge, which requires recognition that:
- All historical writing is in the end an historian's interpretation of the past and this means that it can never be completely unbiased. It contains a subjective element and historians disagree with one another. The Dutch historian, P. Geyl, has said that "History is an argument without end": no agreed or final version is possible.
- Historical interpretation changes in relation to the historian's own standpoint in time and place.
- Sources are used selectively by historians to support an interpretation.

The package contains an extensive GLOSSARY which covers all the main events and personalities referred to and also a CHRONOLOGY of the events covering the period 1929 to 1933 to help you. You can access these files GLOSSARY.HDC and

CHRONOL.HDC from HiDES SCROLL. There is a Block chart which can be accessed from PICTURES (BLCHART.SH~) which offers you an overview of the different activities involved in studying your HiDES Package.

It would be helpful if you had pen and paper to hand to jot down points as you read through the documents. When you come to answer the questions in the HITLER.HQS file there are instructions to help you view the relevant document or section of it with the appropriate question and also help on accessing and using the notepad. [You can also refer to the HiDES Workbook [Lessons 9–12] for help on using the notepad] When comparing your "NOTEPADS" with the response, you will be given some "feedback" information to re-enforce the points under discussion.

(At this point the program contains a list of books which might prove helpful in the study and a Preamble which gives background information on Hitler's accession to power).

Instruction

Go to "SCROLL" and Select 'TEXT-A.HDC' and read 'Document 1'.

Repeat this for TEXT-B, TEXT-C and TEXT-D.

These 4 documents summarise the essentials of the debate on why Hitler became chancellor on 30 January 1933.

Read each document carefully to find the key phrase which summarises the explanation associated with each document cited.

QUESTION 1

How have the 4 commentators referred to in these documents sought to explain Hitler's success in January 1933?

Quote the key phrase(s) to support your answer.

Go to NOTEPAD 1 and enter your answer.

Ask the system to analyse your response.

Instruction

Go to "SCROLL" and refresh your reading of 'TEXT-A'

Document 1 in the HDC file.

Read very carefully Waite's summary of the arguments used by Shirer to support his interpretation of Hitler's success.

QUESTION 2

Examine Waite's summary of the interpretation offered by Shirer. What evidence did Shirer draw upon to reach his conclusion?

Go to NOTEPAD 2 and enter your answer.

Ask the system to analyse your response.

Instruction

Go to "SCROLL", select the HDC file 'TEXT-A'.

Read very carefully the documents 2, 3 and 4 by Grunberger, W. Carr and K.D. Bracher respectively. You are urged to explore the evidence provided in each of these 3 documents cited in the HDC file, which support the views put forward by Shirer, that the forces in Germany hostile to democracy and favourable to National Socialism had deep historical roots. You should quote keywords/phrases from each of the 3 historians which seem to you to support the views expressed by W. Shirer. Quote these in your answer and acknowledge the historian — linking them with Shirer's views. Refer to 'GLOSSARY.HDC' in SCROLL and read the 'WEIMAR CONSTITUTION' for help on features of the Constitution referred to in the texts by W. Carr and K.D. Bracher.

QUESTION 3a

To what extent do these documents support Shirer's view that influences were present in German history which were hostile to democracy and made the failure of the Weimar Republic inevitable?

Go to NOTEPAD 3 and enter your answer.

Ask the system to analyse your response.

QUESTION 3b

Were there any forces in German history referred to in the 3 documents which were not identified by Shirer?

Go to NOTEPAD 4 and enter your answer.

Ask the system to analyse your response.

Chapter 25

The Sygap Package: Its Application in the Practice and Teaching of Historical Demography

Alain Bideau and Guy Brunet

Introduction

Sygap is an original development resulting from research in historical demography undertaken in parallel in France and Quebec. During the 1970s the Programme de Recherche en Demographie Historique (PRDH) of the University of Montreal undertook an exhaustive analysis of parish registers and vital registration data in the province of Quebec extending from the 17th century up to 1850. In this research several hundred thousand birth, marriage, and death records were compiled, interlinked and controlled in order to reconstitute the population. This could only be done with the help of computers. PRDH was a pioneer in using computers, which, at the time, required a large investment of resources (Desjardins *et al.*, 1977; Beauchamp *et al.*, 1977).

The Research Group set up in Lyon at the end of the 1970s to study Rendu-Osler disease contained both historical demographers and medical geneticists (Bideau *et al.*, 1979). This hereditary disease was remarkably widespread in a limited geographical area. To study its transmission, it was necessary to obtain as complete as possible a genealogy of those affected by the disease (about five per cent of the population in the region studied) (Bideau *et al.*, 1989b). This was done by an exhaustive study of parish registers and vital registration data, in which the methods first introduced by Louis Henry were used (Fleury and Henry, 1965). In this region, where homonymy was common, the study of genealogies required complex analyses of kinship and consanguinity, and this, in turn, required the use of computers.

The two teams, therefore, agreed to collaborate in creating an original package which would make it possible to calculate the usual demographic parameters (life tables, fertility rates, distributions of age at marriage, etc.), as well as to construct biographies and genealogies, both in the ascending and descending line. With the development of microcomputers it became possible for most of the research teams to use this software. It was also decided to convert a set of programs which had been developed at the University of Montreal on its main CYBER computer for use on microcomputers (Desjardins, 1985; Bideau *et al.*, 1989a).

Operating Principles of Sygap

Main Features

The main feature that distinguishes Sygap from other programs developed for de-mographic analysis (Hainsworth and Bardet, 1981; Leboutte *et al.*, 1987) is its ability to study kinship links between individuals. This requires a population reg-ister which contains 'family files', reconstituted in accordance with the principles elaborated by L. Henry (Fleury and Henry, 1965). Every individual who appears in the vital registers as subject, spouse of a subject, or kin to a subject is given a bio-graphical entry. This entry is linked to information available for other individuals to whom the subject is related. The entire information in the data base is designed to be available to the researcher on demand, irrespective of whether a reconsti-tuted biography or an ascending genealogy is required.

The population register consists of a set of files which are logically interrelated. Two files assure the consistency of the system. One is the dictionary of variables, and the other the file of parameters. Two other files contain the data, a file of indi-viduals and a file of unions, with their associated index files.

The Individual File

This contains two types of information: genealogical links between individuals and the variables that characterise each of them. Each individual is given a unique code number which makes it possible to identify him or her unambiguously. The code is designed by the user, but its unique nature is part of the design of the system. Thus, the minimum structure of the individual files is:

IDI	N*6	Individual identification code;
SEXE	C*1	Sex ('F', 'M' or 'X');
NOMINATIF	C*30	Individual surname;
DATEN	D	Date of Birth;
XDATEN	C*2	Flag to show source and reliability of date of birth;
LIEUN	C*3	Code for Place of Birth;
DATED	D	Date of Death;
XDATED	C*2	Flag to show source and reliability of date of death;
LIEUD	C*3	Code for Place of Death
PERE	N*6	Identification code of individual's father
MERE	N*6	Identification code of individual's mother
CNGCOEFF	N*9	Coefficient of Consanguinity

('C' Character; 'N' Number; 'D' Date).

The variables XDATEN and XDATED are flags which enable the user to locate the source of the data and the accuracy of the dates of birth and of death. Note that (depending on the specific needs of the research) it is always possible to add fur-ther variables. Such variables will not be recognised by Sygap but can be treated by dBase.

Union Files

These complement the individual files by noting the matrimonial links that exist between individuals. They contain descriptive variables about each union (date, place, etc.). Each union is identified by a unique code number, which is controlled by the system. The system refuses to acknowledge any union in which the male is aged less than 15 years, or the female aged less than 12 years. No individual can be married to more than one living person at the same time. These parameters can be varied by the user, for instance, in societies in which divorce or polygyny is practised. The structure of the union file is as follows:

Union	N*6	Number of Union;
Homme	N*6	Husband's Identification Number;
Femme	N*6	Wife's Identification Number;
DATEM	D	Date of Marriage;
XDATEN	C*2	Flag to show source and reliability of date of marriage;
LIEUM	C*3	Code for Place of Marriage;
DATEFU	D	Date of Dissolution of Union;
XDATEFU	C*2	Flag to show source and reliability of date of dissolution of union;
ENFILL	N*2	Number of Children born before Marriage;
ENFPRENUP	N*2	Prenuptial conception.

('C' character; 'N' Number; 'D' Date).

The variables XDATEM and XDATEFU are flags which enable the user to locate the source of the data and the accuracy of the date of marriage and the date of dissolution of the union respectively. As in the case of individual files, the user can add other relevant social variables specific to the research.

Management of the Population Register

The system operates interactively. The user is faced with a menu and must select the option that corresponds to the required function. The principal menu contains five options: each with several sub-menus. The five main options are:

- 'individual' to consult an individual file, modify some of the characteristics in it, suppress it, or use it to create new files. The system then proposes a data entry form for the information relating to the new individual.
- 'union' the same options as above are offered for union files.
- 'consult' four possibilities are offered: to consult the ascending genealogy of an individual, his or her descending genealogy, his or her biography, or his or her union file(s).
- 'list individuals': to consult the list of individuals who make up the register which is given in alphabetical or numerical order.
- 'list unions:' the same possibilities as above (alphabetical or numerical listing) for unions.

Genealogical, Demographic or Genetic Calculation with Sygap

Five Modules of Analysis

In addition to the system of managing the population register as described above, Sygap suggests a set of modules which make demographic analysis possible, and also establish genetic parameters which relate to the population studied. Each of these modules functions with an interactive menu. The default calculation is undertaken on the total database. The user can create sub-files which make it possible to isolate some groups of individuals or unions (for example, unions which occurred between certain dates in a given place). These selections are necessarily made through the intermediary of dBase. The calculations provide the essential demographic parameters, as defined by Henry (Henry and Blum, 1988), but we cannot pretend that they will provide all parameters which particular researchers may require!

The list of available options is as follows:

Fertility

- Corrected legitimate fertility rates.
- Fertility rates for ever fertile women.
- Interval between marriage and first birth, and between births of different orders.
- Proportion of illegitimate births.
- Frequency of prenuptial births.
- Distributions of twin confinements by age of mother.
- Distribution of unions by type (MF, MO, EF, EO)[1].
- Mean age of mother at last birth.
- Parity progression ratios by size of family.
- Seasonal movements in conceptions or births.
- Sex ratio at birth.

Nuptiality

- Nuptiality tables for single persons.
- Mean age of spouses at marriage.
- Marital status of parties at marriage.
- Ages of spouses in combination.

---

[1] MF: Date of Marriage and Date of End of Union known;
MO: Date of Marriage known. Date of End of Union not known;
EF: Date of Marriage not known. Date of End of Union known;
EO: Date of Marriage and Date of End of Union not known.

- Frequency of remarriage by age at widowhood.
- Measures of the duration of the union.
- Sex of surviving spouse by age difference between spouses.
- Monthly marriages.

Mortality

- Calculation of minimum and maximum life tables (0–99 years).
- Calculation of minimum and maximum life tables for adults (10–99 years)[2].
- Marital status at death.
- Monthly deaths.

Various

- Compilation of births, marriages and deaths for particular periods.
- Model census at date X and distribution of living individuals by five-year sex and age groups.

Genealogical and Genetic Analysis

This more original module is based on a statistical analysis of the data provided by ascending genealogies. The analysis can relate to the genealogy of a single individual or to that of a much larger group. At the individual level the ascending genealogy as reconstituted by Sygap illustrates the addition of an individual into a given population. Thus, the model can provide a listing of all of an individual's ancestors in each generation. At the group level, the coefficient of consanguinity shows the degree to which a population is open to migration, exogamy, etc., as well as its structure, by comparing different groups of individuals. The kinship coefficient makes it possible to measure the frequency of exchanges between different groups of the population over a number of generations. These are the most commonly used indices in population genetics at present. The genetic analysis module depends on four specific calculations:

- Compilation of ascending genealogies.
- Description of an individual's ascending genealogy.
- Calculation of coefficients of consanguinity.
- Calculation of kinship coefficients.

---

[2]   In the 'minimum mortality' life table it is assumed that all individuals whose fate is unknown survive; in the 'maximum mortality' life table it is assumed that such individuals die immediately after the last date when they were mentioned as being alive.

Sygap and its Users

Research

The two research teams which compiled the program were naturally its first users. Before the program was published, it was tested on smaller files, constructed by students. Many others have subsequently adopted Sygap, among them are students (Prost, 1993), or teams of researchers in historical demography, e.g. the team at the Department of History of the Federal University of Parana at Curitiba, Brazil. A translation of the manual into Portuguese and English is envisaged.

Users of the program can obtain a description of the demographic regime of the populations they study within a few minutes; in addition its value lies in its ability to produce data bases with common standards, which can be used in parallel enquiries. Specific programs can be developed which depend on several data bases. The need to produce special algorithms and programs is therefore much reduced, and researchers can have a guarantee that their data will have been produced in the same manner. For instance, we are at present engaged in a comparative study on population renewal in two specific mountain sites (Alps and Jura) over a fairly large number of generations. These two files have been obtained from a study of parish registers and vital registration. Genealogical links have been established by Sygap and common programs in dBase can be used which ensure the production of comparable results.

It is important to remember that in addition to the variables needed for the functioning of the system and which have been described, each user can add more variables that appear useful to him or her. Thus, a researcher who is investigating an ancient population in which there is slavery, or a society in which individuals are distinguished on the basis of their colour or ethnic origin (e.g. Brazil during the 18th century) could introduce a new 'status' or 'ethnic' variable. Though these variables will not be recognised by Sygap, they will be taken into account by dBase and could be used to extract information from files. Sygap therefore has, from its very beginning, been a flexible system which can be modified by its users to meet their specific needs. Historical demographers will find Sygap helpful in organising their data which can extend the calculation proposed for 'union' and 'individual' files in dBase and various other statistical packages (for example, SPSS, STATGRAF or SURPASS). Specialists in other disciplines (sociologists, economists, or anthropologists) can use Sygap to establish the principal parameters which characterise the demographic regime of the populations they are studying, without having to perform the calculations themselves.

Teaching

To learn the basic calculations in historical demography is often a long and difficult process for students, because of the large number of data that need to be treated. Sometimes the student cannot reconcile the different calculations explained by the teacher on data from published sources, given the very limited experience of performing the calculations that students can obtain during their course.

We shall only give one concrete example of the educational possibilities offered by Sygap: the calculation of corrected legitimate fertility rates. Once the method has been explained by the teacher, it is possible to use Sygap to start the procedures on data which have been compiled by the students themselves. For example, in a class of 40 students, each can enter data relating to 10 families. The total calculation for 400 families gives a sufficient number, and will show in succession:

- apparent fertility rates.
- births by age at marriage of mother.
- births that have not been registered in the registers of baptisms, but which have later been found when the child in question either dies or marries.
- births that have not been registered, and which have not been found later. Their number has been estimated by a applying a correction factor.
- sum of the two previous categories.
- woman-years.
- and finally corrected fertility rates, that take account of all births.

Thus Sygap can produce on the computer screen during the teaching period all the calculations that the teacher can explain and gradually develop. He is relieved of the task of having to write the calculations on the blackboard at each stage. This is true for most of the calculations produced by Sygap.

Genealogy

Sygap is of interest to genealogists outside the university system, as it traces family lines. There are a plethora of different software packages in genealogy, but few can deal with so large a volume of data. Moreover, Sygap offers the possibility of going beyond the establishment of family genealogies, and permits analyses of all available genealogical information (number of ascendants, number of founders, completeness of information, number of common ancestors, kinship patterns), together with a description of the genealogical links etc. Studies, such as that on the geographical and social mobility of the French population, based on 3000 families have shown the possibilities of applying quantitative methods to exploit genealogical information (Dupâquier, 1992). We have also recently shown how information from genealogical data can be used to study the evolution and structure of a population (Bideau et al., 1993).

We therefore regard Sygap as a valuable tool, easy to use, responding flexibly to the aspirations of a vast public with different interests: researchers, teachers, and genealogists. Clearly, this means that the version actually proposed will have to be modified and made more complete. Such developments in collaboration with other research teams will bear witness to the value of this package for the whole scientific community.

Chapter 26
IT, ET and Beyond: Rethinking How
Allan Martin

Introduction: Getting Technology in Perspective

Technology is often presented to us amidst an aura of popular mythology. It is presented as something very much of the moment, of today, as a feature of contemporary life which is almost without history. It is presented as amazing, revolutionary, completely changing, in a way that has never occurred before, our way of life. It is presented as being moved forward by the genius of individual inventors, ignoring their historical context to make their breakthrough. It is presented as universally beneficial. As the only authentic value in a faithless age. In all these there is some truth and much untruth.

In fact technology is very old. No one who has seen it can forget the scene in Stanley Kubrick's film *2001* when ape becomes ape-man, when animal becomes tool-user. This represents powerfully the birth of technology. And technology has been with man throughout his prehistory and his history. It is part of the human condition. As humans, we are wielders of technology.

In that prehistory and that history, technolological "revolutions" are not uncommon. A selection of revolutionary breakthroughs, developments which made the human world in some essential way a different place, are shown in Figure 26.1 below. There are probably plenty of others that readers can think of. Our technological environment constantly changes, and the "revolutions" may be processes that occurred over periods of many years, with much trial and error and argument.

Those revolutions in Figure 26.1 are some of the successful ones. But technological failures are also common. Plenty of inventions just didn't catch on, or were even shown to be unsound, sometimes only after repeated failures. Think of the number of people who tried to fly by flapping a pair of wings and jumping off a cliff. Others didn't happen at the right time, and the material or cultural context wasn't right for them to be exploited. Consider Hero of Alexandria's steam device, and Charles Babbage's computing engines. Even the typewriter, listed as revolutionary above, didn't take off very quickly, and the earliest producers went bankrupt because people couldn't see much of a point in it.

Technological advances are culturally constrained, and depend upon contextualisations made by people, especially those with resources to dispose of. Thus the typewriter was originally conceived as a sort of do-it-yourself printing kit to do one-off handbills and such, and typewritten text was initially perceived as inferior to the handwritten word. It was only when it was seen to be able to

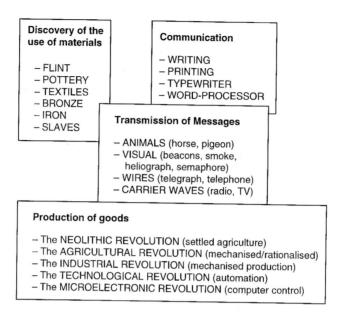

Figure 26.1   Technological Revolutions in History

automate the process of letter-writing, so that only a signature could validate many texts, even created simultaneously, that its potential was opened up and sales took off. But it needed (and helped to create) a perception that the typed word is more official, more part of the due process of interaction in a bureaucratic society, than handwritten notes. By contrast, the telephone took off almost immediately, since people could perceive it as a long-awaited extension of the notion of the telegraph — the ability to transmit voice instead of just beeps and buzzes.

Technological advances are striven for; they very rarely pop up by accident. Investment of funds, from a wealthy patron desirous of the reflected prestige, a government keen for political advantage, or a company intent on keeping its products competitive and hoping to get one step ahead of the competition, is what often makes possible the experimentation, the building and rebuilding, the trial and error that surrounds the emergence of a new technology. Sadly, technological advance is often stimulated by greed and ambition. The perception of potential sales can be more important than the real utility of the object (if one can speak of "real" utility; is utility only found in the eye of the beholder?); the potential for destruction more important than any benefits to humanity.

Technology perpetuates inequality. Technology is sometimes made out to be a leveller, enabling all to benefit. Yet in practice each new technology creates a new social division, between those who have it and those who do not. Possession becomes a source of real power, the access to the functionalities which the technology provides, as well as of symbolic power, the outward demonstration of the wealth to buy it or the political power to have access to it. Even as a technology diffuses further through society, there will remain an expensive leading edge granting access to only a few.

Technology can thus be beneficial, or it can be dangerous. But above all, it is seductive. We are encouraged to believe, to make an act of commitment. Having invested, or bought, commitment is enticing, relieving, liberating. Like lovers, we see only the picture in our mind's eye. And like seduction, it veils the issues of morality that surround it, the choices about the uses of people and things which our actions necessarily involve, whether we perceive them or not.

I've avoided mentioning computers or IT (information technology) in this section, because it's easy to think of the computer as something that's unique, and very special to our age. And it is, up to a point. But it's also just another bit of technology, which we can place in a context that goes back to our dawning.

Technology in Education

Let's now consider how technology has contributed to the development of the process of education. The medium of communication of knowledge and technique has varied over time and place: oral transmission, handwriting, printing, radio, etc. Note that each new development has added to the choice of medium available, rather than casting all the others into oblivion. Oral transmission, whether accompanied by demonstration or not, is still the most widely used and effective mode of interaction between teacher and learner. The range of materials available has increased too: sand, slate, stone, clay, wax, pottery, animal skin, paper, chisel, brush, pencil, steel-nibbed pen, and so on.

The issues that surround education have however remained largely unchanged. A key set of issues is economic: what are the resources available to the educational process, and how are they to be distributed? Another set is ideological: what is suitable to be learned, and who is suitable to learn? Remember that education is about the tranmission of culture including justifications of the status quo.

We can consider the way in which all the revolutions which affected the whole of society have impacted upon education. But there have been, too, breakthroughs in the field of education. Think of the effect of cheap paper and pencils, which allowed writing to be individualised and stored — each pupil could own his/her own products in their own jotter. Systems have been breakthroughs too: the "monitorial" system enabled a single teacher to transmit to a very large number of pupils, effecting a fashioning of education on an industrial model (we are not discussing here the quality of the product).

Modern Resource Technology "Breakthroughs"

A number of "revolutions" in educational technology have been hailed in the last forty years. However, in hindsight we can see that such "breakthroughs" have proved to be valuable in a more limited range of circumstances than was first thought.

Educational television has certainly been able to bring graphic audiovisual images before pupils. However, TV is essentially a passive medium; communication is one-way and there is no interaction with the viewer. The television is essentially a substitute for the traditional dominant teacher, and to develop interactive work, the teacher must make the same effort as she would with traditional visual aids. Handling TV may in fact be more difficult, in that the images shown, or the voice which accompanies them, may speak with the resonance of authority, rendering critical consideration of the content more difficult.

Programmed learning was seen by its supporters as a means of truly individualising learning and making it active. However the crude behaviourist model underlying the "teaching machines" focused on a fixed and limited number of paths of correctness through the material. The quality of interaction between pupil and "teacher" was very poor, particularly as the machines did not have the ability to form any sort of model of the learner, and therefore to respond to genuinely individual learning situations. In its focus on the individual, programmed learning also precluded pupil-pupil interaction, and even made the role of the human teacher problematic. The enterprise was undermined further by the creakiness of the technology used to implement it — handles to wind backwards and forwards and flaps to open and shut. The teaching machine was rather obviously a box containing a textbook on a strip of paper.

Many of the same points might be made about *language laboratories*, which were claimed to revolutionise language teaching — they were individualised, removing the interactive aspect of langauge that is at its heart; they offered little or no response to the learner, with no address to the learner's particular situation unless the teacher happened to be listening in. Those who have used, or rather suffered, language laboratories, will know that the material is often endlessly repetitive, and that the experience is tedious and uninvolving.

Coming closer to home, *simulation-games* were championed in the seventies as a way of involving pupils in the experience of historical decision-making. But in the classroom they were never as successful as their proponents made out, and never took off as a tool to be drawn on by every history teacher. The problem again was creaky technology, the teacher fumbling with packs of cards and laying out little tokens on a board or selecting the right bits of paper to hand out to each team. In a sense, the mechanism was too visible, down to the throwing of dice to determine which way way the wind will blow or whether the public will use a particular train. All this required the suspension of disbelief to be a major act of commitment. And what happened when there was not enough time in a single lesson, and the current situation needed to saved for next week — where can you put a flat board with all those little pieces on it so they will remain unjolted for a week?

It is easy to dismiss developments which patently failed to live up to the hype. But in suitable if perhaps limited circumstances, each of the items considered above can be used successfully as an aid to learning. It is worth drawing attention to a common problem with innovation in educational technology — this is the problem of "creaky technology": an imaginative idea is developed, but is implemented using using such a crude technology that it is unable to deliver the experience which the originators of the idea had envisaged. There are other factors which make implementation more complicated than it might have been:

• The timetable, in most secondary schools at least, is organised in small chunks of time, making it very difficult for any activity which requires complicated setting up, and needs to be run over a long period. This is particularly problematic in a subject like history where lessons may only occur once a week for any class.

- Another problem which particularly affects history is that syllabuses are crammed with content, so that activities which dwell for some weeks on a particular issue or event may be seen as an impossible allocation of time if the syllabus is to be completed.
- A more general difficulty is that of teacher resistance to innovation: anything too different from traditional practice may be regarded as suspect, and even if used, teacher commitment to its success may be lacking.
- Many innovations fall victim to their own publicity: over-hyped ideas arouse excessive expectations, which leave users disappointed and disillusioned when they cannot be met; and simplicity and ease of use may be exaggerated, leading to negative reactions when teachers find that using a new method or a new piece of teaching material takes more time and effort than doing things the way they have always done them.
- Innovation becomes bolted to personal careers, in schools and more widely. Views of the innovation then become tangled with opinions about the people who support them.
- Resources are usually insufficient to realise the potential of innovation: insufficiently refined or untested versions may be released, and research on the full educational effects and implications is replaced by a "let the users find out" approach, which can have very negative results.

The point about all this is that we have to be very cautious about the claims made for any educational innovation. Inflated claims do not guarantee that a new teaching tool will be any use to teachers or to learners.

What does IT Achieve?

We must therefore be cautious in asking what IT offers the history teacher, and we must be prepared to offer qualifications to we do say. So far, it seems that the use of appropriate IT applications can offer:

- A high level of interaction, between student and computer (by contrast with the teaching machine), between student and student (by contrast between teaching machines and language laboratories, and between student and teacher.
- Flexibility: computer programs can offer a variety of responses far in excess of the teaching machine and a variety of stimuli beyod the range of most other media.
- The speed and the sophistication of responses overcomes "creaky technology syndrome": and allow users to focus on what the the application can do rather than how it works.
- Multi-functionality: using IT, one can do a lot of different jobs, often all at the same time. Often data can be straightforwardly transferred between one application and another.
- Sharability: IT facilities can be used by groups as well as individuals, and even dispersed groups can share ideas and products. The spread of networks has made this aspect increasingly important.

But for all of these advantages to be reaped as an enhanced accrual of learning, it is essential that adequate resources are available, that adequate training is provided, and that preparation and IT use in the classroom is supported by technical and auxiliary personnel.

The effect of developments in IT has been to offer teachers the opportunity to reconsider the way teaching is done, although I will immediately qualify this by saying that IT is not the only catalyst of this process. Using IT applications, learning can be:

- Active rather than passive.
- Co-operative/interactive rather than individually-focussed, allowing interaction between pupils in group-based situations.
- Dialogue-based (pupil-teacher interaction) rather than monologue-based.
- Resource-based rather than product-based.
- Pupil-focused rather than teacher-focused.
- Pupil-rather than teacher-controlled/managed.
- Focused on the teacher as manager/facilitator/adviser rather than controller.
- Focused on pupil/student as client rather than subject.

IT can also enable activities to take place which would not previously have been considered possible. Here are some examples which readers may already have encountered:

- Swift interrogation of large or very large bodies of data.
- Rapid generation of graphic presentations.
- Compilation of networked data collections from disparate and distant sources.
- Ongoing reworking of text.
- Manipulation of graphic images.
- Rapid statistical analysis.
- Creation of "publishable-quality" pages of text and graphics.
- Rapid transmission of text and graphics.

This section has been a necessarily very cursory resumé of some of the positive points made with regard to IT in the classroom. But it seems clear that the claims made for IT which can be substantiated do suggest that IT should have a significant impact on educational practice. It does offer the possibility of teaching in a new and different way. Of course, IT can also be used in very traditional ways too. The notion of the "electronic blackboard" suggests a way in which IT can be used in support of the traditional lecturing situation, and graphical presentation packages form one of the most popular forms of software on the market.

History Teaching and IT: Possibilities

In history the use of IT has enabled teachers not only to do what they have always done more effectively, but also to reconsider how history as such may be taught and learned.

One of the major opportunities which IT developments have offered to the history teacher are the possibilities for interrogation of databases, and statistical manipulation and graphical presentation of the data. Questions can now be asked of bodies of data which would not previously have been feasible due to time constraints and creaky technology. Examples in this collection are David Martin's work with ships of the Armada, and Peter Hillis' *Moving House* package. Analysis of census data, formerly a tedious and time-consuming task, can now be an enthralling activity because students can focus on asking and seeking the answers to historical questions rather than spending most of their time on the mechanics of manual searches.

The use of IT facilities has also however made available to the teacher data in quantity and in range of forms (including text, graphics and film) hitherto only obtained with great difficulty or cost. CD-ROM storage possibilities and the use of the Internet are important factors in this development. The CD-ROM has enabled large bodies of information to be available in the ordinary history classroom; even with just one computer such a resource can be effectively used by a whole class. And the Internet not only allows students and faculty to exchange data with colleagues in many parts of the world, but also to search through and to obtain what is relevant amongst the truly vast quantity of data available through the World Wide Web.

Hypertext systems have made it possible to structure large bodies of data in a form in which they can be used effectively by students. Having vast data resources at one's disposal does not mean that they will be necessarily well-used, and it is therefore valuable to be aware of collections in which related data has been well structured and presented. Robin McLachlan and John Messing's *Gallipoli* collection forms an excellent example. But hypertext also forms a tool which students themselves can use to structure data, and in structuring it to strive towards an understanding of the significance of particular items and their relationships to each other. Data can be assembled from a variety of sources, including primary data collected by students themselves, as texts, tables, images, sound or even snatches of video. The Canton Project, described elsewhere in this volume, forms an excellent example of what can be produced. The collection and structuring of the dataset forms a valuable learning experience for students, and the finished dataset becomes a new resource for the classroom, which may be used, or amended and expanded by other students. Setting up such collections is an excellent way of making productive use of the enormous volume of historical data that is available in students' own localities and indeed within their own families.

In contrast to the crude monolinear question and answer of the teaching machines, interactive dialogue on historical questions can be supported. The HiDES Project, described separately by Jane Jenkins and Frank Colson, shows what is possible. We should remember however that the sort of dialogue which can be developed is not a dialogue with a human teacher, but with a programmed system. Such a system can call for response and possesses a number of preprogrammed strategies for making its own response, which can include the system acquiring new knowledge. In this way it can be a valuable stimulus to student thinking. But it is not thereby a replacement for a good teacher, whose ability to comment upon students' output and suggest ways forward will be much more flexible than that of the computer, and, if the teacher knows her class, more directed towards the needs of the particular student.

The employment of IT has enabled simulations to become feasible as classroom exercises. Computer support, in speeding up the supply of responses to actions, in performing ongoing calculations and in generally managing all the bits and pieces that previously had to be managed on bits of paper, cards and tokens, enables students to engage in a simulation run and to consider the experience rather than being distracted by the management of the event. The fact that the model underlying the simulation is part of a program means that the model too can be manipulated and variables changed more easily than with many manual simulations. A simulation is not a simple application, and there has been much debate over the value of simulations for historical learning; but this debate has only been stimulated because of the very popularity of simulations among computer-using history teachers. In fact, all that we do as history teachers is subject to the caveat that, as Alaric Dickinson reminds us, the nature of learning in history is still very little understood.

We should finally not forget that, using everyday generic computer applications — the word-processor, database, spreadsheet, and drawing program — pupils can carry out many valuable historical learning activities. Writing accounts or dramatisations of historical events or discussions of historical questions, recording research on particular epochs or cultures, assembling collections of texts, lists, and pictures, creating presentations to be delivered to fellow students, creation and reworking of pupils' accounts of and researches into historical epochs, preparing wall-displays, posters, portfolios of material or historical magazines — all of these activities are possible using a very limited set of common software. Specialist historical programs are not always necessary.

Ways Forward

The chapters in this volume show that IT has a role in the teaching of history. But the consideration of what IT can offer can permit realistic rethinking to be done about educational technology as such, that is, the way in which educational activity is structured as a dynamic and interactive system of resources and processes. Changes in the learning situation which IT allows need to be adopted more widely in history teaching generally. This entails firstly breaking down the schizophrenic attitude which compartmentalises IT and non-IT activities, so that IT use becomes an everyday and taken-for-granted part of work in history classrooms, rather than being presented as a special treat offered in addition to the "normal work". This will not be easy because it has still to happen in most curricular areas in most schools, not just history. Using the computer is still perceived by most pupils and most teachers as a special activity, and any computer-involved activity seems to have a positive motivational effect. A corollary of integrating IT use into normal classroom activities is that IT provision needs to be integrated into whole resource provision for teaching and learning. Too often computers are seen as special objects lying outwith normal funding arrangements, and are purchased from special grants, or money realised through Parent Teacher Association fund-raising events, or even by collecting vouchers from a particular supermarket chain. The attitiudes of teachers are important here and even in the British Isles we are still far from a situation in which all or even most history teachers readily embrace IT. In contrast to the rosy picture presented by government statistics (a good demonstration of what can be achieved through "cosmetic statistics"), the situation in the classroom is much more tentative, with regular IT use still dependent on the presence of enthusiastic individuals.

The second aspect of this process is to extend to the teaching process gains which seem to have been achieved with IT, set out earlier in this chapter, into other teaching/learning situations. It would be churlish to say that this is not happening already, and not to admit that teaching process advances made with IT have been themselves stimulated by the changes in the methodology of hsitory teaching which have been going on over the past twenty years. But the interactions are mutual, and experience with IT can now be a stimulus for more general methodological advance.

Finally, can we move "beyond How" by asking whether the use of IT enables a move beyond *how* we teach to *what* we teach, a reconceptualisation of what we mean by teaching history (not just the teaching but the history as well). Current resources enable activities to be performed which were not possible in pre-IT era — the interrogation of large databases, simulations, on-line data searches. But do the activities made possible by IT have implications for what we mean by "teaching history", i.e. What sorts of activities are legitimate for the history classroom? We can now ask students to carry out activities which twenty years ago would have been inconceivable for either school pupils or undergraduates. IT has undoubtedly played a major part in making it possible for school pupils and undergraduates to do the sorts of things which previously only historians could do.

Conclusion

In looking both at the history of technology and our use of technology in history, we must be conscious of the danger of misapprehension of technology. It is easy to regard technology as a force which exists independently of people, which determines events, which is always beneficent, and which has nothing to do with morality. But, as indicated at the beginning of this chapter, we have to recognise that the nature and the effect of technology depends on what people do with it. Technology is culturally shaped: it is what we make it. And development and use carries a moral responsibility: we make conscious choices about it. We cannot say that "we are only scientists" or "we are only users".

These points are especially relevant here as history and technology are both "hot" cultural products. They are both influential areas of culture with high public profiles. As such both will be subject to close political manipulation and control. Through national curricula in history governments attempt to shape the way chidren are inducted into their past; through technology policies they attempt to present themselves as responsive to political needs (which may not even overlap with educational needs). In both areas the majority of us who are not in government may have to work hard to influence the public debate and policy-making in both areas. On the other hand, both history and technology offer ways to change society, history by offering models of change and of the alternatives available, technology by providing means by which changes can be effected and by which alternative situations can be sustained. But it is the actions of individuals and groups which bring about change, and which determine the direction which changes take. History and technology are ours to reflect upon, to comment upon, to make and to remake.

Bibliography

Almond, J. and Tomlinson, P. (1990) "Teacher Perceptions of the Microcomputer in the History Classroom" in Martin & Blow, 29–42.

Ashby, R. and Lee, P.J. (1987a) "Children's Concepts of Empathy and Understanding in History" in Portal, 62–88.

Ashby, R. and Lee, P.J. (1987b) "Discussing the Evidence", *Teaching History*, **48**, 13–17.

Avalanche Vol. 2: HyperStacks for Education (1993) Sydney, Apple Computer, Australia (CD-ROM).

Baker, C. (1990) "Keynote Address to the First International Conference on Computers in the History Classroom", in Martin & Blow, 17–28.

Baker, C. and Paterson, I. (1989) "Computers in Secondary School History Teaching: an HMI View", *Teaching History*, No. 54 (January).

Bean, C. (1921) *The Story of Anzac*, Sydney, Angus & Robertson.

Beauchamp, P., Charbonneau, H., Desjardins, B. and Legare, J. (1977) "La Reconstitution Automatique des Families: un Fait Acquis", *Population*, 32, (special issue): 375–400.

Beetsma, J. and Beetsma, Y. (1990) "Development and Evaluation of Computer-Aided Case-Studies" in Martin & Blow, 201–210.

Bennett, S. (1990) *Rewriting History*, Coventry, NCET.

Benton, P. (Ed.) (1990) *The Oxford Internship Scheme: Integration and Partnership in Initial Teacher Education*, Gulbenkian Foundation.

Bideau, A., Plauchu, H. and Jacquard, A. (1979) "Démographie Historique et Génétique de Population: la Concentration Géographique d'une Maladie Héréditaire Rare" *Annales Economie, Sociétés, Civilisations*, **34**, 85–105.

Bideau, A., Desjardins, B., Brunet, G. and Legare, J. (1989a) "Démographi Historique et Génétique de Population. Collaboration franco-québécoise autour de la Constitution de registres de Population." *Population et Cultures*: 9–20.

Bideau, A., Plauchu, H., Brunet, G. and Robert, J.M. (1989b) "Etude épidémiologique de la Maladie de Rendu-Osler en France: Répartition géographique et Prévalence", *Population*, **44**, 9–28.

Bideau, A., Brunet, G., Plauchu, H. and Heyer, E. (1993) Histoíre généalogique ou généalogie historique. Constitution de la population de la vallée de la Valserine in *Mesurer et Comprendre*. Paris, P.U.F.: 33–44.

Bitter, M-E. (1987) "Developments and Perspectives of CAL in the Dutch Humanities Classroom", in Kent & Lewis, 31–38.

Bitter, M-E. (1990) "An Ambitious Approach to In-Service Training on CAL for Dutch History Teachers", in Martin & Blow, 222–231.

Blow, F. and Dickinson, A. (ed.) (1986) *New History and New Technology*, London, The Historical Association.

Blow, F. (1989) *Using Computer Simulations in History*, Coventry, NCET.

Blow, F. (1990) "Computers, Simulation and Empathy", in Martin & Blow, 144–152.

Booth, M. (1990) "National Curriculum History: Interim Report", *Teaching History*, No. 58, (January).

Brewer, W.F. (1987) Schemas versus mental models in human memory in Morris, P. (ed.) *Modelling Cognition*. London. John Wiley & Sons.

Briggs, J.H. (1988) *Learning with Expert Systems*, Hartfield, Advisory Unit for Microtechnology in Education.

Cerman, M. (1990) "Computing and History in Austrian Schools: Concepts and Aims", in Martin & Blow, 57–62.

Copeland, W.D. (1985) "Teaching Students to 'do' History: The Teacher and the Computer in Partnership", *The History Teacher*, 18(2), 189–197.

Copeland, W.D. (1987) "Potentials for Technology in the Pursuit of Knowledge", California Public Schools Forum, 2, 32–47.

Davis, V., Denley, P., Spaeth, D. and Trainor, R. (ed.) (1993) *The Teaching of Historical Computing: an International Framework*, St. Katharinen, Scripta Mercarurae Verlag/Max Planck Institut für Geschichte.

Denley, P. and Hopkin, D. (ed.) (1987) *History and Computing*, Manchester UP.

Denley, P., Fogelvik, S. and Harvey, C. (ed.) (1989) *History and Computing II*, Manchester UP.

Department of Education and Science (1977) *Curriculum 11–16: a Working Paper*, London, HMSO.

Department of Education and Science (1985) *Better Schools*, London, HMSO.

Department of Education and Science (1985) *History in the Primary and Secondary Years: an HMI View*, London, HMSO.

Department of Education and Science (1988) *History from 5 to 16*, London, HMSO.

Department of Education and Science (1989) *National Curriculum History Working Group: Interim Report*, London, HMSO.

Department of Education and Science (1989) *Information Technology in Initial Teacher Training*, (The Trotter Report), London, HMSO.

Department of Education and Science (1989) *Initial Teacher Training: Approval of Courses*, Circular 24/89, London, HMSO.

Department of Education and Science (1990) *National Curriculum History Working Group: Final Report*, London, HMSO.

Department for Education (1993) *Statistical Bulletin 6/93: Survey of Information Technology in Schools*, London, HMSO.

Desjardins, B. (1985) Quelques éléments de l'expérience informatique du PRDH in *Informatique et Prosopographie*, Paris, CNRS: 159–177.

Desjardins, B., Beauchamp, P. and Legare, J. (1977) "Automatic family reconstitution: the French Canadian 17th century experience", *Journal of Family History*, 2, 56–76.

Dicks, B. (1985) "Choice and Restraint: Further Perspectives of Socio-Residential Segregation in the 19th Century Glasgow" in Gordon, G. *Perspectives of the Scottish City*, Aberdeen University Press.

Dickinson, A.K. and Lee, P.J. (1978) "Understanding and Research", in Dickinson and Lee, 90–120.

Dickinson, A.K. and Lee, P.J. (Eds) (1978) *History Teaching and Historical Understanding*, London, Heinemann Educational.

Dickinson, A.K. (1990) "New Technology within Initial Teacher Training" in Martin & Blow, 213–221.

Dickinson, A.K. (1993) "Information Technology in the Process of Teaching and Learning History", in Guerra, 9–38.

Driver, R. and Easley, J. (1978) "Pupils and paradigms: a review of literature related to concept development of adolescent science students", *Studies in Science Education*, **5**, 61–8.

Dupaquier, J. (1992) *La société française au XIX° siècle. Tradition, Transition, Transformations*, Paris, Fayard.

Eder, F. (1989) "EDV im Geschichtsunterricht?" in Fischer, 220–242.

Fischer, G. et al. (1989) *Geordnete Welten*, Vienna, Verlag für Gesellschaftskritik.

Fleury, M. and Henry, L. (1965) *Nouveau manuel de dépouillement et d'exploitation de l'état civil ancien*, Paris, I.N.E.D.

Galpin, B. (1989) *Expert Systems in Primary Schools*, London, British Library, Reseach paper 73.

Goodall, S. (1990) "The Development of the Use of Expert Systems in a Primary Classroom: its Contribution to the National Curriculum" *Modus Newsletter*, No 3.

Government Statistical Service (1993) *Statistical Bulletin*, 6/93, Department for Education, London, February.

Greenstein, D. (1994) *A Historian's Guide to Computing*, Oxford University Press.

Guerra, M. (ed.) (1993) *Història e Informática*, Lisbon, Gulbenkian Foundation.

HABET (1991) "Responses to the Final Report of the History Working Group", *Teaching History*, No. 62, (January) 30–31.

Hainsworth, M. and Bardet, J-P. (1981) *Logiciel CASOAR. Calculs et analyses sur ordinateur appliqués aux reconstitutions*, Paris, S.D.H.

Hassell, D.J. and Webb, M.E. (1990) "Modus: the Integrated Modelling System", *Computers in Education*, **15**, 265–270.

Haydn, T. (1996) "IT in History Classrooms in Britain: Myth and Reality" in Lehners et al.

Henry, L. and Blum, A. (1988) *Techniques d'analyse en Démographie Historique*, Paris, I.N.E.D.

Her Majesty's Inspectorate for Schools (1989) *Curriculum Matters: Information Technology 5–16*, London, HMSO.

Hughes, M. (ed.) (1995) *Teaching and Learning in Changing Times*, Oxford, Blackwell.

Information Technology: A Cross Curricular Theme (1989) Report to the Parliamentary under Secretary of State for Education.

Journal of Computer Assisted Learning, published four times a year by Basil Blackwell Scientific Publications.

Kent, A. and Lewis, R. (ed.) (1987) *Computer-Assisted Learning in the Humanities & Social Sciences*, Oxford Blackwell.

Leboutte, R., Alter, G. and Gutman, M. (1987) "Analysis of Reconstituted Families: a Package of SAS Programs", *Historical Methods*, 20, 29–34.

Lee, P.J., Dickinson, A.K. and Ashby, R. (1995) " 'There were no facts in those days': Children's Ideas about Historical Explanation", in Hughes.

Lehners, J-P., Hendrickx, F. and Werne, A. (eds) (1996) *Proceedings of the Fourth International Conference on Computers in the History Classroom*, Luxembourg, Centre Universitaire de Luxembourg.

Lincoln, Y.S. and Guba, E.G. (1985) *Naturalistic Enquiry*, Newbury Park California, Sage Publications.

McLachlan, R. (1990) "The Australian Biographical Dictionary Database", in Martin & Blow, 63–71.

McLachlan, R. (ed) (1990) *Discovery Gallipoli*, Canberra.

McLachlan, R. and Starick, W. (1991) *Gallipoli 75 The Database*, Adelaide, Satchel Software.

MacLeod, D. (1876) *Norman Macleod*, London, Dalby, Isbister & Company.

Martin, A. (1987) "Computers and Simulation in the Humanities", in Kent & Lewis, 80–86.

Martin, A. (1988) "An Adaptable Microworld for the History Classroom", *Computers & Education*, 12, 169–172.

Martin, A. (1989) "Informationstechnologie und 'New History' an Britischen Schulen", *Beiträge zur Historischen Sozialkunde*, **19**, 7–11.

Martin, A. and Blow, F. (ed.) (1990) *Computers in the History Classroom*, Leeds University Press/CHC Publications.

Martin, A. (ed.) (1992) *Teaching National Curriculum History with IT*, London, The Historical Association, Occasional Paper No. 4, 2nd Ed.

Martin, A. (1992) "Over the Horizon: the Future for IT in the History Classroom", *Teaching History*, No. 69, (October), pp. 34–35.

Martin, A. (1993) "Simulation and the Teaching of History in Schools", in Guerra, 299–325.

Martin, A. (1995) "Portability as a Catalyst for Cross-Curricular IT Permeation", in Tinsley, D.J. and van Weert, T.J. (eds) *World Conference on Computers in Education VI*, London, Chapman & Hall, pp. 645–653.

Martin, A. (1996) "Portable Computers in the History Classroom", in Lehners *et al.*, 43–55.

Martin, C. (1975) *Full Fathom Five*, London, Chatto & Windus.

Martin, C. and Parker, G. (1988) *Spanish Armada*, London, Penguin.

Mawdsley, E. and Munck, T. (1993) *Computing for Historians*, Manchester, University Press.

Messing, J. and McLachlan, R. (1993) *History and Hypermedia: Gallipoli from a New Perspective*, ACEC 93 Australian Computers in Education Conference, Nepean, July, (conference paper).

Muir, J. (1901) Glasgow in 1901. Glasgow: William Hodge.

National Curriculum Council (1990) *Non-Statutory guidance: Information Technology Capability*, York, NCC.

National Curriculum Council (1990) *Core Skills 16–19 (a Response to the Secretary of State)*, York, NCC.

National Curriculum Council (1991) *Information Technology in the National Curriculum*, York, NCC.

Needham, R. (1987) *Teaching Strategies for Developing Understanding in Science*. Children's Learning in Science Project, University of Leeds.

Nichol, J., Briggs, J. and Dean, J. (eds.) (1988) *Prolog, Children and Students*, London, Kogan Page.

O'Shea, T. and Self, J. (1983) *Learning and Teaching with Computers*, Brighton, Harvester Press.

Peacock, M. (1989) *Information Technology in the TVEI Curriculum 14–18*, Sheffield, Training Agency.

Portal, C. (ed.) (1987) *The History Curriculum for Teachers*, Lewes, Falmer Press.

Primary History and Teaching History, published by The Historical Association, 59a Kennington Park Road, London SE11 4JH.

Prost, M. (1993) *L'isolat de la Vallouise. Etude des structures démographique d'une communauté des Alpes Briançonnaises (1540–1851) et essai d'anthropologie physique*, Ph.D. thesis, Paris, E.H.E.S.S.

Robb, J.E. (1983) "Suburb and Slums in Gorbals: Social and Residential Change 1800–1900", in Gordon, G. and Dicks, B. *Scottish Urban History*, Aberdeen, University Press.

Robins, K. and Webster, F. (1989) *The Technical Fix: Education, Computers and History*, London, Macmillan.

Schick, J. (1990) *Teaching History with a Computer*, Chicago, Lyceum Books.

School Examinations and Assessment Council (1990) *Examinations Post-16: Developments for the 1990s*, London, Central Office of Information.

School Examinations and Assessment Council (1993) *Pupils' Work Assessed: Information Technology Capability*, London, SEAC.

Shemilt, D. (1980) *History 13–16 Evaluation Study*, Edinburgh, Holmes McDougall.

Smart, L. (1988) "The Database as a Catalyst", *Journal of Computer Assisted Learning*, **4**, 140–149.

Smart, L. and Parker, C. (ed.) (1992) *Making Links*, Coventry, NCET.

Smart, L. (1995) *Using IT in Primary School History*, London, Cassell.

Smith, J. (1846) *The Grievances of the Working Classes and Pauperism and Crime of Glasgow with Their Causes, Extent and Remedy*, Glasgow.

Somekh, B. (1992) *Initial Teacher Education and New Technology*, (Project INTENT), Coventry, National Council for Educational Technology.

Spaeth, D. (1996) "Computer-Assisted Teaching and Learning", in Booth, A. & Hyland, P. (ed.) *History in Higher Education*, Oxford, Blackwell, pp. 155–177.

Technical and Vocational Education Initiative, *Developments 10: Flexible Learning*, London, The Training Agency, n.d.

Times Educational Supplement (1992) *The price of advice*, April 23, p. 18.

Tressell Publications (1993) *The Spanish Armada Database*, Brighton, Tressell Publications.

Waterhouse, P. (1988) *Supported Self-Study: an Introduction for Teachers*, Coventry, NCET.

Watson, D. (1993) *The Impact Report: an Evaluation of the Impact of Information Technology on Children's Achievements*, Kings College London.

Webb, M.E. and Hassell, D.J. (1988) "Opportunities for Computer Based Modelling in Secondary Education", in Lovis, P. and Tagg, D. (eds.) *Computers in Education*, Amsterdam, Elsevier.

Wellington, J. (1989) *Education for Employment: The Place of Information Technology*, Windsor, NFER-Nelson.

Wilkes, J. (ed.) (1985) *Exploring History with Microcomputers*, London, Council for Educational Technology.

Wills, S. (1990) "History is not spoon fed to us any more!: The Computing History Project as a Professional Development", in Martin & Blow, 232–240.

Wolff, J-M. (1990) "Computers and History in Secondary School Teaching in France: Bilan et Perspectives", *History & Computing*, 2, 36–39.

Yeomans, D., Martin, A. and Williams, R. (1995) "From Vertical to Horizontal? A Longitudinal Study of Information Technology in Ten Schools", *Journal of Information Technology for Teacher Education*, **4**, 329–350.

INDEX

Adoption of IT by History Teachers, 3, 97–103

CAL (Computer Assisted Learning) in History, 69, 167–174, 203–209, 219–223
CAL Evaluation, 205–209
Canton Project, 175–178
Causality, 111–125
CD-ROM, 3, 14, 18–28, 61, 64–65, 164, 179–190, 239
CHATA Project, 110–111
CHC (Computers in the History Classroom) conferences, 29, 41, 92, 116, 147–148
Changes in History Teaching, 2–3, 14–18, 147–148, 167–174, 241
Classroom Management, 105–107, 141–142
Computer-Assisted Case Studies, 203–209

Database Work, 3, 40–41, 48–50, 66, 139–146, 191–201, 225–231, 239
Desktop Publishing, 31, 51–52
Developments in:
    Australia, 5, 127–131, 179–190
    Austria, 4
    Denmark, 10, 63–68
    France, 5, 10, 57–62, 225–231
    Luxembourg, 4, 9, 37–44
    Netherlands, 4–5, 97–103, 167–174, 203–209
    Portugal, 4–5, 45–55
    Scotland, 191–201
    UK, 4–5, 9, 29–35, 69–73, 75–81, 83–93, 105–107, 133–138, 139–153, 155–161, 211–218, 219–223
    USA, 13–28, 175–178
Drawing, 47–48

Educational Technology, 235–237
Electronic Mail, 61
Empathy, 67–68, 109
Expert Builder, 165, 211, 214
Expert Systems, 76–81, 214–218

Future Trends, 14–18, 165–174, 240–242

Gallipoli Stacks, 179–190, 239
Graphs, 50–51, 59–60

HiDES Project, 76–81, 165, 219–233, 239–240
Historical Demography, 225–231
History Curriculum, 3–6, 37–38, 63–65, 70–73, 134
History and IT in Higher Education, 7, 175–178, 225–231
History and IT in Primary Education, 7, 133–138, 216
History and IT in Tertiary Education, 75–81, 127–131, 219–223
HyperCard, 128–130, 178–181, 188–189, 194
Hypermedia, 177
Hypertext, 43, 128–130, 168, 177–190, 194–201, 239

Implementation of Change, 97–103, 147–153
Implementation Programmes, 4–5, 45, 58–59
Information Retrieval, 65–66
Information Systems Approach to Learning, 166–167, 170
Initial Teacher Education, 155–161, 194, 201
IT Courses in Schools, 80–88
IT Culture in Schools, 10

IT and Historical Culture, 10–11
"IT Threshold", 6

Justifications for IT Use, 84–85

Learning Strategies, 175
Levels of IT Usage in Schools, 32–33, 88
Local History, 43, 51, 133–138, 175–178

Map-Making, 47, 60–61
Materials Development, 4–5, 203, 219–223
Mental Models, 212–213, 217–218
Methodology of History, 144–145
Minerva Project, 5, 45
Modelling, 211–218
Models of IT Development, 4–6, 86
Moving House, 164, 191–201
Multimedia, 3, 164, 179–190

National Curriculum for England and Wales, 2, 70–72, 75, 133–134, 211, 215–216

Oral History, 43
Oxford Internship Scheme, 155–156

Programmed Learning, 236
Progression in History, 109–126
Pupil Activities, 31–32
Pupil Perceptions of IT in History, 42–43, 80–81, 208–209, 220–221

Resources, 4–5, 9, 18–28, 58–59, 72, 189–190

Role of Government, 6, 164–165

School Expenditure on IT, 30–31
School IT Co-ordinator, 88–91
School IT Strategy, 69–73, 83–93
Simulations and Simulation Games, 31, 41–42, 67–68, 105, 127, 211, 240
Software Evaluation, 203–209
Spanish armada Database, 139–146
Spreadsheet Work, 60
Stakeholders in History, 1–2
Statistics, 60
Study of History, xvii, 1, 109
Sygap Package, 225–231

Teacher Competence, 5, 7, 9–10, 35, 69
Teacher Perceptions of IT in History, 33, 97–103, 106, 157
Teacher-Pupil Relationship, 54–55
Teachers' Usage of IT, 92, 97–103
Teaching Methods, 14–18, 45–46, 76–79, 149–153
Teaching Strategies, 51–52, 98, 105–107, 127–131, 133–138, 139–146
Technology and History, 241–242
Toolbook, 177–178
Training of Teachers, 5, 33–34, 39–40, 52–53, 61, 91–92, 147–153, 155–161
TVEI Project, 75, 83–84, 93, 194

Understanding in History, 109–126, 133–134, 155–161, 212–213, 220–221
Urban Migration, 191–201

Word Processing, 31, 51, 240